Communist Logistics
in the Korean War

Recent Titles in
Contributions in Military Studies

The 1,000 Hour War: Communication in the Gulf
Thomas A. McCain and Leonard Shyles, editors

U.S. Domestic and National Security Agendas:
Into the Twenty-First Century
Sam C. Sarkesian and John Mead Flanagin, editors

The Military in the Service of Society and Democracy
Daniella Ashkenazy, editor

The Italian Navy in World War II
James J. Sadkovich

Scientific Information in Wartime:
The Allied-German Rivalry, 1939–1945
Pamela Spence Richards

Marching Toward the 21st Century:
Military Manpower and Recruiting
Mark J. Eitelberg and Stephen L. Mehay, editors

The Changing Face of National Security: A Conceptual Analysis
Robert Mandel

United States Army Logistics: The Normandy Campaign, 1944
Steve R. Waddell

Passchendaele and the Royal Navy
Andrew A. Wiest

The Founding of Russia's Navy: Peter the Great and the Azov
Fleet, 1688–1714
Edward J. Phillips

The Specht Journal: A Military Journal of the Burgoyne Campaign
Helga Doblin, translator

Collective Insecurity: U.S. Defense Policy and the New World Disorder
Stephen J. Cimbala

Communist Logistics in the Korean War

Charles R. Shrader

Contributions in Military Studies, Number 160

Greenwood Press
Westport, Connecticut • London

Library of Congress Cataloging-in-Publication Data

Shrader, Charles R.
    Communist logistics in the Korean War / Charles R. Shrader.
      p. cm.—(Contributions in military studies, ISSN 0883–6884
; no. 160)
    Includes bibliographical references and index.
    ISBN 0–313–29509–3 (alk. paper)
    1. Korean War, 1950–1953—Campaigns. 2. Korean War, 1950–1953—
Logistics. 3. Korea (North). Chosŏn Inmin'gun. I. Title.
II. Series.
DS918.S515   1995
951.904′2—dc20   95–9753

British Library Cataloguing in Publication Data is available.

Library of Congress Catalog Card Number: 95–9753
ISBN: 0–313–29509–3
ISSN: 0883–6884

First published in 1995

Greenwood Press, 88 Post Road West, Westport, CT 06881
An imprint of Greenwood Publishing Group, Inc.

Printed in the United States of America

The paper used in this book complies with the
Permanent Paper Standard issued by the National
Information Standards Organization (Z39.48–1984).

P

In order to keep this title in print and available to the academic community, this edition
was produced using digital reprint technology in a relatively short print run. This would
not have been attainable using traditional methods. Although the cover has been changed
from its original appearance, the text remains the same and all materials and methods used
still conform to the highest book-making standards.

He who has a thorough knowledge of the conditions of the enemy as well as his own conditions is sure to win in all battles.

—Sun Tzu

Contents

Contents *ix*

Illustrations

CHARTS

DIAGRAMS

Preface

For the United States and its South Korean and United Nations allies, the Korean War consisted of a series of shocking surprises. The violent and fast-moving attack of the North Korean People's Army (NKPA) on 25 June 1950 and the subsequent retreat of Republic of Korea and United States forces to the Pusan Perimeter defense line was but the first of these shocking surprises. The unanticipated intervention of Communist Chinese forces (CCF) in the war in October-November 1950 and the subsequent retreat of battered United Nations Command (UNC) forces below the 38th Parallel was the second such event, and the unexpected devolution of the conflict after mid-1951 into a static war of trenches, small patrols, and limited offensives also came as a surprise to many participants and observers. Perhaps no aspect of the war in Korea came as a greater shock to UNC commanders and staff officers than the amazing ability of the NKPA and CCF to maintain a steady stream of supplies to their forces in Korea in the face of a massive and determined UNC air interdiction campaign of an intensity rivaling that of the Allied effort against Germany in World War II. American logisticians at the time expressed their admiration for the ability of the NKPA and CCF to sustain their forces in the field despite the many natural and operational obstacles, an achievement which one historian of the Korean War has described as "one of the minor miracles achieved by the *Inmun Gun*."[1]

The question addressed in this study is how the North Korean and Chinese Communists were able to sustain their forces in the field for three years against the relatively well-equipped and technologically sophisticated forces of the United Nations Command. Accordingly this study is focused on the logistical organization, methods, requirements, and operations of the North Korean People's Army and the Chinese Communist Forces during active operations in Korea between 25 June 1950 and 27 July 1953. The emphasis here is on what has been called the "operational level of war"; the political and grand strategic aspects of enemy logistics in Korea, as well as details of combat service support at the lowest levels, thus receive only minimal attention. Inasmuch as the most vulnerable link in the Communist logistical system appears to have been the distribution segment of that system, lines of communications, Communist transportation organizations and assets, and the movement of men and supplies, as well as UNC efforts to interdict the flow of matériel to Communist combat forces and the corresponding efforts by the NKPA and CCF to counter UNC interdiction efforts, are described in some detail. Other aspects of operational logistics, such as maintenance and medical services, consequently receive only cursory examination.

This study is based primarily on the declassified documentation of NKPA-CCF logistical activities assembled by UNC intelligence agencies during and immediately after active combat operations in Korea, 1950–1953. The postwar analyses of Western scholars have also been used extensively. For the most part, access to North Korean and Communist Chinese sources remains difficult. The one-sided nature of the sources used in this study requires that the results be used with some caution in that a reliance on friendly intelligence estimates of enemy capabilities and intentions does not permit a thorough assessment of enemy logistical plans and performance with respect to their own perceptions of requirements and goals. Until North Korean and Communist Chinese documents on their Korean War logistical activities are opened to Western scholars, we must continue to rely on such one-sided sources.

Given its restricted scope, this study is important mainly as a means of demonstrating what an enemy force of a given size and level of technical and organizational sophistication was capable of doing under a given set of conditions of terrain, opposing forces, and effort. Nevertheless, a number of useful conclusions may be derived from the story of NKPA-CCF logistical activities in Korea between 1950 and 1953, particularly with regard to the difficulties of interdicting with modern airpower an enemy logistical system with relatively low overall requirements, a low level of mechanization, and a lean organizational structure operated by a determined and resourceful enemy.

I am indebted to a number of individuals who provided invaluable assistance in the completion of this project. The entire staff of the United States Army Military History Institute at Carlisle Barracks, Pennsylvania, were unflagging in their support. I am especially grateful to my daughter, Sheila L. Bixby, who proofread the entire volume; to Mrs. Diane R. Gordon, who did the index; and to Colonel (USAF Retired) Jim Enos, who did the photographic work. Special thanks are also due to Mr. Sterling S. Hart of Chevy Chase, Maryland, who arranged the production of maps and charts, carefully reviewed the manuscript, and offered a number of helpful suggestions. My wife, Carole, also deserves a special bouquet of love and thanks for her unending support and her tolerance of my preoccupation over several months with events in a distant land long ago to the exclusion of pressing domestic duties.

NOTE

1. T. R. Fehrenbach, *This Kind of War: A Study in Unpreparedness* (rev. ed., New York: Bantam Books, 1991), 162.

Part I
The Logistics Environment

1

Introduction

For the North Korean People's Army (NKPA) and the Chinese Communist Forces (CCF), the war in Korea from June 1950 to July 1953 was above all a war of logistics. Communist strategy, operational decisions, and prospects for success were based largely on logistical considerations throughout the war, and questions of supply, storage, and distribution weighed heavily in the councils of the NKPA and CCF. Such questions also preoccupied the thoughts of United Nations Command (UNC) commanders and intelligence analysts seeking to determine Communist capabilities and intentions.

The Korean War can be divided into three distinct periods from the point of view of NKPA-CCF logistics, the first of which extended from 25 June 1950 to July 1951. The NKPA forces which invaded the Republic of Korea (ROK) on 25 June 1950 were well trained and well equipped but unprepared for an extended campaign or the intensive interdiction effort mounted against them by UNC air forces. Initially they achieved great success, driving the ROK and supporting US forces southeast into the Pusan Perimeter (shown on Map 1.1). However, the effort exhausted NKPA supplies and exposed their extended supply lines to increasingly effective UNC air interdiction. The NKPA offensive was decisively halted by the coordinated landing of UNC forces at Inchon and the breakout from the Pusan Perimeter in September 1950. Following UNC seizure of the key transportation hub of Seoul, the North Koreans were forced to retreat north in great disorder. The rout of the NKPA continued until the intervention of Chinese Communist forces in October-November 1950. The CCF also achieved initial success with their unexpected counterattack on forward UNC ground forces, but they too were unprepared logistically to support a large force over long lines of communications in the face of an intensive UNC air interdiction campaign. Consequently, the Communist offensives in early 1951 were limited in duration, and UNC ground forces were ultimately able to force the Communists to the conference table in July 1951.

In the second period, from July 1951 to the end of 1952, the NKPA-CCF acted forcefully to strengthen their logistical support capabilities by reorganizing and reinforcing their supply and transportation systems and by increasing the anti-aircraft artillery protecting their supply lines. Effective passive defense measures were supplemented by an increasing ability to repair railroads, highways, and other key distribution facilities rapidly and thus maintain the flow of essential supplies to frontline units. The improvements in logistical organization and methods made between July 1951 and December 1952 brought the NKPA-CCF in early 1953 to a point at which they were capable not only of providing sufficient logistical support for a strong static defense but were also increasingly capable of stockpiling sufficient supplies in forward areas to permit the conduct of sustained offensive operations.

Efforts to improve further the NKPA-CCF logistical systems continued in the final period of the war from January through July 1953. By July 1953 the Communist forces had on hand in forward areas sufficient food, fuel, ammunition, and other supplies to support a general offensive of seventeen to twenty-four days, in contrast to their limited ability in 1950 and early 1951 to sustain offensive operations for only six to eight days at a time. When an armistice was signed on 27 July 1953, the logistical prospects of the NKPA-CCF had never looked better.

Throughout the war the NKPA-CCF distribution system was the most vulnerable aspect of their overall logistical system and was consequently the focal point of UNC efforts to degrade Communist combat potential. UNC air forces enjoyed air superiority over much of the Korean area of operations and conducted an intensive air interdiction program designed to cut NKPA-CCF supply lines and deny to the enemy the supplies and equipment necessary for the conduct of sustained operations. However, the UNC air interdiction program, while it certainly degraded Communist logistical support to frontline forces, was never able to achieve its objective of bringing about a decisive defeat of the NKPA and CCF. The lack of adequate technology for detecting and targeting enemy movements at night and in periods of reduced visibility and the lack of adequate numbers of suitable aircraft which could be applied to the effort restricted the UNC air interdiction program. Moreover, the steady improvement of NKPA-CCF air defense capabilities and the presence of significant numbers of Communist MIG-15 fighters flying from Manchurian bases immune to UNC attack further hampered the effectiveness of the UNC air interdiction program, as did the failure of UNC ground forces to maintain a high tempo of operations after July 1951, which allowed the Communist forces to initiate or break off contact at will, resting and replenishing supplies as they wished and stockpiling supplies for future operations.

A number of factors contributed to the resilience of the NKPA-CCF logistical systems in Korea. In the first instance, the logistical requirements of both the NKPA and the CCF in Korea were very low in comparison to those of UNC forces; and while the minimal provision of food, clothing, and medical support to frontline Communist troops sometimes caused great hardship and suffering, it apparently did not cause a significant deterioration of morale and discipline. Although both the NKPA and the CCF made maximum use of captured supplies and supplies (particularly foodstuffs) requisitioned in areas near the frontlines, both armies relied principally on formal, albeit relatively lean, logistical systems. The flexibility of the relatively lean NKPA and CCF logistical organizations, which evolved in the direction of the more rigid but more efficient Soviet model during the course of the war, also contributed to the ability of the Communist forces to maintain an adequate flow of supplies to their frontline troops.

The NKPA and CCF transportation systems relied principally on rail movement supplemented by motor transport at intermediate levels. However, the Communists lacked motor transport at lower echelons and thus made extensive use of carts, pack animals, and human bearers for unit movements and for the movement of supplies in the immediate area of the front, around destroyed sections of railroad and highway, and locally in the rear areas. The inadequacy of NKPA-CCF motor transport at lower echelons was an important defect in the Communist logistical system inasmuch as reliance on less efficient animal and man-pack transport restricted Communist tactical mobility and flexibility in combat operations. However, the NKPA and CCF in Korea demonstrated great ingenuity and determination in protecting what transport they did have from UNC attempts to interdict their lines of communications and to destroy their trains, trucks, and other scarce logistical resources. They were particularly adept at passive air defense measures, including camouflage and the use of natural cover and concealment, and at the rapid restoration of destroyed and damaged fixed transport facilities such as bridges, rail lines, and highways.

Although the Communists were never strong enough logistically to employ their maximum combat manpower to defeat the UNC forces and eject them from the Korean peninsula, they were able to maintain a flow of supplies to frontline units sufficient to enable them to conduct a static defense strong enough to prevent a UNC victory and, in the last months of the war, to mount strong sustained offensive actions. Despite over one quarter of a million UNC air interdiction sorties directed against their lines of communication, transport equipment, supply installations, and industrial facilities over a period of three years, the NKPA and CCF were stronger than ever when the armistice was signed on 27 July 1953.

Map 1.1
Korea, 1950–1953

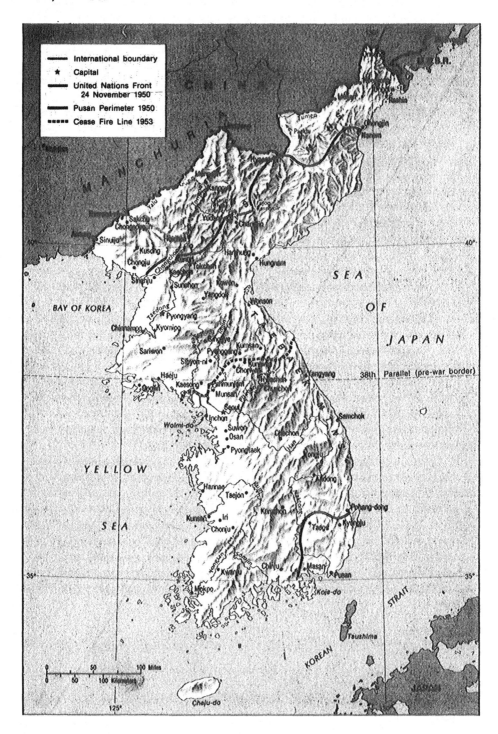

2

The Physical Environment

Historical events occur in a unique set of physical and temporal circumstances which give the events their own peculiar attributes. The Korean War of 1950–1953 took place in just such a unique physical environment, which did much to determine the scope and scale of logistical operations on both sides. Military operations in Korea were particularly sensitive to the geography on which they took place, and the movement of men and supplies as well as the tactical employment of weapons were determined in large part by the topography and climate of the Korean peninsula.[1] This physical environment, insofar as it consisted of human-made facilities, changed significantly over the three-year course of the war, but the unchanging geography and climate of the Korean peninsula did much to limit the impact of such changes as well as the overall logistical options available to both the NKPA-CCF and UNC forces.

THE GEOGRAPHY OF THE KOREAN PENINSULA

The Korean peninsula, shaped somewhat like a squat, thick S, lies on a roughly north-south axis and separates the Yellow Sea from the Sea of Japan.[2] Lying between 124° 11' and 130° 56' east longitude and 33° 7' and 43° 1' north latitude, Korea is approximately 525 miles in length and is widest in the north (about 200 miles) and narrowest in its waist (about 125 miles). With an area of just over 85,000 square miles, it has 5,800 miles of coastline and includes some 3,500 offshore islands. Only a few locations in the far northern part of the peninsula are more than 100 miles from the sea. The Korean peninsula is bounded on the west by the Yellow Sea, on the south by the Korean Strait, and on the east by the Sea of Japan. The northern boundary is shared with the northeastern provinces (formerly Manchuria) of the People's Republic of China for 500 miles along the Yalu River and with Siberia for about 11 miles along the Tumen River some 75 miles south of Vladivostok.

The topography of Korea resembles that of Italy. Most of the country is mountainous and rugged. The northern section of Korea is dominated by the Pai Shan Range, which slopes from northeast to southwest. Elevations are not extreme, but much of the range lies above 3,000 feet; only Paektu Mountain exceeds 9,000 feet. The Pai Shan Range, which separates Korea from Manchuria and the Russian Maritime Provinces, is broken by three principal corridors, the most important of which is the western corridor along the lower reaches of the Yalu River.[3] Another gap is formed in central North Korea by the valleys of the Tongno and Chongchon Rivers, and in the far northeastern corner access is available from eastern Manchuria and the Vladivostok region via several narrow valleys and a coastal strip.

From the eastern end of the Pai Shan mountains, the Taebaek Range extends south from the Yalu River nearly to the southern port of Pusan, paralleling the east coast and dividing the country into eastern and western coastal sections. The Taebaek Range includes peaks of 5,000 to 6,000 feet and constitutes a natural barrier between the two coasts. Its extremely rugged terrain presents formidable obstacles to military movements. The eastern coastal strip is narrow and rugged while the western section of Korea broadens toward the south and consists of numerous foothills giving way to relatively flat, muddy river plains.

Korea is well watered and well drained by eleven principal rivers, most of which flow generally from northeast to southwest and thus form a series of substantial barriers to north-south movement. The Yalu (or Amnok, as it is known to the Koreans) rises in the northern mountains and forms the boundary of Korea with Manchuria. The Yalu is Korea's longest river, flowing southwestward some 500 miles into the Yellow Sea. The Tumen is the major river of northeastern Korea and flows eastward into the Sea of Japan. In southeastern Korea, the Naktong and Somjin rise in the Taebaek Mountains and flow generally southward into the Korea Strait. The principal rivers of western Korea rise in the Taebaek Range or the northern mountain barrier and flow westward into the Yellow Sea. From north to south the western rivers are the Chongchon, the Taedong, the Yesong, the Imjin, the Han, the Kum, and the Yongsan. For the most part they are long and winding and have extensive tidal flats at their mouths. In the mountainous regions in which they rise, these rivers are relatively swift and narrow and provide abundant potential for hydroelectric power. In the coastal plains they are somewhat slower, broader, usually navigable for small boats, and important for irrigation.

Many of the principal towns and cities of Korea lie along the major river systems, and the major ports are at their mouths.[4] Sinanju on the west coast at the mouth of the Chongchon River is an important junction of the western and central passages from Manchuria. Sixty miles south of Sinanju lies the important port of Chinnampo, which serves the northern mining and industrial region at the mouth of the Taedong River. Korea's largest iron and steel works are at

Kyomipo, 15 miles upstream from Chinnampo, and another 30 miles upstream is the North Korean capital of Pyongyang. One of the most important of Korea's rivers, the Han, together with its tributaries, the Imjin and the Pukhan, drains a major portion of central western Korea. The Han passes the South Korean capital of Seoul and empties into the Yellow Sea just north of the main west coast port of Inchon. Kunsan, the major port for the agricultural area of southwestern Korea, lies some 90 miles south of Inchon at the mouth of the Kum River, along which is also located the important central town of Taejon. In the southwestern corner, the port of Mokpo lies near the mouth of the Yongsan River, along which is situated the important town of Kwangju. The greatest port in Korea, Pusan, lies near the mouth of the meandering Naktong River in southeastern Korea. The important town of Taegu also lies near the Naktong. Farther north on the east coast lie the important port cities of Wonsan and Hungnam. The ports of Chongjin and Unggi are in the far northeastern corner of the country.

Despite its extent, the Korean coastline is not particularly hospitable. The proximity of steep mountains to the shore on the eastern coastline limits the extent of the useful coastal plain, which is divided into small, isolated compartments. Broad, shallow, muddy estuaries on the western coast likewise limit development, as does the unusually high tidal reach. The tidal range on the east coast is 1 to 2 feet, but on the west coast it is from 20 to 36 feet.[5] The key port of Inchon is well known for its 30-foot variation between high and low tide, one of the greatest ranges on earth for a major port.

THE KOREAN CLIMATE

In general, the monsoonal Korean climate can best be described as inhospitable, with extreme variations between summer and winter and between the mountainous north and the south. Although Korea lies in the same latitudes as the eastern seaboard of the United States from northern New York to North Carolina, the variations in climate are much more extreme. The seasonal shift of the prevailing winds significantly affects temperature, precipitation, humidity, and visibility. The Korean climate is continental in winter, and the flow of air is from Siberia and Mongolia. The summer climate is maritime, and the prevailing winds are from the south and southwest off the Pacific Ocean. Spring and autumn are transitional seasons.

Summers are generally hot and humid. Summer temperatures reach the nineties in the south but are more moderate in the higher elevations of the north. Summertime high temperatures of over 100° F are not uncommon in the lower elevations. Summer is also the rainy season, and the average annual rainfall throughout most of Korea is 40 to 50 inches, varying from less than 25 inches in the upper Yalu River basin to over 80 inches in the south. Most of the country receives from 8 to 10 inches of rain in July, and the southern highlands sometimes get more than 16 inches. Typhoons form in the Marianas Islands in late summer and early fall and move northwest across the East China Sea, skirting southeastern Korea or passing directly across the country. Korea experiences one to five typhoons per year, with heavy rains, high winds, and extraordinary tides.

Winters in the higher elevations of the northern interior are extremely cold, ranging from less than 0° F to 10° F with extremes as low as minus 45° F. However, the average monthly winter temperatures in the southeast are generally above freezing and range from 30 to 40° F at night and 40 to 45° F in the daytime on the southern coast. The number of frost-free days per year in the northern interior average 130, compared to 170 in the central region around Seoul and 226 in the south around Pusan. The winter winds sweeping down from Mongolia are often strong but serve to maintain a relatively low humidity. Winter precipitation is generally light, with less than 1 inch of snow per month in the north and 2 to 3 inches per month in the lowlands of the east coast.

TRANSPORTATION FACILITIES

Korea's basic transport infrastructure in 1950 reflected the country's topography and its political development as well. Port facilities were poorly developed by Western standards, and the modern railroads and highways that existed had been constructed during the period of Japanese dominance from 1910 to 1945. These routes were most fully developed in the relatively moderate terrain of the western section of Korea, and the capital city of Seoul was the focal point. Lines of communication in Korea were generally oriented north-south, and communications between the eastern coastal strip and the western section of Korea were limited. For the most part, the mountainous north and interior of Korea boasted little in the way of adequate transportation facilities.

Water Transport

Before the Korean War, only a small percentage of Korea's transport needs were met by water transport. The lack of well-developed ports and related domestic industries as well as a small merchant marine were contributory factors.[6] Korea had few good ports (Pusan in southeastern Korea was the best). The extensive mud flats and extremely high tidal ranges of the west coast limited development of west coast ports. The principal western port, Inchon, was notorious for its 30-foot tidal range, restricted approaches, and small tidal basin. Other west coast ports such as Kunsan, Yosu, Mokpo, and Chinnampo were little more than fishing villages. The northeastern ports of Wonsan and Hungnam had significant potential but were not fully developed. Table 2.1 outlines the characteristics of the main Korean ports as they existed in 1950. Coastal

Table 2.1
Korean Ports ca. 1950[7]

| Port | Berths | | | Estimated Military Discharge Capacity (ST/day) | Storage Area | | Remarks |
	Along-side	At Anchor	Lighter (feet)		Open (acres)	Covered (sq ft)	
Changjon			2,500	3,000			Very shallow but good lighterage port
Chinhae		10-15	5,500	4,500			Major coal port
Chinnampo	4	ample		3,000	10	630,000	Second in importance to Pusan
Chongjin	17	unlimited		19,700	11	200,000	Major northeast industrial port
Hungnam	12	unlimited		8,300	10	608,000	Well developed; 30-ft tides; restricted basin
Inchon	5	poor		8,000	45	740,500	Principal southwestern agricultural port
Kunsan	5	9+		2,400			
Masan	4	47		4,600		390,000	Small; strong currents; 50 mi. to Yellow Sea
Mokpo		10	2,100	1,500			Unsheltered and poor holding ground; 210,000-barrel petroleum storage
Najin	11	poor		9,000		400,000	Small and shallow fishing port
Pohang		unlimited	3,800	5,000		60,000	Largest/best Korean port; highway clearance capacity poor; 340,000-barrel petroleum storage
Pusan	18	34	6,000	30,000		830,000	Fishing and minor industrial port
Songjin	2	unlimited		3,500	59	223,000	Northernmost port on west coast; 21-ft tides
Tasado	5	unlimited		3,000		525,000	Limited clearance capacity
Tongyong		19		1,800	10	126,000	
Unggi	4	unlimited		5,100	30	120,000	Major east coast port
Wonsan	3	unlimited		7,400		240,000	Developed to supplement Pusan
Yosu	5	38		4,700	4.3	200,000	

ST = short tons.

Table 2.2
Navigable Rivers of Korea[8]

River	Length (miles)	Navigability			Obstacles
		Small Ocean-Going Vessels	Junks	Small Native Craft	
Chongchon	121			92 miles to Huichon	Shallow and rocky beyond Anju
Han	320	40 miles to Seoul		250 miles to Yongchun	Iced over from December to March
Imjin	154			50 miles to Sangnyong	Strong currents and numerous shoals
Kum	248	10 miles above mouth			Approach from sea difficult due to shoals and tidal range
Naktong	323			215 miles to Andong	Narrow and winding, experienced pilots required
Somjin	131			22 miles	Boulders in riverbed make navigation difficult; heavy summer rains cause flooding
Taedong	273	63 miles to Pyongyang		161 miles to head of navigation	Irregularly iced over from December to March; floods in July and August cause 10-ft rises
Tumen	325		72 miles	211 miles to Songhak-tong	Iced over from November to March
Yalu (Amnok)	490	25 miles to Simuiju	221 miles to Chian	436 miles to Hyesanjin	Iced over from November to March; channel and shoals subject to rapid changes; mouth obstructed by bars
Yesong	106			38 miles	Irregularly iced over from December to March

shipping was also of some importance but was limited by the extensive irregular coastline and the lack of good ports.

In 1950, Korea's inland waterways were undeveloped and played little role in the Korean economy. The mountainous terrain and shallow rivers generally precluded such development. The total navigable length of Korea's inland waterways was about 1,540 miles, of which only about 138 miles were navigable by ocean-going vessels.[9] The remainder could be negotiated only by small craft (of less than 1-ton capacity and less than 2-foot draft) and were generally of only local importance. Table 2.2 outlines the principal navigable waterways.

Railroads

The Korean railway system was constructed by the Japanese beginning early in this century.[10] Before the Korean War, the railroads carried about 80 percent of all commercial traffic and the Korean railroad system had a capacity of approximately 20,000 short tons (ST) per day.[11] Originally well built, by 1950 the capacity of the Korean railroad system was limited by poor maintenance of fixed facilities, motive power, and rolling stock as well as by shortages of materials and trained personnel. In 1950, the system comprised over 3,000 miles of standard-gauge (4 feet, 8.5 inches) track, of which about 310 miles was double tracked. In addition, there were about 523 miles of narrow-gauge (2 feet, 6 inches) track. Stations were located 3 to 6 miles apart, and some 400 of them were of sufficient importance to have buildings. The largest terminals were at Seoul, Pyongyang, and Pusan. The principal repair shops were at Seoul, Pusan, Pyongyang, Wonsan, and Chongjin and were capable of repairing some 1,300 locomotives, 2,000 passenger cars, and 3,000 freight cars each year. In 1950, about 1,500 locomotives were available, but only about 500 of them were operable. There were about 2,000 passenger cars, including 150 narrow-gauge passenger cars, 70 percent of which were in poor condition. The more than 7,000 freight cars, including 1,000 narrow-gauge freight cars, were mostly of about 30 ST capacity.[12]

Seoul was the focal point of the Korean rail network, with four of the five main lines radiating outward from the city. The fifth main line linked the east and west coasts of the peninsula. Numerous standard-gauge and narrow-gauge feeder lines linked the ports and larger towns with the main railroad lines. These lines were for the most part well built, with heavy ballast and bridges and tunnels of modern construction. Generally the railways followed the river valleys and tunneled through rather than topped the many ridges. During the course of the war, most of these rail lines, as well as the available motive power and rolling stock, were subjected to both ground and air action, and considerable construction was also undertaken. The situation as it existed in mid-1950 is displayed in Table 2.3.

Table 2.3
Korean Rail Lines ca. 1950[13]

Line No.	Points Connected	Distance (miles)	Track	Min. Curve Radius (feet)	Ruling Grade (%)	Est. Haul (ST)	Estimated No. of Trains/Day		Bridges		Tunnels	
							Troops	Supplies	No.	Total Length (feet)	No.	Total Length (feet)
I	Pusan-Seoul	270	Double	1,312	1.1	400	5	25	460	64,104	63	75,376
II	Pusan-Seoul	310	Single	985	2.5	200	2	8	311	44,573	96	118,850
IIA	Pohang-Kyongju	23	Single	985	1.7	150	6	2	25	2,380	5	?
III	Taejon-Mokpo	160	Single	1,312	1.3	400	2	5	153	19,232	9	7,101
IV	Iri-Yosu	125	Single	985	2.5	200	2	8	105	11,921	7	9,373
V	Seoul-Sinuiju	310	Single Double	650 (N) 990 (S)	1.3	400	2	8	100	26,856 *	15	12,123 *
VI	Seoul-Inchon	19	Double Single	1,312	1.0	400	2	8	9	1,020	None	0
VII	Seoul-Chunchon	60	Single	985	2.5	200	2	8	67	9,207	12	6,984
VIII	Seoul-Najin	740	Single	990	2.5	200	2	8	490 **	59,081 **	108 **	132,734 **
IX	Pyongyang-Manpojin	220	Single	990	2.5	200	2	8	?	?	?	?
X	Chinnampo-Sunchon-Kowon	157	Single	820	2.0	300	2	8	13	?	13	53,700

* Between Seoul and Pyongyang only
** From Seoul to Milepost 490 only

The principal line (Line I), and the first to be constructed, was double tracked and ran from Seoul to the southeastern port of Pusan via Suwon, Chonan, Chochiwon, Taejon, Kumchon, and Taegu. Feeder lines left the main Seoul-Pusan line at Taejon (Line III) and ran southwest to Iri, where they divided into three lines running west to Kunsan; southeast via Chonju, Namwan, and Sunchon to Togyang (Yosu) (Line IV); and south via Chongup and Songjong to Makpo (Line III), with an extension southeast from Songjong via Kwangju, Pesong, and Pongnim to connect with the Iri-Togyang line at Sunchon. Another southwestern extension left the main line at Chonan and ran through Hannae to Sudong across the Kum River mouth from Kunsan. Shorter extensions left the main line at Samnangjin running southwest via Masan to Samchonpo and at Kumchon running north to beyond Sangju. A short line linked Seoul with the port of Inchon (Line VI).

The principal line to the north (Line V) originated at Seoul and ran by way of Munsan, Kaesong, Sariwon, Pyongyang, Sinanju, Chongju, and Sonchon to cross the Yalu into Manchuria at Sinuiju. Originally double tracked, some 67 miles of track were removed shortly before the Korean War, leaving the northern portion of the route single tracked. The main Seoul-Sinuiju line was joined at Chongju by a line which crossed the Yalu below the Suiho reservoir near Sakchu. Another line (Line IX) coming from Manpojin on the upper reaches of the Yalu by way of Kanggye and the Tongno-Chongchon gap joined the main Seoul-Sinuiju line at Sinanju. Feeder lines connected Seoul to Chunchon (Line VII) and Pyongyang to the port of Chinnampo, to Tokenon, and to Kusong (via Sunchon and Taechon).

A third main line (Line II) connected Seoul with Pusan via Wonju, Chechon, Yongju, Andong, Yongchon, and Kyongju, with extensions from Kyongju northeast to Pohang on the east coast (Line IIA) and from Yongju northeast to Samchok. The fourth main line radiating from Seoul (Line VIII) ran to Wonsan via Uijongbu and connected the lines in the western part of Korea with the main east coast line, which extended from Yangyang on the central coast north via Wonsan, Kowon, Hamhung, Hungnam, Songjin, Kilchu, Yongan, Chongjin, and Hoeryang to Namyang (Tumen) on the Manchurian border. An eastward extension ran from Namyang to Hunyung, and another extension of the mainline ran from the vicinity of Suwon-dong (Chongjin) northwest via Najin and Unggi to the Siberian border, with a spur northwest along the Tumen River border via Aoji and Sinansan to Yongbuktong. Other extensions of the main east coast line ran northwest from Kilchu to Hyesan on the Yalu River and northwest from just north of Komusan to Musan also on the Yalu. There was a gap of about 45 miles from the southern end of the main east coast line just above the 38th Parallel at Yangyang to Samchok. The fifth main line (Line X) ran across the peninsula and through the Taebaek Range and connected the west coast port of Chinnampo with Kowon via Sunchon, Unsan, Sinchang, Chahasan, and Songnae.

In 1950, the Korean rail system was connected to that of Manchuria at five places and to that of the Soviet Union in one. The principal crossings from Manchuria were (west to east) at Antung/ Sinuiju; at the foot of the Suiho Reservoir near Chongsongjin and Sakchu; at Manpojin; at Tumen/ Namyang; and near Hunyung. The single connection with the Russian maritime provinces, completed during the Korean War, was north of Unggi. An extension of the main east coast lines ran from Kilchu to Hyesan on the Yalu, but no connecting railroad existed on the Manchurian side of the border. Similarly, a Korean line extended from Suwon-dong on the east coast to Musan on the Yalu without a Manchurian connection. The Manchurian rail system also had a line which terminated at Linchiang, but no rail line existed on the Korean side.

Although immune to UNC attack, the railroad systems of Manchuria, north China, and the Soviet Union were extremely important to the logistical support of North Korean as well as Chinese Communist troops in Korea. The inset on Map 2.1 depicts the more important Chinese and Soviet railroad lines serving Korea. In 1945, the railway system in China itself covered approximately 16,000 miles, but by 1948 less than 5,000 miles were operational due to destruction during the civil war.[14] Manchuria had just over 6,000 miles of railroads.[15] There were five connections from Siberia south to China, Mongolia, and North Korea. The Russian lines were broad (5-foot) gauge, and thus freight had to be transferred at the change-of-gauge stations at the Chinese and North Korean borders.[16] Estimates in October 1954 rated the capacity of Soviet railroads feeding China and North Korea at approximately 17,500 tons per day. Restrictions on the capacity of the Chinese eastern railroad across Manchuria were more critical and reduced the deliverable tonnage to approximately 13,000 tons per day less necessary local traffic, or as much as 339,000 tons per month.[17] These connections were, of course, linked to the key Trans-Siberian Railroad, which was rated in July 1952 as capable of handling thirty-six trains per day each way.[18] When subtractions are made for necessary maintenance cargo, minimum civilian needs, and Soviet military requirements, a maximum of sixteen trains (16,000 metric tons) each way per day, or about 5.8 million metric tons each way per year, might have been available for other purposes, such as the supply of the Chinese and North Koreans.[19]

Map 2.1
Korean Transportation Facilities, 1950

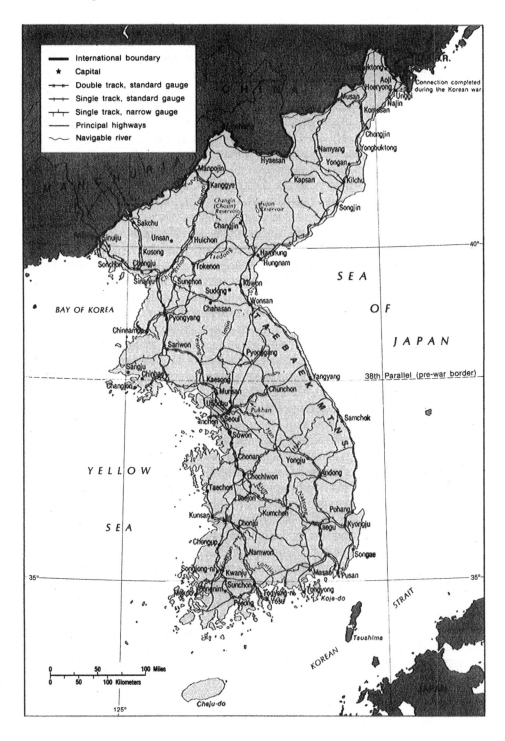

Highways

In 1950, Korea had about 20,000 miles of highways, almost all of which were considered poor secondary roads by U.S. standards.[20] Built for the most part in the twentieth century, most of Korea's roads were unpaved but well founded and surfaced with crushed rock and gravel. Few met the 22-foot-wide standard for a two-lane highway, and the best roads were only about 18 feet wide, with numerous bottlenecks at narrow bridges and 11- to 13-foot bypasses. Sharp curves and steep grades, particularly in the mountainous areas, further restricted the highway net. These roads were particularly susceptible to the effects of summer rains and winter ice and snow and were not well suited to heavy military traffic.

The Korean highway system, like the Korean rail system, was oriented north-south and had few through lateral routes connecting the east and west coasts. Seoul was the focal point of the highway net, and the two main highway routes were laid out in an X. One leg ran approximately 600 miles southeast from Sinuiju on the Yalu to Pusan on the southeast coast. The other leg ran about 840 miles southwest from Hunyung on the northeastern border to Mokpo on the southwestern coast. There were, of course, numerous feeder roads, connections, and extensions. Usable roads were more numerous in the lowland areas of western and southern Korea and scarcer in the mountainous north and west. Characteristics of the principal routes are described in Table 2.4.

The Korean highway system was linked to that of Manchuria at Sinuiju, Chongsongjin, Manpojin, Linchiang, and a number of places in the northeast (Musan, Hoeryong, Namyang, Hunyung, and in the vicinity of Aoji) and funneled through Chongjin on the northeastern coast. The two most important Manchurian routes connecting directly with Korea were Route M-6 from Suifenho to Tumen and Route M-7 from Mukden to Antung.[21] Route M-6 was 214 miles long, two to three lanes wide, and surfaced with sand and gravel. The Suifenho segment was a well-maintained all-weather road suitable for heavy military vehicles. It provided a shortcut from the vicinity of Vorshilov in the Soviet Union to northeastern Korea via Namyang and carried a considerable amount of traffic during the hostilities in Korea. Its rated capacity in March 1954 was between 500 and 1,500 short tons per day. Route M-7 was a vital strategic highway of about 155 miles in length, two to three lanes wide, surfaced with asphalt, and provided with ferro-concrete bridges over all major streams. It connected the important rail and industrial center of Mukden with Antung on the Korean border and was used extensively during the Korean War. Its rated capacity in March 1954 was between 1,500 and 4,000 short tons per day. Overall, during the Korean War the Manchurian highway system was capable of transporting approximately 48 percent of the supply tonnage normally moved by rail.[22] Of course, the Manchurian highways were subject to the same seasonal restrictions as those in Korea itself.

Table 2.4
North Korean Highway Capacities ca. 1953[21]

Route No.	Terminals	Distance One Way (miles)	Type	Lanes	Unrestricted Capacity		Remarks
					Normal (ST)	Maximum (ST)	
1	Sinuiju-Pyongyang	156	Gravel Dirt	1 to 2	8,000	9,600	Entry route
2	Chongsongjin-Chongju	75	Gravel	1 to 1.5	7,000	8,400	Entry route
3	Manpojin-Kumu-ri	208	Gravel	1 to 2	7,000	8,400	Entry route
4	Linchiang-Wonsan	198	Gravel Dirt	1 to 1.5	5,000	6,000	Entry route
5	Chongjin-Wonsan	300	Paved Gravel	1 to 2	6,000	7,200	Entry route connecting with Musan, Hoeryang, Namyang, Hunyung, and Unggi
	Total Capacity of Entry Routes				**33,000**	**39,600**	
6	Pyongyang-Kaesong	113	Gravel	1 to 2	8,000	9,600	Best route from 39th Parallel to front
7	Pyongyang-Sibyon-ni	97	Gravel	1 to 2	5,000	6,000	Follows streams
8	Sariwon-Haeju	40	Gravel	1 to 2			
9	Yangdok-Singye	66	Gravel Dirt	1 to 1.5	5,000	6,000	Narrow, winding, and mountainous; one-way in some areas
10	Majon-ni-Sibyon-ni	80	Gravel	1 to 2	4,500	5,400	Narrow and winding; many defiles
11	Wonsan-Pyonggang	65	Gravel Dirt	1 to 1.5	4,000	4,800	Few bridges or defiles; parallels Wonsan-Pyonggang railroad
12	Wonsan-Kumsong	65	Gravel Dirt	1 to 1.5	4,000	4,800	Runs along coast to Tongchon, then through mountains to Kumsong
13	Hwachon-ni-Marhwi-ri	30	Dirt	1 to 1.5	4,000	4,800	Main route to front east of Pukhan River
14	Pyongyang-Haeju	120	Gravel	1 to 2			
15	Pyongyang-Wonsan	132	Gravel Paved	1 to 2	5,000	6,000	Major all-weather route across peninsula; mountainous; many defiles

Air Transport

The Japanese constructed a number of small airfields in Korea during their occupation of that country, and the North Korean and Communist Chinese had a small number of Soviet-built transport aircraft.[24] However, Communist air movement of troops and supplies during the Korean War was insignificant. Undoubtedly, some critical items were imported by air from China and the Soviet Union, but the tonnage of such movements cannot be determined and was probably negligible.[25]

MILITARY IMPLICATIONS OF THE PHYSICAL ENVIRONMENT

The principal military implications of Korea's physical environment concern the degree to which the terrain and climate serve to restrict the ground communications and reduce trafficability during significant portions of the year. The northern mountains restrict the routes of passage between southern Manchuria and northern Korea, and the central Taebaek Range severely limits east-west communication in Korea itself. The rugged terrain of most of the country limits the construction and operation of railroads and highways and requires numerous tunnels, bridges, defiles, and steep grades. Consequently, the best fixed transportation routes are found in the gentler terrain of the western section of the country. The east-west river systems act as obstacles to north-south movement, and the mountains serve to channelize north-south communications and limit the degree to which forces operating on one north-south axis can be reinforced or supplied from parallel axes. The overall effect of such restrictions of the lines of communication is to impede military logistical and tactical movements and make them more vulnerable to ground and air interdiction.

Seasonal weather conditions in Korea limit observation and air operations, but their most important effect on ground operations is to limit trafficability. Snow, ice, and poor visibility in winter and mud and dust in summer adversely affect highway operations and the maintenance of both rail lines and highways. Heavy rains from June to September create poor trafficability conditions throughout most low-lying areas. Cross-country mobility is further limited by the extensive rice paddies, which are flooded from March to October in the north and from May to October in the south. The most favorable season for cross-country movement is from late September to late November. Chart 2.1 portrays the seasonal trafficability conditions of the roads in North Korea.

Chart 2.1
Seasonal Trafficability of Highways in North Korea[26]

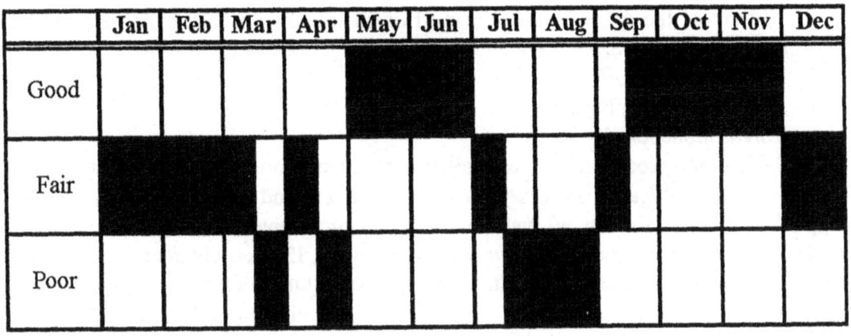

	Jan	Feb	Mar	Apr	May	Jun	Jul	Aug	Sep	Oct	Nov	Dec
Good	□	□	□	□	■	■	■	□	■	■	□	□
Fair	■	■	□	■	□	■	□	■	□	□	□	■
Poor	□	□	■	□	■	□	■	□	□	□	■	□

As any veteran of the Korean War will attest, the terrain and climate of the Korean peninsula can also take their toll on soldiers and matériel. Winter cold and summer heat adversely affect the performance of weapons and vehicles and produce numerous personnel casualties. In winter, the grease in weapons freezes, vehicles refuse to start, and soldiers suffer frostbite, hypothermia, and other cold injuries. In summer, dust clogs air filters and erodes weapons while high temperatures and humidity spoil supplies and produce heat stroke and other heat injuries. The mountainous terrain also generally limits the use of motor vehicles and pushes people and animals to the limits of their stamina. In general terms, the Korean peninsula is one of the least favorable places on earth for conducting modern mechanized warfare. The rugged terrain in particular tends to offset any advantage that a modern, technologically sophisticated army might have over an enemy with few complicated weapons or vehicles, a fact which was demonstrated definitively during the Korean War of 1950–1953.

NOTES

1. James A. Field, Jr., *History of United States Naval Operations: Korea* (Washington: USGPO, 1962), 90.

2. Sources for the description of Korean geography and climate include Field; Headquarters, Department of the Army, *Area Handbook for Korea* (DA Pamphlet No. 550-41; Washington: USGPO, November 1964); Headquarters, Department of the Army, Office of the Assistant Chief of Staff, G-2, *Korea—Basic Intelligence Summary (Tentative)* (Intelligence Research Project No. 5809, Washington: Headquarters, Department of the Army, Office of the Assistant Chief of Staff, G-2, 18 July 1950); Headquarters, Department of the Army, Office of the Assistant Chief of Staff, G-2, *Korea Handbook* (Washington: Headquarters, Department of the Army, Office of the Assistant Chief of Staff, G-2, September 1950); and Robert Frank Futrell, *The United States Air Force in Korea, 1950–1953* (rev. ed., Washington: Office of Air Force History, 1983).

3. Field, 91.

4. The description of Korean towns and ports is based on Field, 91–94.

5. Field, 96–97.

6. "Effect of the Armistice on Enemy Logistics in North Korea, Part I: Enemy Transport Facilities," *USAFFE Intelligence Digest*, IV, no. 6 (August 1954), 15.

7. *Korea Handbook*, Figures 17 and 18.

8. *Korea Handbook*, Figure 16.

9. *Korea Handbook*, 49–50.

10. The description of the Korean rail system is based on Field, 94–95; Futtrell, 63; *Korea—Basic Intelligence Summary (Tentative)*, 12–25; and *Korea Handbook*, 41–43. Map 2.1 depicts the Korean rail system as it existed circa September 1950.

11. *Korea—Basic Intelligence Summary (Tentative)*, 12; Headquarters, United States Army Forces Far East and Eighth United States Army, Office of the Assistant Chief of Staff, G-2, *Intelligence Estimate Korea* (APO 343: Headquarters, United States Army Forces Far East and Eighth United States Army, Office of the Assistant Chief of Staff, G-2, 3 March 1955), F-1.

12. *Korea—Basic Intelligence Summary (Tentative)*, 23–24. There were 660 locomotives in South Korea, 300 of which were operable, and 870 in North Korea, 200 of which were operable. Of 880 passenger cars in North Korea, only about 150 were operable.

13. *Korea Handbook*, Figure 14; *Korea—Basic Intelligence Summary (Tentative)*, Figure T-3.

14. "Chinese Rail Net—Still a Major Military Weakness," *USAFFE Intelligence Digest*, V, no. 7 (July 1955), 1.

15. James A. Huston, *Guns and Butter, Powder and Rice: U. S. Army Logistics in the Korean War* (Selinsgrove, PA: Susquehanna University Press, 1989), 37.

16. "Capability of the Soviet Far Eastern Rail Net," *USAFFE Intelligence Digest*, VI, no. 4 (April 1956), 15.

17. "Capability of the Soviet Far Eastern Rail Net," 15; Huston, 38.

18. "Capability of the Soviet Far Eastern Rail Net," 12.

19. "Capability of the Soviet Far Eastern Rail Net," 12.

20. Description of the Korean highway system is based on Field, 95; Roy E. Appleman, *South to the Naktong, North to the Yalu* (Washington: Office of the Chief of Military History, Department of the Army, 1961), 116–117; and "Military Supply in North Korea," *USAFFE Intelligence Digest*, V, no. 10 (October 1955), 35. Map 2.1 depicts the major Korean highway routes as they existed circa 1950.

21. For details, see "Manchurian Highway Logistic Capabilities," *USAFFE Intelligence Digest*, IV, no. 1 (March 1954), 55–57.

22. "Communist China's Logistical Hurdle: The Sino-Soviet Frontier," *USAFFE Intelligence Digest*, V, no. 9 (September 1955), 2.

23. "Railroads and Highway Transport in North Korea and Their Impact on Enemy Logistics," *USAFFE Intelligence Digest*, I, no. 13 (2 July 1953), 36 and 38; "Effect of the Armistice on Enemy Logistics in North Korea, Part I: Enemy Transportation Facilities," 11. See Map 2.1.

24. Headquarters, Department of the Army, *Handbook on the Chinese Communist Army* (DA Pamphlet No. 30-51; Washington: USGPO, 1952), 122–123 and 130–131. The transport aircraft available to the North Koreans and Chinese Communists were the IL-2, a Soviet version of the twin-engine U. S. DC-3 (C-47) with a range of about 570

nautical miles; and the IL-12, which was very similar. In July 1950, the PLA had about 150 transports of all kinds (see Headquarters, Eighth United States Army, Office of the Assistant Chief of Staff, G-2, *Intelligence Estimate, 27 July 1953* [APO 301: Headquarters, Eighth United States Army, Office of the Assistant Chief of Staff, G-2, 27 July 1953], 8–9).

25. Futrell, 64; "Effect of the Armistice on Enemy Logistics in North Korea, Part I: Enemy Transport Facilities," 16.

26. "Railroads and Highway Transport in North Korea and Their Impact on Enemy Logistics," 35.

3

NKPA-CCF Logistical Doctrine
and Organization

Several myths and misconceptions surround the logistical support of the Communist forces in Korea. One of the more persistent misconceptions is that the logistical doctrines, organizations, and methods of both the North Korean People's Army and the Chinese Communist Forces in Korea were extremely primitive and thus incapable of supporting large formations in modern warfare. By Western standards the logistical doctrine and support organizations of the NKPA and the CCF in Korea from 1950 to 1953 may indeed be considered rudimentary, but on closer examination it is clear that both the NKPA and the CCF had a logistical doctrine of some complexity and formed a variety of organizational structures, often complex and capable of providing adequate logistical support to their forces in the field. NKPA-CCF logistical doctrines and methods were characterized by flexibility and innovation, which allowed them to compensate for their comparative lack of material resources and modern technology as well as for such restrictions to their freedom of action as the UNC forces were able to impose. NKPA and CCF logistical organizations were equally flexible and often exhibited great variation in form, strength, and equipment of the assigned service units.

NKPA-CCF LOGISTICAL DOCTRINE

In view of the fact that both the NKPA and the CCF were equipped primarily with Soviet military equipment and relied heavily on Soviet advisors, it is not surprising that their logistical doctrine was based on World War II Soviet Army doctrine modified to suit the peculiar strategic and tactical situation in Korea as well as their peculiar national traditions and political imperatives.[1] However, the logistical doctrine of the NKPA differed from that of the CCF in several respects, the most important being that the NKPA system generally followed the Soviet model more closely. NKPA doctrine, organization, and methods thus tended to be more uniform and more rigid, with greater centralized control and fewer local variations than the CCF system, which allowed senior commanders considerable latitude in organizing their forces and prescribing how they would be supported logistically.[2] For the most part, the NKPA was organized along conventional lines with a normal proportion of logistical support units. The CCF, on the other hand, had barely emerged from its guerrilla past and relied on a flexible supply doctrine and only a few supporting units for its lightly armed combat forces.[3]

NKPA and CCF logistical doctrine, insofar as it was codified, agreed on a number of key points. In both armies, as in the United States Army, logistics was a command responsibility.[4] In the NKPA, the chief of rear services at each echelon was in fact a deputy of the commander and was next in line of command after the chief of staff.[5] The commander at each level was held accountable for all aspects of the support of the troops and units under his supervision and was expected to utilize every available resource, including civilian equipment and labor, to meet the logistical needs of his unit. Combat unit commanders were also expected to control their logistical units directly and to give high priority to the logistical estimate of the situation in making their operational decisions.[6] Once the operational decisions were made, the commander was supposed to assign immediately the supporting mission of his rear service organizations. Accordingly, the commander had to understand the following problems:

a. The consumption estimate calculated by higher headquarters for operations in combat.

b. The amount of supplies held in reserve by the various subordinate units in the command.

c. The quantity of supplies and time of issue scheduled by the higher headquarters.

d. The standard transportation equipment situation, its biggest supply problem concerning its sphere of operations.

e. The quantity of auxiliary transportation equipment, composition, and capabilities.

f. The general conditions pertaining to the operational sphere of its regular units, the rear area service units and its agencies.

g. The location of the service of supply command in a higher headquarters.

h. The condition of the base section area including the following factors:
whether the base section headquarters is conveniently located or not,
whether it is properly camouflaged and secured, the availability of roads to
the front and rear in order to facilitate the transportation of supplies and the
distance on the roads, the availability of local equipment and the political
influences of the inhabitants.[7]

U.S. Army doctrine in 1950 prescribed that an officer on the commander's
staff, the S-4 or G-4, was responsible for formulating logistical plans to support
operations, establishing logistical policy, estimating logistical requirements, and
overseeing the execution of support to the combat forces. However, both the
NKPA and CCF in Korea took a much different doctrinal approach. In both
Communist armies, the rear service organization at each echelon was responsible for most routine matters of supply and administration, thus leaving the
commander and staff free to focus almost exclusively on operational concerns.[8]
The commander of the rear services organization at each level was both staff
officer and operator. As a logistical staff officer, he was responsible for all
classes of supply and provided instructions to subordinate units of the command
regarding

a. The ammunition and petroleum consumption of each subordinate unit;

b. The quantity of reserve supplies that the various subordinate units are
supposed to retain towards the termination of hostilities;

c. The main routes of transportation leading to the front and rear;

d. Warehouses and their locations;

e. The delivery procedure for the supplying of front line units;

f. In the event of a shortage of transportation facilities a procedure ... to
determine the priority of supplies.[9]

As a logistical operator, the commander of the rear services organization at
each echelon controlled storage and issue facilities, allocated and controlled
transport, operated maintenance facilities, administered matters of finance including payment for supplies requisitioned in the local area, and exercised administrative control over unit medical and veterinary services.[10] He was also
responsible for rear area security.[11]

Both the NKPA and the CCF subscribed, as did the U.S. Army, to the principle that the impetus of supply should be from the rear.[12] That is, higher echelons
were responsible for supporting lower echelons by delivering supplies and other
logistical support down to subordinate units. With respect to the movement of
supplies down to subordinate units, however, it was not unusual for the chief of

the rear services at a higher echelon to direct subordinate units to pick up supplies at depots located well to the rear.

Both the NKPA and CCF made it a matter of principle to make maximum use of captured matérial following the ninth of Mao Tse-tung's "Ten Commandments" of strategy: "Replenish ourselves by the capture of all enemy arms and most of his personnel. The source of men and material for our army is the front."[13] Both armies also practiced preplanned supply to the maximum extent possible, but here NKPA doctrine differed substantially from that of the CCF in Korea. The NKPA followed the Soviet model closely in insisting on a rigid system of priorities to regulate the flow of supplies to the front, with ammunition and fuel taking priority over all other classes of supply.[14] These priorities were determined by the importance of the mission assigned to the unit involved, and frontline combat units had absolute priority over units of the second and rear echelons.[15] The CCF system, on the other hand, took a much more flexible approach which afforded the commander at each level much greater leeway in providing support to his forces. The execution of plans, including logistical plans, was decentralized, although adherence to the established plan was demanded, at least in the initial phases of an operation.[16] Indeed, CCF commanders did not hesitate to modify existing methods to meet changing conditions.[17]

With respect to transport doctrine, the NKPA generally followed the Soviet model while the CCF had no agreed-on logistical doctrine at all concerning the employment of transport units. However, both the NKPA and the CCF in Korea emphasized the use of railroads for the movement of supplies to forward units.[18] Motor transport was reserved for logistical movements in the rear areas. Administrative and tactical movements of units was normally carried out by road marches using organic unit transport. Frontline transport, both tactical and logistical, was accomplished primarily by animal transport and porters.

NKPA-CCF LOGISTICAL ORGANIZATION

During the Korean War, determining the organization of NKPA and CCF units, either combat or support, was difficult for United Nations Command intelligence agencies, and accurate description of NKPA and CCF organizations remains a difficult problem today in the absence of access to definitive North Korean and Chinese documents. The task is made more complex by the fact that apparently until late in the war neither the NKPA nor the CCF attempted to standardize the organization of their combat units, and support units remained until the end somewhat "catch-as-catch-can." Moreover, there was considerable variation in the number of men, animals, and equipment as well as in the organizational structure of similar type units of both armies throughout the war.[19]

NKPA Logistical Organization

The logistical organization of the NKPA closely followed the Soviet pattern, with several variations to account for the particular traditions and needs of the North Korean government and armed forces. At each echelon of command from the Ministry of Defense to the infantry regiment, three key organizations provided logistical support: the technical services, the Ordnance Section of the separate artillery organization (department or section) at each level, and a Rear Service Department (RSD) or Rear Service Section (RSS) at each level.[20] The supply and maintenance of technical equipment (e.g., radios and medical supplies) was the responsibility of the technical service (e.g., Signal Corps or Medical Department) concerned. The requisition, storage, issue, and maintenance of arms and ammunition was a responsibility of the Ordnance Section in the artillery organization at each echelon. The RSD/RSS at each level was the primary logistical organization and was responsible for the procurement and distribution of all supplies (except for technical equipment, weapons, and ammunition) as well as for the operation of supply depots, the control of transport and service units, the maintenance of lines of communications, and rear area security. As one of the three deputy commanders at each echelon of the NKPA, the chief of the RSD/RSS both commanded the assigned and attached logistical support units and functioned as the staff officer for logistics. He was required to render logistical support to all forces stationed in or passing through his assigned geographical area and controlled the movement of supplies to supported units and forward depots. He assigned or attached transport and other logistical units to subordinate commands as necessary and usually retained direct control of a portion of the available transport. Operational planning at each echelon was closely coordinated among the Chief of Staff (for tactical plans), the chief of the Artillery Section (for required arms and ammunition), and the chief of the Rear Service Department.[21]

The North Korean Ministry of National Defense

At the beginning of the Korean War, the North Koreans attempted to control national economic affairs through a National Planning Committee. The Committee failed to function satisfactorily and the Ministry of National Defense (MND) under Marshal Choe Yong Gun soon assumed full control of the procurement, both internal and external, of all military supplies without regard to the needs of the civilian economy.[22] The MND (depicted in Diagram 3.1) took over the subordinate agencies of the National Planning Committee and created several new agencies to oversee logistical planning, production, transportation, and the purchase and distribution of war matériel. Two of these agencies were the Trade Branch Office, responsible for the purchase of arms and equipment from the Soviet Union, and the Antung Military Affairs Committee, a liaison office of the Sinuiju Military Affairs Committee, which coordinated with the

Chinese Communist government for the acquisition of supplies and their movement into North Korea through the town of Antung.

Diagram 3.1
North Korean Ministry of National Defense (June 1950)

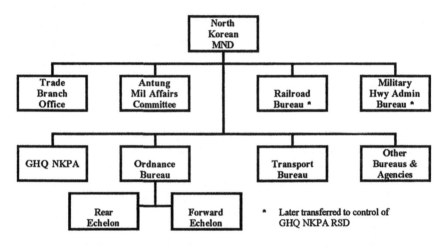

Once supplies were acquired and delivered to North Korea, they came under the control of one of several bureaus in the MND responsible for logistical matters. In June 1950, the four most important of these bureaus were the Ordnance Bureau, the Transportation Bureau, the Railroad Bureau, and the Military Highway Administration Bureau. Smaller bureaus subordinate to the MND (for example, the Food and Clothing Bureau) handled less important logistical functions.[23] The Railroad Bureau soon achieved the status of an independent ministry, and the Military Highway Administration Bureau as well as important parts of the Transportation Bureau were transferred to the control of the Rear Services Department (RSD) of NKPA General Headquarters (GHQ NKPA).[24]

The Ordnance Bureau of the MND was responsible for the procurement, production, maintenance, and distribution of all ordnance equipment and munitions.[25] The Ordnance Bureau was divided into a Rear and a Forward Echelon. The Rear Echelon, consisting of Planning, General Affairs, Arms and Equipment, Ammunition, Transportation, and Repair Departments, determined requirements and allocations for the combat units; arranged procurement, storage, and issue of arms and ammunition; and arranged for the movement of such supplies to the ordnance depots of the Ordnance Bureau and the NKPA corps. The Forward Echelon of the Ordnance Bureau was divided into four sections (Planning, Arms and Equipment, Ammunition, and General Affairs) and acted as an intermediary between the Rear Echelon and the ordnance battalions organic to the NKPA corps, receiving, processing, and passing on to the Rear Echelon the requisitions from the corps. The Forward Echelon was purely a staff agency and did not control depots, repair facilities, or transportation. All major ordnance storage and repair facilities and the transportation of ordnance items were managed by the Rear Echelon.

The Transportation Bureau of the MND was organized into ten departments: Planning and Organization, Rear Supply, Forward Supply, Repair and Maintenance, Inspectorate, Transportation, Officer Personnel, Administration, Finance, and Statistical.[26] In general the Transportation Bureau was responsible for all matters having to do with military highway transportation and motor vehicles, but many of its more important functions were assumed by the Transportation Bureau of GHQ NKPA after June 1950. The Planning and Organization Department controlled requisitions for motor vehicles and allocated vehicles in accordance with established tables of organization. The Forward Supply Department processed requests for vehicles received from the combat units and passed them to the Rear Supply Department which handled distribution of the vehicles to the combat units. The Repair and Maintenance Department inspected and repaired vehicles prior to their delivery to using units.[27] Such work was accomplished in the Department's repair shop in Pyongyang or by private garages under contract. The Inspectorate Department enforced regulations regarding the care and maintenance of vehicles by the combat units through a system of inspectors in the field. The Transportation Department coordinated transportation requests from the various departments of the Transportation Bureau and other MND agencies.

NKPA General Headquarters

The General Headquarters, North Korean People's Army (GHQ NKPA), was the highest level of command for the North Korean armed forces and controlled a subordinate Front (Army Group) headquarters, corps in reserve, and various combat support and combat service support units not organic to corps and divisions.[28] The GHQ NKPA was located in Pyongyang at the beginning of the war but retreated to Manchuria during the rout of the NKPA after the UNC landing at Inchon. It returned to North Korea in December 1950 and was subsequently located at Sopo near Pyongyang for the duration of the war. The logistical structure at GHQ NKPA level (depicted in Diagram 3.2) replicated that of the Ministry of National Defense. An Ordnance Bureau subordinate to the GHQ NKPA Artillery Department operated a major ordnance depot and handled matters pertaining to arms and ammunition. The GHQ NKPA Rear Services Department, commanded by General Choe Hong Kup, managed other supply and transportation matters and operated the main depots of the NKPA.[29]

Diagram 3.2
NKPA General Headquarters

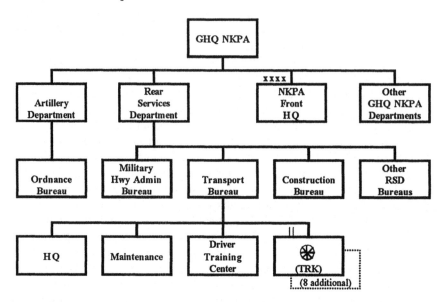

The GHQ NKPA Rear Services Department controlled three major logistical bureaus (Transportation, Construction, and, after 1950, Military Highway Administration) and a number of smaller ones.[30] The Transportation Bureau of GHQ NKPA consisted of a headquarters element, a maintenance unit, a driver training center, and nine independent truck battalions. Each of the independent truck battalions was authorized approximately 120 task vehicles and was normally utilized under direct GHQ NKPA Rear Service Department control to supplement the North Korean railroad system in the movement of supplies from the Manchurian border to NKPA rear area supply installations, to move supplies from railheads to depots, and to carry out interdepot movements.[31] In some cases, one or more of the independent truck battalions was placed under the operational control of lower echelon headquarters. The Military Highway Administration Bureau was responsible for highway security and maintenance, bridge repair, and traffic control and consisted of a headquarters and a number of military highway administration regiments.[32] The Construction Bureau carried out military construction and engineering tasks and consisted of a headquarters and three construction brigades, each of which had a headquarters and eight construction battalions.

NKPA Front Headquarters

The GHQ NKPA planned and directed the invasion of South Korea from Py-ongyang during the early stages of the war, but the advance of the NKPA into the Republic of Korea necessitated the creation of a Front Headquarters to con-trol the two committed NKPA corps.[33] The NKPA Front Headquarters was first reported at Seoul in July 1950 and subsequently directed the operations on the Pusan Perimeter from Kumchon. During the retrograde movement and collapse of the NKPA after Inchon, the Front Headquarters remained in the Yangdok-Kumwha area with remnants of the NKPA II Corps to direct guerilla operations. The Front Headquarters reemerged again in June 1951 and controlled the NKPA II, III, V, and VII Corps on the eastern portion of the front. It subsequently controlled a varying number of committed NKPA corps in the eastern sector until the end of the war. The highest tactical command echelon of the NKPA, the Front Headquarters corresponded to an army group headquarters. It repli-cated the logistical structure of the Ministry of National Defense and GHQ NKPA, with an Ordnance Section subordinate to the Front Artillery Department and a Rear Service Department, both of which operated army group level depots and performed the usual logistical functions.[34]

The NKPA Corps

At corps level, NKPA logistical functions were planned, executed, and super-vised by the Ordnance Section of the corps Artillery Section and by a corps Rear Service Section (depicted in Diagram 3.3), which consisted of a guard company, a transportation battalion, a field hospital and associated evacuation battalion, and a staff element consisting of a political section, a supply section, and ten staff sections responsible for various categories of supply as well as the pro-curement and supervision of civilian labor.[35] The corps Ordnance Section proc-essed requisitions for weapons and ammunition and operated the corps ammuni-tion dump and ordnance maintenance facility. The Supply Section of the corps Rear Service Section staff element operated a corps supply dump and each of the staff element's ten staff sections (Organization and Planning, Administra-tion, Provisions, Clothing, Ordnance, Food Service, Transportation, Intendance and Finance, Vehicle Maintenance, Road Maintenance, Medical, and Fuel), each of which managed the requisition, receipt, storage, transport, and issue of the supplies for which it was responsible in much the same way as was done at higher echelons.[36] The NKPA corps transportation battalion probably had 120 trucks.[37]

Diagram 3.3
NKPA Corps Logistical Organizations

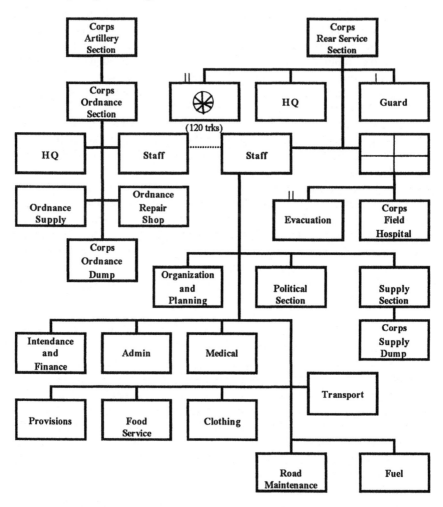

The NKPA Infantry Division

   The NKPA infantry divisions which participated in the invasion of South Korea in the summer of 1950 were organized as shown in Diagram 3.4. Following the rout of the NKPA in September 1950 after the UNC landings at Inchon and the break-out from the Pusan Perimeter, the surviving NKPA forces were reorganized and a slightly smaller NKPA infantry division emerged, albeit one with a heavier support component. The organization of this new type NKPA infantry division as it existed in 1953 is shown in Diagram 3.5. In both types of division, the commander of the artillery regiment was responsible for the supply of all

Diagram 3.4
NKPA Infantry Division (1950)

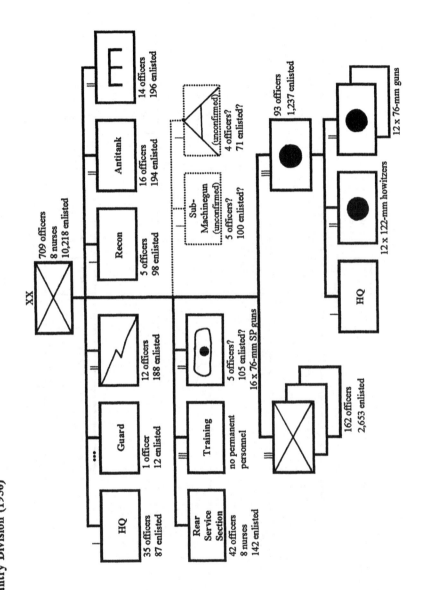

XX

709 officers
8 nurses
10,218 enlisted

HQ
35 officers
87 enlisted

Guard
1 officer
12 enlisted

12 officers
188 enlisted

Recon
5 officers
98 enlisted

Antitank
16 officers
194 enlisted

E
14 officers
196 enlisted

Sub-
Machinegun
(unconfirmed)
5 officers?
100 enlisted?

(unconfirmed)
4 officers?
71 enlisted?

Rear
Service
Section
42 officers
8 nurses
142 enlisted

Training
no permanent
personnel

5 officers?
105 enlisted?
16 x 76-mm SP guns

162 officers
2,653 enlisted

93 officers
1,237 enlisted

HQ

12 x 122-mm howitzers

12 x 76-mm guns

Diagram 3.5
NKPA Infantry Division (1953)

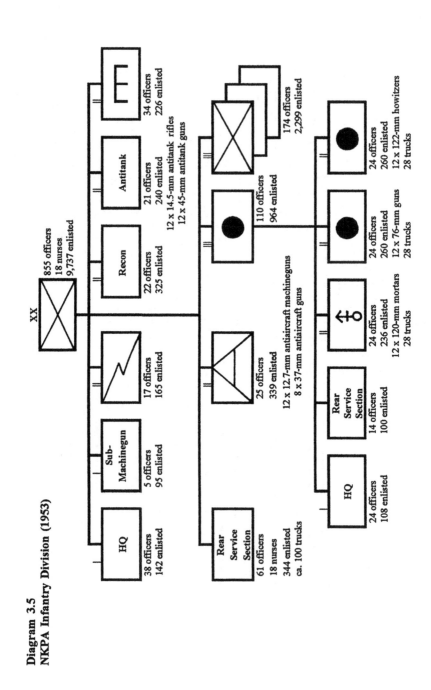

XX

855 officers
18 nurses
9,737 enlisted

HQ

38 officers
142 enlisted

Sub-
Machinegun

5 officers
95 enlisted

17 officers
165 enlisted

Recon

22 officers
325 enlisted

Antitank

21 officers
240 enlisted
12 x 14.5-mm antitank rifles
12 x 45-mm antitank guns

E

34 officers
226 enlisted

Rear
Service
Section

61 officers
18 nurses
344 enlisted
ca. 100 trucks

25 officers
339 enlisted
12 x 12.7-mm antiaircraft machineguns
8 x 37-mm antiaircraft guns

110 officers
964 enlisted

174 officers
2,299 enlisted

HQ

24 officers
108 enlisted

Rear
Service
Section

14 officers
100 enlisted

24 officers
236 enlisted
12 x 120-mm mortars
28 trucks

24 officers
260 enlisted
12 x 76-mm guns
28 trucks

24 officers
260 enlisted
12 x 122-mm howitzers
28 trucks

weapons and ammunition as well as the maintenance and evacuation of ordnance matériel, while the Assistant Division Commander for Rear Services supervised the operations of the division Rear Service Section.

The Rear Service Section of the 10,935-man June 1950 NKPA infantry division was authorized forty-two officers, eight female nurses, and 142 enlisted
men, organized as shown in Diagram 3.6.[38] The Supply Section was the heart of
the Rear Service Section's operational capability. Although charged with operating the division supply dump, the Supply Section was essentially a staff element responsible for the requisition, storage, and distribution of all equipment
and supplies (other than arms and ammunition) and for the supervision of transport, medical, and finance matters. The divisional transportation company consisted of six officers and sixty-four enlisted men and was authorized about fifty
trucks, ten horse-drawn wagons, six or seven motorcycles, and about twenty ox-
carts.[39] The divisional medical company consisted of fourteen officers, eight
female nurses, and forty-two enlisted men at full strength.[40] The medical company operated a divisional field hospital and provided field medical personnel to
the combat units and other elements of the division. The guard platoon of one
officer and twenty-three enlisted men, a part of the divisional guard company,
provided security for supply installations.

Diagram 3.6
Rear Service Section, NKPA Infantry Division (1950)

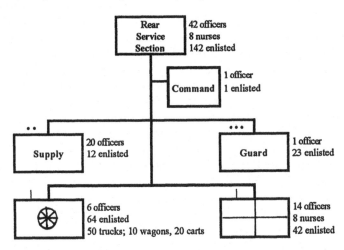

The structure of the Rear Service Section of the later (April 1953) 10,610-
man NKPA infantry division was considerably larger, with sixty-one officers,
eighteen nurses, and 344 enlisted men organized as shown in Diagram 3.7. The
Rear Service Section transportation company was authorized approximately 100

trucks, and the medical battalion operated the division hospital and also provided a medical company (seven officers and fifty enlisted men) to support each of the division's infantry regiments.[41]

Diagram 3.7
Rear Service Section, NKPA Infantry Division (1953)

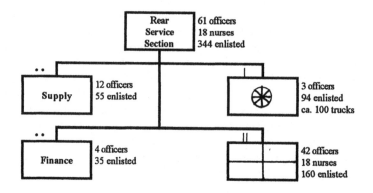

The Rear Service Section of the 1950 NKPA infantry regiment was authorized fourteen officers and 107 enlisted men organized in a finance section, an intendance section, a rations and forage section, a clothing section, a general affairs section, a veterinary section, a medical section, a supply platoon, and a transportation platoon.[42] Some authorities reported that the regimental Rear Service Section also included a thirty-man maintenance platoon, a twenty-man regimental band (probably used as litter bearers), and twenty-three trucks.[43] The Rear Service Section of the 1953 NKPA infantry regiment had an authorized strength of seven officers and fifty-six enlisted men and consisted of a finance section, a supply section, a transportation section, and a medical company attached from the Division Rear Service Section medical battalion.[44] In addition, the divisional artillery regiment had an organic Rear Service Section of fourteen officers and 100 EM.

The supply and transportation organization at the NKPA infantry battalion level was minimal, consisting of one officer and five enlisted men (a supply sergeant, an ammunition and weapons sergeant, two cooks, and a barber/messenger).[45] The infantry battalion was not authorized any transport but probably had a few animal-drawn carts and levied the civilian population for porters as necessary. Principal functions of the battalion supply section were to supervise delivery of food, ammunition, and other supplies from higher echelons, to operate the battalion supply distribution point, and to forage for food in nearby villages.

CCF Logistical Organization

The logistical organization of the CCF in Korea differed from that of the NKPA in that all logistical services and supplies, including weapons and ammunition, were managed by a rear services organization at each echelon. These rear services organizations were responsible for logistical planning, procurement, the operation of storage facilities, maintenance, and transportation. However, as with the U.S. system, medical supplies were generally handled in medical rather than supply channels.[46]

Ministry of Defense, People's Republic of China

At the highest level, the logistical support of the CCF in Korea was controlled by the Ministry of Defense in Peking. This control was exercised through a General Rear Services Department (GRSD) responsible for establishing logistical policy and overseeing the planning and operations of the rear services organizations of all ground, sea, and air forces.[47] Within the Ministry of Defense, two additional departments provided independent controls on military logistical support. The Finance Department administered and distributed funds for military purposes, and the General Military Equipment Department was responsible for construction and the production of munitions.

Rear Services Department, People's Liberation Army

The General Staff of the People's Liberation Army (PLA) was not deeply involved with matters of logistics and focused instead on intelligence, operations, and personnel administration.[48] The Rear Services Department (RSD) of the PLA, located in Peking, was the agency responsible to the General Rear Services Department of the Ministry of Defense for the logistical support of the military units subordinate to GHQ PLA.[49] During the Korean War period, the GHQ Rear Services Department was headed successively by Chang Ling-pu and Chan Ch'un-ch'uan. The six major departments of the GHQ Rear Services Department were Political, Transportation, Finance, Supply, Ordnance, and Health.[50] The general logistical structure of the PLA also included a Motor Transport Corps and a Railway Corps separate from the regular combat forces. These organizations were of considerable size and regulated highway and rail transport throughout China.[51]

Rear Services Department, PLA Field Army

In 1949, following the Chinese Civil War, China was divided into six geographical military areas and two autonomous regions to facilitate military and administrative control. The four Field Armies into which the PLA had been reorganized in the fall of 1948 were deployed in four of the military regions

(Northwest, Southwest, Central/South, and East China).[52] The PLA Field Army was a flexible organization, and its size and composition varied according to its mission, the anticipated threat, and the nature of the region to which it was assigned.[53] Each Field Army controlled one or more Army Groups, each of which was subdivided into Armies (corps equivalents) of two to four (usually three) divisions each. In addition to its assigned Army Groups, each Field Army controlled a number of independent combat support and combat service support units and each had its own Rear Services Department, which advised the commander on logistical policy, conducted logistical planning, operated logistical facilities, and controlled logistical troops assigned or attached to the Field Army. Each Field Army Rear Services Department had two major subordinate elements: a Health Department and a Supply Department. Service units controlled by the Field Army included truck regiments, Railway Corps elements, engineer units, and medical units as well as a variety of military and civilian labor units and quasi-military transportation organizations, some of which could be attached to subordinate Army Groups. When operating independently, the Field Army was allocated sufficient service troops to establish a logistical command capable of supporting as many as 750,000 troops. Normally, the Field Army commander retained under his direct control only those service troops required to support the Field Army headquarters and those forces not assigned to the subordinate Army Groups. Thus, most logistical tasks in a theater of operations were carried out in the Army Group or Army rear areas, and large logistical formations directly subordinate to the Field Army were not required.

Rear Services Department, GHQ, CCF in Korea

The Chinese Communist forces deployed in Korea after October 1950 in effect constituted a Field Army for which a suitable logistical support structure had to be created from scratch. Consequently, given the normal flexibility in organization of the PLA, the logistical structure supporting the CCF in Korea was different in some ways from that found in the four static Field Armies in China (which themselves varied) and exhibited considerable internal variation as well.[54] Moreover, the logistical organization of the CCF in Korea underwent several major revisions during the course of the Korean War, each of which tended toward closer approximation of the Soviet pattern.[55]

Initially, the Chinese Armies deployed in Korea were responsible for their own logistical support, but early in 1951 the GHQ CCF in Korea organized a Rear Services Department similar to that of a PLA Field Army.[56] This organization was apparently located in Mukden, Manchuria, and was operated by the headquarters of the North East China Military Area throughout the Korean War.[57] The GHQ CCF Rear Services Department assumed responsibility for the procurement, movement, storage, and issue of all supplies for the CCF in Korea and was commanded by General T'ao Ying, who was both the commander of the Rear Services Department and the principal logistics staff officer of the

GHQ CCF.[58] The GHQ CCF Rear Services Department was initially organized with a command section, a staff section, a Transportation Department, which controlled a number of independent truck regiments, and a Supply Base, which controlled three Branch Units (each of which was responsible for the support of three CCF armies).[59]

A major change in the structure of the GHQ CCF Rear Services Department occurred in January 1951, when the responsibility of the Branch Units was shifted from the support of designated tactical units to an area basis. The number of Branch Units was then increased from three to seven and the scope of their responsibilities was enlarged.[60] The resulting organization of the GHQ CCF Rear Services Department is shown in Diagram 3.8. Only five of the seven new Branch Units created in January 1951 were actually located in Korea.[61] The 1st, 2nd, and 3rd Branch Units were located at Samdung, Yangdok, and Sariwon, respectively, and supported CCF tactical units and installations in the forward and intermediate rear areas. The 4th Branch Unit at Kujang-dong and

Diagram 3.8
Rear Services Department, GHQ, CCF in Korea (post-1950)

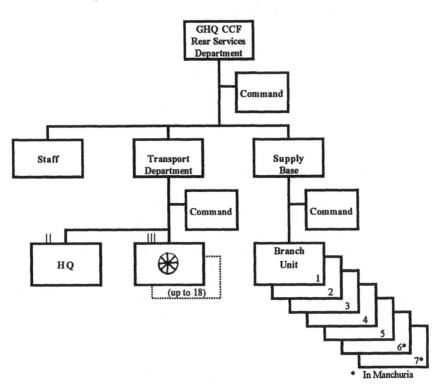

the 5th Branch Unit at Pyongyang served in a general support role, servicing CCF reserve armies and service units in the rear areas and supporting the three forward Branch Units. The 6th and 7th Branch Units also served in a general support role but were located in Manchuria.

The Transportation Department was also reorganized in January 1951, with a headquarters battalion and eight truck regiments (each of which had a complement of about 111 officers, 1,206 enlisted men, and 318 trucks organized in six truck companies, a maintenance company, a guard company, a labor company, a supply platoon, and a medical section).[62] Some of these truck regiments were attached to the Branch Units, and all were generally employed in the movement of supplies in the rear areas.

The Branch Units were not supply depots but rather were administrative centers responsible for the processing of supply requisitions, the allocation of supplies, and the compilation of supply data.[63] However, personnel from the Branch Unit staff sections did operate a supply receiving point (usually located at a railhead or highway terminal, the function of which was to receive supplies and route them via the Main Depots to the Sub-Depots normally within twenty-four hours of receipt), and the Branch Unit's own Rear Services Section provided support to the personnel of the Branch Unit itself.[64] In 1953, the typical Branch Unit (depicted in Diagram 3.9) was authorized 6,750 personnel organized into a command section, a political department, a staff department (with operations, communications, reconnaissance, administrative, medical, military affairs, ordnance, finance, food, clothing, transportation, cryptographic, and rear service sections), a labor battalion, a security regiment, an organic transportation regiment, an attached transportation truck regiment, and a supply department.[65] The Branch Unit Supply Department consisted of approximately 3,464 personnel organized in a command section, a political section, and a staff section. Each Branch Unit Supply Department controlled three to six Main Depots, each of which had a strength of approximately 689 personnel and in turn controlled three to six Sub-Depots.

Each Main Depot was organized along lines similar to that of the Branch Unit and consisted of a command section, an administrative unit, a field hospital, a labor group composed of personnel from the Branch Unit labor battalion, and a security unit composed of personnel from the Branch Unit security regiment.[66] The Main Depot was primarily an administrative entity, and the actual receipt, storage, and issue of supplies was accomplished by one of its three to six subordinate Sub-Depots, each of which was authorized a strength of approximately three officers, six accountants, six statistical clerks, six warehousemen, six supply men, three messengers, a guard platoon (about twenty-four men), and a labor team detailed from the Main Depot to load or unload supplies.[67] Each Sub-Depot was capable of supporting a division of 13,000 men and also supplied units located in or passing through its assigned geographical area.[68]

Diagram 3.9
Typical CCF Rear Services Department Branch Unit (ca. 1953)

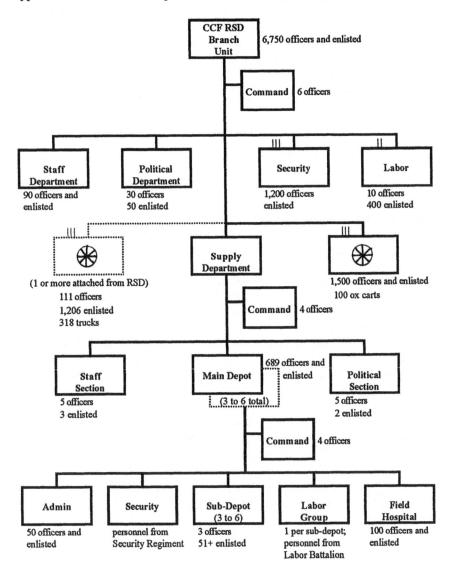

Rear Services Department, CCF Army Group in Korea

Ordinarily the PLA Army Group was a tactical organization and was not responsible for the logistical support of its subordinate Armies, which were supported directly by the Rear Services Department of the PLA Field Army. However, the special conditions in Korea prompted the CCF Army Groups in Korea (initially the XIIIth, with headquarters at Yangdok, and the IXth, with headquarters at Sohung) to create full-fledged Rear Services Departments and to assume responsibility for the support of their subordinate armies.[69] As organized in 1953, the CCF Army Group Rear Services Department (depicted in Diagram 3.10) was authorized 121 officers and 637 enlisted men in a command section, a supply section, a medical section, and a transportation section consisting of an animal transport company and two truck companies used to supplement the organic transport of the subordinate armies.[70] The personnel of the Supply Section operated a supply point supporting the Army Group headquarters and units in its area not assigned to the subordinate armies.

Rear Services Department, CCF Army in Korea

Each CCF Army in Korea had a Rear Services Department (depicted in Diagram 3.11), which controlled service units assigned or attached to the Army and which operated Army supply depots. The 1953 CCF Army Rear Services Department had an authorized strength of 233 officers and 1,227 enlisted men and was organized in a Command Section and three main sections: a Medical (or Sanitation) Section, a Supply Base, and a Miscellaneous Section.[71] The Medical Section was organized with a command and staff element, two litter units, and a field hospital capable of providing a company-sized medical unit to support personnel of the Army headquarters as well as four branch hospitals, each of which could be broken down further into four medical teams. The Supply Base was organized as shown in Diagram 3.12. The Supply Base operated an Army supply point co-located with the Branch Unit Main Depot supporting the Army. This supply point handled all requisitions from the Army Rear Services Department to the supporting Branch Unit, coordinated the movement of supplies to the Army and its subordinate divisions, and generally acted as a liaison office between the Army Rear Services Department and the supporting Branch Unit.[72] Its three mobile supply bases were usually designated the Rear Base, Central Base, and Forward Base, although their location and functions were somewhat flexible. Each Supply Base also had an attached security platoon of sixty to seventy-five men, who guarded the depots and supplies in transit and acted as air-spotters.[73] The organization and functions of the Miscellaneous Section remain unclear.[74]

Diagram 3.10
CCF Army Group in Korea (1953)

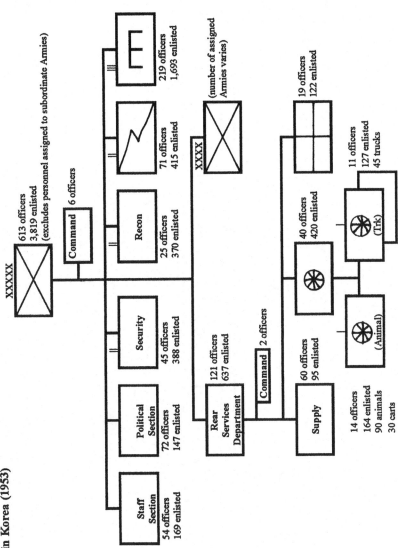

Diagram 3.11
CCF Army in Korea (1953)

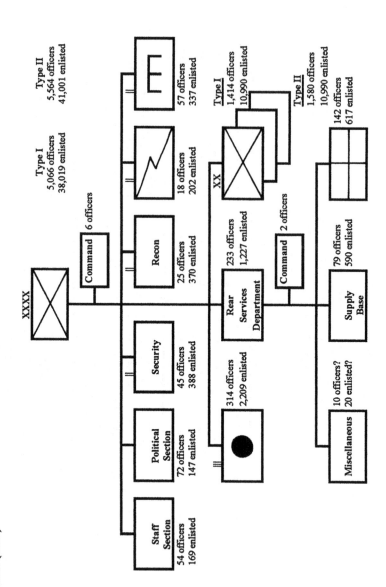

Diagram 3.12
Supply Base, Rear Services Department, CCF Army in Korea (1953)

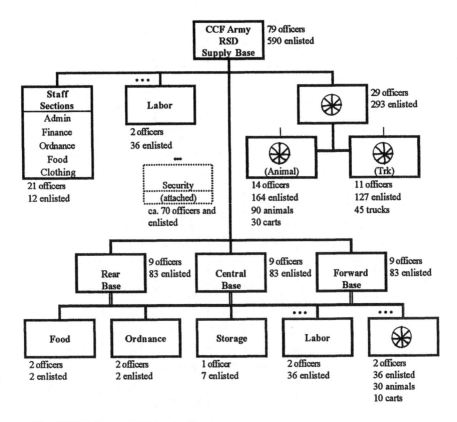

The CCF Infantry Division in Korea

As was the case at higher echelons, the logistical support structures of the two types of CCF infantry division in Korea (depicted in Diagram 3.13) seem to have varied in size and organization from time to time and place to place.[75] However, the basic structure is clear. Each CCF infantry division in Korea had a Rear Services Section responsible for the requisition of food, ammunition, and other supplies through the CCF supply system and for the procurement of food and other resources on the local market.[76] Normally the command post of all CCF combat units from Army down to regiment was divided into two groups: a Forward Tactical Command Post and a Rear Service Command Post commanded by the commander of the Rear Services Department/Section.[77] Only a few supply personnel were present at the forward tactical command post, primarily for liaison, advice to the commander, and support of command post personnel.[78]

Diagram 3.13
CCF Infantry Division

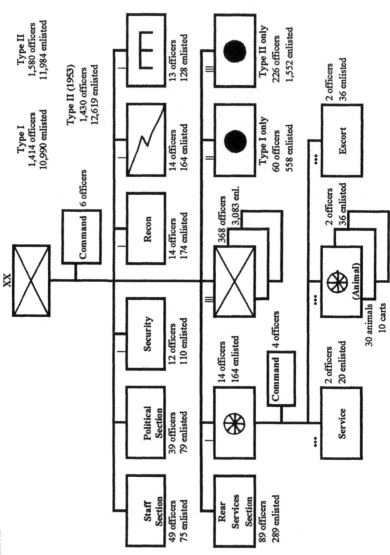

The Rear Services Section was identical in both types of CCF infantry division and consisted of eighty-nine officers and 289 enlisted men organized as shown in Diagram 3.14.[79] Personnel assigned to the various staff sections of the divisional Rear Services Section were responsible for logistical planning, estimates, records, requisitions, issues, and records. The division normally did not maintain depots but may have had temporary supply distribution points operated by personnel from the Rear Services Section.

Diagram 3.14
Rear Services Section, CCF Infantry Division (1953)

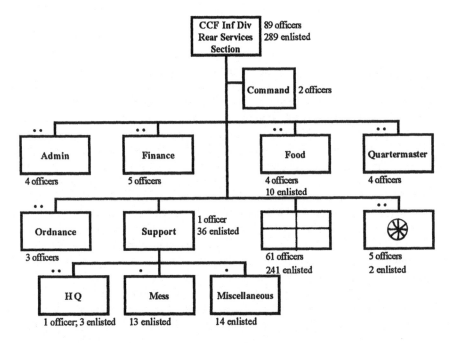

The infantry regiment was the lowest echelon of the CCF in Korea to have a separate rear services organization. In April 1953, the Rear Services Section of the CCF infantry regiment was authorized forty-three officers and 140 EM organized in a command section (five officers), an administrative section (five officers and five EM), a quartermaster section (five officers and two EM), an ordnance section (nine officers and ten EM), a finance section (five officers and two EM), a medical unit (six officers and twenty-eight EM), a litter company (eight officers and 116 EM) attached from the division Rear Services Section litter battalion, and a transportation company (eight officers, ninety-three EM, fifteen carts, and forty-five animals).[80]

Supply procedures at both the battalion and company level were simple and apparently did not require an extensive formal organizational structure. However, the CCF battalion did have a number of officers and men engaged in logistical tasks. A supply office in the battalion headquarters was manned by a supply officer in charge, an assistant supply officer, an officer in charge of food, and an officer in charge of ammunition and equipment.[81] Two enlisted clerks supported the battalion supply officer. The battalion headquarters itself had an organic mess (nine EM, one cart, and two animals) and medical support (one officer and six EM) and may also have had a service platoon, which provided porters.[82]

CONCLUSION

The logistical doctrine, methods, and organization of the North Korean and Chinese Communist forces in Korea changed substantially over the course of the Korean War, constantly adapting effectively to the changing operational environment. As the number of Communist troops in Korea increased after October 1950, the NKPA and CCF in Korea organized a logistical system fully capable of meeting the requirements of a large-scale static defense and limited offensive action. The modern mechanized army with which North Korea attacked South Korea in June 1950 was almost totally destroyed after the UNC Inchon landings in September 1950, and the reorganized North Korean forces which emerged during the winter of 1950-1951, as well as the newly introduced Chinese Communist forces, at first had only the barest essential supporting elements and relied on relatively small and primitive supply and transport elements. But as the war progressed, both the NKPA and the CCF in Korea developed logistical organizations of greater strength and mechanization at all echelons. The resulting NKPA and CCF logistical systems exhibited considerable flexibility and innovation as well as a great deal of internal variation in size, structure, and equipment, which often baffled UNC intelligence analysts. By early 1953, the Communist combat forces were being well supported by numerous logistical units fully capable of providing all that was needed for a prolonged static defense and limited offensive actions. By the end of the war in July 1953, the NKPA and CCF logistical systems were on the verge of being able to support a massive and extended offensive campaign, which would have constituted a serious threat to the United Nations forces.

NOTES

1. "Chinese Communist Army and North Korean Army Logistics and Class Supply," *USAFFE Intelligence Digest*, VI, no. 4 (April 1956), 50; "The Enemy Supply System in North Korea," *USAFFE Intelligence Digest*, II, no. 4 (2 September 1953), 15–16; Head-

quarters, Department of the Army, Office of the Assistant Chief of Staff for Intelligence, *Logistical Data for the Chinese Communist Army* (Washington: Headquarters, Department of the Army, Office of the Assistant Chief of Staff for Intelligence, 1959), 1.

2. General Headquarters, Far East Command, Military Intelligence Section, Allied Translator and Interpreter Service, "Interrogation Reports—North Korean Forces: North Korean Logistics," *ATIS Research Supplement,* Issue No. 1 (19 October 1950), 17–27; "The Enemy Supply System in North Korea," 16.

3. Eliot A. Cohen and John Gooch, *Military Misfortunes: The Anatomy of Failure in War* (New York: Vintage Books, 1991), 177.

4. "Interrogation Reports—North Korean Forces: North Korean Logistics," 17; "The Chinese Communist Field Army," *USAFFE Intelligence Digest,* V, no. 10 (October 1955), 3.

5. "Interrogation Reports—North Korean Forces: North Korean Logistics," 17.

6. Avrosimov Chilimuniya and Shih-ku-li-tieh-tzu, *Chinese Communist General Principles of Army Group Tactics* (2 volumes, Manila: General Headquarters, Far East Command, Military Intelligence Section, General Staff, 1951), I, 39. This was a Chinese translation and adaptation of a Soviet doctrinal manual and was translated into English by the Military Intelligence Section, Far East Command.

7. *Chinese Communist General Principles of Army Group Tactics,* I, 39–40.

8. "Interrogation Reports—North Korean Forces: North Korean Logistics," 17. The functions of the various staff departments at each echelon in the NKPA forces are described in General Headquarters, Far East Command, Military Intelligence Section, Allied Translator and Interpreter Service, "Enemy Documents, Korean Operations," *ATIS Research Supplement,* Issue No. 5 (13 December 1950), 4–7. The document cited is an English translation of a manual entitled "Staff Department Field Manual" issued by the National Defense Bureau, North Korean Democratic Republic, in 1949 and captured near Tuksong-dong on 12 August 1950.

9. *Chinese Communist General Principles of Army Group Tactics,* I, 41.

10. "Interrogation Reports—North Korean Forces: North Korean Logistics," 17. The technical branches retained responsibility for maintenance of specialized equipment pertaining to their branch, and medical units had their own channels for supply and technical matters.

11. *Chinese Communist General Principles of Army Group Tactics,* I, 41–42.

12. "Interrogation Reports—North Korean Forces: North Korean Logistics," 18; "Chinese Communist Army and North Korean Army Logistics and Class Supply," 53; James A. Huston, *Guns and Butter, Powder and Rice: U.S. Army Logistics in the Korean War* (Selinsgrove, PA: Susquehanna University Press, 1989), 353.

13. From Mao's *The Turning Point in China* (circa 1946), cited by Edgar O'Ballance, *The Red Army of China: A Short History* (New York: Frederick A. Praeger, 1963), 221; Robert B. Rigg, *Red China's Fighting Hordes* (rev. ed., Harrisburg, PA: The Military Service Publishing Company, 1952), 184. Rigg (p. 184) cites the adage of the ancient Chinese philosopher of war Sun Tzu to the effect that "one cartload of the enemy's provisions is equivalent to twenty of one's own."

14. "Interrogation Reports—North Korean Forces: North Korean Logistics," 18; General Headquarters, Far East Command, Military Intelligence Section, Allied Translator and Interpreter Service, "Interrogation Reports—North Korean Forces: Typical North Korean Infantry Division," *ATIS Research Supplement,* Issue No. 1 (19 October 1950), 11.

15. *Chinese Communist General Principles of Army Group Tactics*, I, 41.

16. "The Chinese Communist Field Army," *USAFFE Intelligence Digest*, V, no. 10 (October 1955), 3.

17. Headquarters, Eighth United States Army, Assistant Chief of Staff G-2/Headquarters, United States Fifth Air Force, Assistant Chief of Staff A-2, *Supply and Transportation System of the Chinese Communist and North Korean Forces in Korea* ([Tokyo]: Headquarters, Eighth United States Army, Assistant Chief of Staff G-2/Headquarters, United States Fifth Air Force, Assistant Chief of Staff A-2, 23 September 1951), 12, 27, and 44.

18. "Interrogation Reports-North Korean Forces: North Korean Logistics," 17–18.

19. UNC intelligence agencies devoted a great deal of effort in trying to determine the composition of various types of NKPA and CCF units. That effort is reflected in the series of organizational diagrams which follow. These diagrams, which must be considered only suggestive, were compiled from five main sources: *Supply and Transportation System of the Chinese Communist and North Korean Forces in Korea*; Headquarters, Department of the Army, Office of the Assistant Chief of Staff, G-2, *North Korean Order of Battle* (Intelligence Research Project No. 5942, Washington: Headquarters, Department of the Army, Office of the Assistant Chief of Staff, G-2, 1 September 1950); General Headquarters, Far East Command, Military Intelligence Section, Theater Intelligence Division, Order of Battle Branch, *Order of Battle Information: Chinese Communist Forces in Korea, Table of Organization and Equipment* ([Tokyo]: General Headquarters, Far East Command, Military Intelligence Section, Theater Intelligence Division, Order of Battle Branch, 30 October 1951); General Headquarters, Far East Command, Military Intelligence Section, General Staff, *History of the North Korean Army* ([Tokyo]: General Headquarters, Far East Command, Military Intelligence Section, General Staff, 31 July 1952); and Headquarters, United States Army Forces, Far East (Advanced), Office of the Assistant Chief of Staff, G-2, *Chinese Communist Ground Forces in Korea: Tables of Organization and Equipment* (APO 500: Headquarters, United States Army Forces, Far East (Advanced), Office of the Assistant Chief of Staff, G-2, 1 March 1953).

20. "Chinese Communist Army and North Korean Army Logistics and Class Supply," 55. Compared to their U.S. counterparts, NKPA and CCF units at all levels had a much lower ratio of service to combat troops, but both the NKPA and the CCF in Korea employed large numbers of nonmilitary personnel, both paid and conscripted, to perform necessary logistical tasks.

21. "Chinese Communist Army and North Korean Army Logistics and Class Supply," 57.

22. *Supply and Transportation System of the Chinese Communist and North Korean Forces in Korea*, 45–46.

23. *Supply and Transportation System of the Chinese Communist and North Korean Forces in Korea*, 52–53.

24. The Railroad Bureau (Ministry) and the Military Highway Administration Bureau are discussed later and in Chapter 6.

25. *Supply and Transportation System of the Chinese Communist and North Korean Forces in Korea*, 51–52.

26. *Supply and Transportation System of the Chinese Communist and North Korean Forces in Korea*, 46–48.

27. *Supply and Transportation System of the Chinese Communist and North Korean Forces in Korea*, 47. Such repair was necessary in that most newly acquired vehicles

were in poor condition. Perhaps 7 percent of the vehicles received from the Soviet Union were not in operating condition, and vehicles requisitioned from private North Korean firms usually had to be overhauled before they could be issued to NKPA units.

28. *History of the North Korean Army*, 84; "Chinese Communist Army and North Korean Army Logistics and Class Supply," 56.

29. Headquarters, United States Army Forces, Far East (Advanced), Office of the Assistant Chief of Staff, G-2, *Chinese Communist Ground Forces in Korea: Unit and Personality List* (APO 500: Headquarters, United States Army Forces Far East (Advanced), Office of the Assistant Chief of Staff G-2, 30 November 1953), 79.

30. Headquarters, United States Army Forces, Far East, and Eighth United States Army, Office of the Assistant Chief of Staff, G-2, *Intelligence Estimate Korea—March 1955* (APO 343: Headquarters, United States Army Forces Far East and Eighth United States Army, Office of the Assistant Chief of Staff, G-2, 3 March 1955), 12–13. The smaller bureaus (Finance, Ration Supply, Clothing Supply, POL Supply, Organization and Planning, Billeting, Accounts and Supply, Munitions Production, and Rear Services Administration) provided administrative services and support. In the post-Korean War period (March 1955), the GHQ NKPA RSD had a strength of 41,977 personnel, including 4,040 in the Transportation Bureau, 8,480 in the Military Roads Administration Bureau, and 29,297 in the Construction Bureau. Its strength in May 1953 was probably about the same.

31. "Enemy Motor Transport In North Korea," *USAFFE Intelligence Digest*, I, no. 9 (2 May 1953), 34. Each battalion also had about thirty trucks used for internal administrative purposes.

32. Discussed in greater detail in Chapter 6.

33. *History of the North Korean Army*, 84.

34. "Chinese Communist Army and North Korean Army Logistics and Class Supply," 56.

35. *History of the North Korean Army*, Chart 3b. The authors of *Supply and Transportation System of the Chinese Communist and North Korean Forces in Korea*, writing in 1951, maintained (pp. 53–58) that the NKPA corps did not have a composite organization to control all supply and transportation matters, but that these functions were performed by several sections of the Corps Rear Command Post. It appears that either the intelligence information available in 1950–1951 was incorrect or that the NKPA corps organization was modified at the time NKPA units were reorganized in Manchuria in late 1950. In any event, it is clear that the NKPA Corps in 1952 and after indeed had a Rear Services Section and that the functions of its various elements were substantially the same as those prescribed by the authors of *Supply and Transportation System of the Chinese Communist and North Korean Forces in Korea* in 1951 for the equivalent separate elements. Furthermore, the Korean War-era U.S. corps was a more purely tactical organization and handled only minimal logistical matters.

36. "Chinese Communist Army and North Korean Army Logistics and Class Supply," 56; *History of the North Korean Army*, Chart 3b.

37. "Enemy Motor Transport in North Korea," 34 (Chart 4). However, the authors of *Supply and Transportation System of the Chinese Communist and North Korean Forces in Korea* (p. 55) described a corps transportation section consisting of two companies of thirty trucks each at full-strength supplemented as necessary by ox carts and human porters, and the authors of "Petroleum, Oils and Lubricants Requirements for Communist Ground Forces, Far East," *USAFFE Intelligence Digest*, V, no. 4 (April

1955) (p. 71, Table III) indicated that each of the seven NKPA corps headquarters controlled only eighty-one wheeled vehicles as late as 1955.

38. "Interrogation Reports—North Korean Forces: Typical North Korean Infantry Division," 10; *History of the North Korean Army*, Chart 4f; *Supply and Transportation System of the Chinese Communist and North Korean Forces in Korea*, 59–60.

39. "Interrogation Reports—North Korean Forces: Typical North Korean Infantry Division," 10 and 13. The exact numbers and types of vehicles authorized are uncertain. NKPA divisions accumulated and used trucks and other vehicles captured from UNC forces or requisitioned as needed from civilian sources. The June 1950 NKPA infantry division is thought to have had a total of 194 trucks, including those in the combat regiments.

40. *History of the North Korean Army*, Chart 4f, but see also *Supply and Transportation System of the Chinese Communist and North Korean Forces in Korea*, 61.

41. Headquarters, United States X Corps, *Organization Charts, Strength of Units, Weapons Tables, Korea, April 1953* ([Korea]: HQ, United States X Corps, April 1953), chart entitled "North Korean Infantry Division."

42. *History of the North Korean Army*, Chart 5b. The authors of *Supply and Transportation System of the Chinese Communist and North Korean Forces in Korea* (p. 61) reported the strength of the NKPA regimental RSS as one officer and thirty-six enlisted men plus a transportation platoon consisting of one officer and twenty-three enlisted men.

43. "Interrogation Reports—North Korean Forces: Typical North Korean Infantry Division," 8.

44. *Organization Charts, Strength of Units, Weapons Tables, Korea, April 1953*, chart entitled "North Korean Infantry Division."

45. *Supply and Transportation System of the Chinese Communist and North Korean Forces in Korea*, 62–63.

46. Headquarters, Department of the Army, *Handbook on the Chinese Communist Army* (DA Pamphlet No. 30-51; Washington: USGPO, 1952), 66.

47. *Logistical Data for the Chinese Communist Army*, 12.

48. Rigg, 73.

49. *Supply and Transportation System of the Chinese Communist and North Korean Forces in Korea*, 2.

50. Rigg, 72–73.

51. For the PLA Transport Corps, see O'Ballance, 201–202.

52. *Logistical Data for the Chinese Communist Army*, 21. The Fourth Field Army, commanded by Marshal Lin Piao, was subsequently redeployed to the North East China Military Area which had its headquarters in Mukden, Manchuria. Both organizations played key roles in the Korean War.

53. "The Chinese Communist Field Army," 2–6.

54. *Chinese Communist Ground Forces in Korea: Tables of Organization and Equipment*, 1. There were apparently no established Tables of Organization and Equipment for the CCF in Korea until late in the war (see *Handbook on the Chinese Communist Army*, 32).

55. *Supply and Transportation System of the Chinese Communist and North Korean Forces in Korea*, 3; Rigg, 74; *Handbook on the Chinese Communist Army*, 32.

56. Huston, 353. In *The United States Air Force in Korea, 1950–1953* (rev. ed., Washington: Office of Air Force History, 1983, 337), Robert F. Futrell noted that in 1951 (presumably before the creation of a separate RSD for GHQ CCF in Korea) the

RSD of the PLA Fourth Field Army, commanded by General Tao Chu, was located at Antung, Manchuria, and supervised the flow of troops and supplies into Korea (probably for the XIIIth Army Group), and the RSD of the PLA Third Field Army, commanded by General Wang Chieu-An, was located at Chian, Manchuria, across the Yalu River from Manpojin (probably supporting the IXth Army Group).

57. "Chinese Communist Army and North Korean Army Logistics and Class Supply," 49.

58. "The Enemy Supply System in North Korea," *USAFFE Intelligence Digest*, II, no. 4 (2 September 1953), 16.

59. *Supply and Transportation System of the Chinese Communist and North Korean Forces in Korea*, 4.

60. *Supply and Transportation System of the Chinese Communist and North Korean Forces in Korea*, 11–12; *Handbook on the Chinese Communist Army*, 66; Futrell, 337. The change permitted the armies subordinate to CCF GHQ to be shifted from place to place without disrupting the established system of supply.

61. "The Enemy Supply System in North Korea," 17; *Intelligence Estimate Korea— March 1955*, 12; "Chinese Communist Army and North Korean Army Logistics and Class Supply," 50; *Supply and Transportation System of the Chinese Communist and North Korean Forces in Korea*, 8. The Branch Units have also been called Logistical Bases, Logistical Commands, and Rear Services Branch Headquarters. For the sake of clarity, they are all referred to in this book as Branch Units regardless of the time and place under consideration.

62. *Chinese Communist Ground Forces in Korea: Tables of Organization and Equipment*, Chart No. 2; *Supply and Transportation System of the Chinese Communist and North Korean Forces in Korea*, 10–11. By the end of the war there were eighteen such truck regiments in Korea. The CCF truck regiments are discussed in greater detail in Chapter 6.

63. *Supply and Transportation System of the Chinese Communist and North Korean Forces in Korea*, 8.

64. *Supply and Transportation System of the Chinese Communist and North Korean Forces in Korea*, 8–9.

65. *Chinese Communist Ground Forces in Korea: Tables of Organization and Equipment*, Chart No. 3. The 1953 structure probably represents a refinement of the original January 1951 structure. *Handbook on the Chinese Communist Army* (p. 66) notes that in 1952 the strength of the Branch Unit was about 10,000 operational personnel, mostly conscripted civilians. According to Futrell (p. 337), each Branch Unit was organized with an ordnance section, a supply base with a variable number of Main Depots and Sub-Depots, a transportation section controlling four truck regiments (each with 150 GAZ-51 trucks), a porter battalion, and a 1,200-man aircraft spotter unit. Huston (p. 353) states that the commander of a Branch Unit was a civilian equivalent in rank to a division commander (Major General). Moreover, at various times the operating units of the Branch Unit, particularly the labor battalion, included large numbers of Chinese civilians as well as military personnel.

66. *Chinese Communist Ground Forces in Korea: Tables of Organization and Equipment*, Chart No. 3; *Supply and Transportation System of the Chinese Communist and North Korean Forces in Korea*, 9 and 25. The chief of the Main Depot was equivalent in rank to a regimental commander. Futrell (p. 337) indicated that the supply section

within the Main Depot administrative unit controlled two organic motor transport companies, each of which had sixty-five trucks.

67. *Supply and Transportation System of the Chinese Communist and North Korean Forces in Korea*, 9–10. The Chief of the Sub-Depot was equivalent in rank to a company commander.

68. *Supply and Transportation System of the Chinese Communist and North Korean Forces in Korea*, 10. Futrell (p. 337) indicated that each Sub-Depot was usually supported by an organic truck company and several porter teams.

69. "Chinese Communist Army and North Korean Army Logistics and Class Supply," 50 and 53; *Supply and Transportation System of the Chinese Communist and North Korean Forces in Korea*, 14–15. The available evidence for a logistical role being played by the CCF Army Groups in Korea is unclear. This is probably due to the inaccuracy of intelligence information available at various times and the usual inherent flexibility of CCF tactical and logistical organizations. The authors of *Supply and Transportation System of the Chinese Communist and North Korean Forces in Korea* (pp. 14–19) particularly confuse the issue by citing the CCF XIXth Army Group as a special case of an Army Group with full logistical functions. The best conclusion seems to be that by 1953 all CCF Army Groups in Korea performed the normal range of logistical functions encountered at other levels.

70. *Chinese Communist Ground Forces in Korea: Tables of Organization and Equipment*, Chart No. 4. The authors of *Supply and Transportation System of the Chinese Communist and North Korean Forces in Korea* (pp. 14–15) stated that the Army Group supply point had a complement of 300 men and (p. 17) that the transportation section of the XIXth Army Group had 500 trucks in five companies. They are probably in error.

71. *Chinese Communist Ground Forces in Korea: Tables of Organization and Equipment*, Chart No. 5; *Supply and Transportation System of the Chinese Communist and North Korean Forces in Korea*, 20–21.

72. *Supply and Transportation System of the Chinese Communist and North Korean Forces in Korea*, 26. As noted earlier, the so-called Miscellaneous Section of the Army RSD may have provided the personnel to operate the Army supply point.

73. *Supply and Transportation System of the Chinese Communist and North Korean Forces in Korea*, 22.

74. *Chinese Communist Ground Forces in Korea: Tables of Organization and Equipment*, Chart No. 5; *Supply and Transportation System of the Chinese Communist and North Korean Forces in Korea*, 21. It perhaps had ten officers and twenty enlisted men and may have constituted either (or both) a liaison element for coordination of supply requisitions and movements with the supporting Branch Unit or an organization to operate the Army supply point.

75. The infantry battalions, regiments, and divisions of the CCF in Korea were reorganized and reequipped beginning in late 1951 with a resulting increase in firepower and motorization. Thus, the CCF infantry division of late 1952 bore little resemblance to that of October–November 1950. See Samuel B. Griffith II, *The Chinese People's Liberation Army* (New York: McGraw-Hill Book Company for the Council on Foreign Relations, 1967), 178.

76. *Supply and Transportation System of the Chinese Communist and North Korean Forces in Korea*, 36.

77. *Supply and Transportation System of the Chinese Communist and North Korean Forces in Korea*, 30.

78. The staff section of the CCF infantry division (both types) also had a service platoon of two officers, thirty-six enlisted men, and twelve animals for internal support. See *Chinese Communist Ground Forces in Korea: Tables of Organization and Equipment*, Chart No. 7.

79. There was considerable uncertainty among UNC intelligence agencies as to the organization and strength of the CCF infantry division Rear Services Section at various times during the war. According to the compilers of *Chinese Communist Ground Forces in Korea: Tables of Organization and Equipment* (Chart Nos. 9 and 17), the RSS was identical in the two types of CCF infantry divisions. However, the G-2 Section of U.S. X Corps, the authors of *Organization Charts, Strength of Units, Weapons Tables, Korea, April 1953* (chart entitled "Chinese Communist Infantry Division"), maintained that the RSS of the April 1953 CCF infantry division (Type II) was authorized seventy-six officers and 554 enlisted men organized in a headquarters (four officers and ten EM), an administrative platoon (ten officers and twelve EM), a finance section (five officers and seven EM), a food section (two officers and three EM), a support section (two officers and ten EM), an ordnance section (three officers and five EM), a quartermaster section (three officers and five EM), a communications section (three officers and five EM), a sanitation section (one officer and four EM), a transportation company (eight officers and 120 EM), and a medical unit (thirty-five officers and 373 EM) composed of an aid station (one officer and five EM), a divisional field hospital (ten officers and twenty EM), and a litter battalion (twenty-four officers and 348 EM) capable of being attached by company to the infantry regiments of the division. The various authorities also differed significantly on the size and organization of the organic logistical units supporting the CCF infantry division. According to the author of "Chinese Communist Army and North Korean Army Logistics and Class Supply" (p. 53), the division RSS transportation company perhaps had fifteen carts and forty-five animals. The authors of *Chinese Communist Ground Forces in Korea: Tables of Organization and Equipment* (Chart No. 15) and *Supply and Transportation System of the Chinese Communist and North Korean Forces in Korea* (pp. 2–3 and 35) seem to indicate that transportation support for both the 12,404-man Type I (with organic artillery battalion) and 13,564-man Type II (with organic artillery regiment) CCF infantry division was provided by an organic animal transportation unit consisting at full authorized 1953 strength of fourteen officers, 164 enlisted men, thirty carts, and ninety animals organized as shown in Diagram 3.14. The transportation unit of the CCF horse-drawn artillery division (*Chinese Communist Ground Forces in Korea: Tables of Organization and Equipment*, Chart No. 30) was the same, but in the motorized artillery division (*Chinese Communist Ground Forces in Korea: Tables of Organization and Equipment*, Chart No. 26) a truck company with eleven officers, 127 enlisted men, and forty-five trucks was substituted. The structure of the transport unit differed from division to division. The RSS of the CCF artillery division was slightly smaller (see *Chinese Communist Ground Forces in Korea: Tables of Organization and Equipment*, Charts Nos. 26 and 30). The motorized artillery division had eighty-three officers and 223 enlisted men in its RSS and included a labor platoon (one officer and thirty EM); the horse-drawn artillery division had eighty-three officers and 236 enlisted men and included a fifteen-truck truck platoon (one officer and thirty-three EM). Both types of artillery division had a much larger ordnance section (ten officers and

twenty EM). The small transportation section established priorities for the division transportation group and coordinated the use of division transportation assets.

80. *Organization Charts, Strength of Units, Weapons Tables, Korea, April 1953*, chart entitled "Chinese Communist Infantry Division." The Rear Services Section of the earlier (1950) CCF infantry regiment had only twenty-four officers and 118 enlisted men.

81. *Chinese Communist Ground Forces in Korea: Tables of Organization and Equipment*, Chart No. 18; *Supply and Transportation System of the Chinese Communist and North Korean Forces in Korea*, 39–40. The regimental heavy weapons battalion had an ammunition platoon (two officers, thirty EM, six carts, and twelve animals) in the artillery company and an ammunition squad in each of the two sections of the heavy mortar company (each with twelve EM, two carts, and eight animals). See *Chinese Communist Ground Forces in Korea: Tables of Organization and Equipment*, Chart No. 19.

82. *Chinese Communist Ground Forces in Korea: Tables of Organization and Equipment*, Chart No. 18; "Chinese Communist Army and North Korean Army Logistics and Class Supply," 53.

4

NKPA-CCF Supply, Maintenance, and Storage Systems

The North Korean People's Army and the Chinese Communist forces in Korea each maintained their own supply and maintenance installations as well as separate systems of supply requisition and issue, maintenance, medical evacuation and treatment, and transport.[1] Neither North Korea nor the People's Republic of China was capable of producing sufficient quantities of war matériel; thus both the NKPA and the CCF in Korea relied heavily on captured equipment, locally obtained supplies, and the support of the Soviet Union. Although the logistical systems of both armies were based on the Soviet model, the principles and methods, as well as the organization of the responsible support units, were somewhat different in the two forces. The NKPA systems tended to be more standardized and rigid than those of the CCF, which varied considerably from unit to unit. Moreover, the logistical systems of the two armies changed considerably over time during the Korean War, mostly in the direction of greater efficiency and less cumbersome procedures. Although the North Korean and Chinese systems were formally linked and coordinated only at the General Headquarters level, undoubtedly some degree of "socialist solidarity" and cooperation existed at lower levels. In all probability, NKPA and CCF units at all levels cooperated by providing logistical support to each other's units when required by the tactical situation.

SOURCES OF SUPPLY

In general terms, the military supplies and equipment used by the NKPA and CCF in Korea, 1950–1953, were obtained by one of five methods. Primary reliance was placed, of course, on internal production, although the manufacture of military matériel was inadequate in most categories in both North Korea and Communist China. Consequently, both the NKPA and CCF relied heavily on arms and equipment captured from their enemies. The pre-1950 Chinese People's Liberation Army (PLA) was largely equipped with weapons captured from the Japanese during and immediately after World War II and with American armaments captured from the Nationalist Chinese during the Chinese Civil War. Some of these armaments found their way to the North Koreans before 1950, and during the Korean War both the North Koreans and the Chinese Communists were frequently resupplied with food, weapons, ammunition, medical supplies, and other matériel captured from U.S., ROK or other UNC forces. Both armies also relied on supplies requisitioned locally in the areas in which they operated. This was particularly true of foodstuffs. In some cases, the original owners were paid or otherwise reimbursed; in other cases, the goods were simply taken. The principal external source of military matériel was the Soviet Union, which provided aircraft, tanks, vehicles, communications equipment, heavy artillery, and ammunition. Finally, a small proportion of the war matériel utilized by the NKPA and CCF in Korea came from third country suppliers.

Internal Production

North Korea had a broad range of natural resources, including abundant water power, timber, rare strategic materials such as tungsten and zinc, large graphite reserves, and substantial deposits of iron ore, copper, lead, cobalt, asbestos, molybdenum, nickel, gold, and silver.[2] Reserves of both bituminous and anthracite coal were large but of poor quality, and almost all coking coal had to be imported from Communist China and Sakhalin. In 1950, Korea had no proven oil fields or shale oil deposits, although there was limited production of synthetic oil from coal. Manpower was also in short supply.

Such industry as existed in North Korea in 1950 was primarily the result of Japanese development of the Korean economy from 1910 to 1945. Korea originally served mainly as a source of food and raw materials and as an outlet for Japanese manufactured goods, but beginning in the late 1920s the Japanese began to develop Korean industry to complement their own. The availability of raw materials and abundant hydroelectric power led to the concentration of most heavy industry in the North, while the South remained primarily agricultural with some light industry. Korea was an important source of both raw materials and industrial goods for Japan during World War II. The division of Korea at the 38th Parallel in 1945 left most of Korea's heavy industrial facilities (perhaps 75 percent) in the North, but industrial production was much reduced in the postwar period due to wartime destruction and deterioration, Soviet exactions, and the substitution for experienced Japanese managers of less capable Koreans. The North Korean Communist government sought to restore production to pre-

World War II levels through a series of one-, three-, and five-year plans, but the established industrial production goals were only partially realized by the beginning of the Korean War.

Before 1950, North Korean heavy industry remained limited. North Korea never met even its own needs in iron and steel production, but in 1949 North Korea produced 166,000 tons of pig iron, 144,000 tons of steel ingot, and 116,000 tons of finished steel. In 1950, there were only six small iron and steel plants operating in North Korea, all of which subsequently suffered destruction or heavy damage from UNC bombing. The strength of North Korean industry was in chemicals. Some 401,000 tons of chemical fertilizer, 136,000 tons of calcium carbide, 9,000 tons of caustic soda, and 538,000 tons of cement were produced in 1949. North Korean refineries (using imported oil) were reported to be capable of producing about 80 percent of the petroleum products required for wartime operations even though the two largest plants, at Hungnam and Pongung, were obliterated by UNC bombing during the war.[3]

The industrial plant inherited from the Japanese included adequate hydroelectric power facilities, a large chemical industry, considerable oil refining capacity, and a small iron and steel industry, but North Korea had few metal fabricating plants, and consumer industries, particularly cotton textiles, were inadequate for even domestic needs. During World War II, Korea had produced small arms and small arms ammunition, light artillery and shells, armor plate, gunpowder, and even aircraft and aircraft engines for the Japanese war machine. However, in 1950 North Korea had only twelve machine-building plants of various types and three shipyards. North Korea remained incapable of producing tanks, trucks, and artillery pieces but did have some capacity for producing small arms and small arms ammunition, military uniforms, and certain other military supplies.

In 1950, UNC air intelligence focused on five major North Korean industrial centers: Wonsan, Pyongyang, Hungnam, Chongjin, and Najin (Rashin).[4] All of these cities, except for Pyongyang, were on the northeast coast. Hungnam was the center of the Korean chemical industry and was the location of the Chosen Nitrogen Fertilizer Company, the Chosen Nitrogen Explosives Factory, and the Bogun (Motomiya) Chemical Plant. Chongjin was an important iron and steel center, with the Japan Iron Works and the Mitsubishi Iron Company. North Korea's petroleum refining industry was centered in Wonsan. The Chosen Oil Refinery on the south edge of Wonsan harbor was the largest in Korea, and the Rising Sun Petroleum Company 5 miles northwest of the city was also important. Second in size only to the Mukden Arsenal in Manchuria, Pyongyang's arsenal produced rifles, automatic weapons, ammunition, some artillery shells, grenades, bombs, and mines as well as aircraft parts. Pyongyang and Sinuiju were also important centers for the production of various goods such as chemicals, textiles, rubber shoes, bicycles, aluminum, and electrical equipment. Other important industrial facilities in North Korea included the Chosen Riken Metals Plant (aluminum and magnesium), the Japan Mining Company Smelter (copper and low-grade zinc), and the Kyomipo Steel Plant (pig iron and steel), all in or near Chinnampo on the west coast. Chongjin and Songjin on the east coast were other key metals-producing areas.

Although Korea was a food-exporting area under the Japanese, only the coastal plains and winding inland valleys were suitable for agriculture. The division of Korea in 1945 left the major food-producing areas in the South, and only about 20 percent of the land in North Korea was arable. North Korea, like the other Communist countries of East Asia, had a long history of food deficiency despite intensive efforts to increase agricultural production through collectivization, mechanization, and the use of chemical fertilizers.[5] The principal grain crops in North Korea were rice, wheat, barley, and millet, and commercial farming of fruits and vegetables was somewhat more important in the North than in the South. The lack of good pasturage did not encourage livestock raising in Korea, although cattle were important as draft animals. Most farming activities were carried out on small plots worked by individual farmers and their families.

The industrial and agricultural production of China, and particularly that of Manchuria, was of course available to the NKPA before as well as after the CCF intervention in October 1950. With respect to the production of munitions, however, Communist China could not meet its own needs much less the added requirements of the NKPA. In 1950, the Chinese munitions industry was all but nonexistent and, like the North Koreans, the Chinese Communists were largely dependent on outside sources of supply, primarily the Soviet Union.[6] The two arsenals at Mukden (Manchuria) and that at Taiyuan (Shansi Province) became available to the Chinese Communists at the end of the civil war in 1949 and were major producers of small arms, automatic weapons, mortars, ammunition, and some light artillery.[7] However, in 1950 Red China (including Manchuria) produced only enough small arms ammunition to provide about five cartridges per day for 250,000 men and only 90,000 rounds of artillery ammunition per year, a quantity sufficient for only about three to five months at the rate used during the Korean War.[8] Even so, the two Mukden arsenals produced about 65 percent of Red China's light munitions in 1950, an amount estimated sufficient to maintain six to ten CCF divisions in combat.[9]

Captured Matériel

Both the NKPA and CCF in Korea made maximum use of food, weapons, ammunition, vehicles, petroleum products, and other supplies captured from their enemies. In 1950, both armies were amply supplied with arms and equipment captured from or surrendered by the Japanese Imperial Army during and after World War II and American weapons taken from the Nationalist Chinese during the Chinese Civil War. The North Koreans obtained considerable quantities of Japanese small arms and light artillery pieces from the Soviets, who turned over stocks captured from the Japanese Kwantung Army to the newly formed NKPA.[10] The NKPA also received some of the equipment captured by the Chinese Communists from their Nationalist opponents. In the first ninty days of the Korean War, the NKPA captured enough matériel to outfit several divisions.[11] The fall of Seoul alone yielded 1,500 American vehicles, 20,000 gallons of gasoline abandoned in the American embassy motorpool, and the entire U.S. July liquor ration.[12] Initially the NKPA leaders prohibited the use of matériel captured from the ROK and UNC forces in order to avoid confusion. The usual procedure was to move such captured matériel to the rear for subsequent disposition. As UNC air interdiction made the resupply of forward NKPA units more difficult, captured American weapons and ammunition were issued to replacements and at least one division, the 7th, traded its Japanese equipment for modern American arms wholesale; even captured Republic of Korea Army (ROKA) uniforms of American manufacture were utilized after July 1950 as regular NKPA stocks became depleted.[13]

The Chinese Communist army had from its beginning considered arms and equipment captured from its enemies as a major source of supply. Enormous quantities of war matériel were obtained from the Japanese during World War II and through the good offices of the Soviet Army after 1945. Even larger quantities of American-produced weapons and supplies were captured from the Nationalist Chinese during the civil war. In just the four battles of Tsinan, the Liaoning Corridor, Chiang-chun, and Mukden in 1948, the Nationalists lost thirty-three divisions, eight of which were 85 percent equipped with U.S. matériel. A month later the toll stood at "17 originally US-equipped divisions," and after the fall of Manchuria, the Nationalists estimated that approximately 80 percent of the arms and equipment supplied to their forces by the United States had fallen intact into Communist hands.[14] Overall the Chinese Communists claim to have captured the following from the Nationalists between 1 July 1946 and 30 June 1950: 3,161,912 rifles and pistols, 319,958 machineguns, 54,530 artillery pieces, 622 tanks, 389 armored cars, 5,527,400 artillery shells, 507,984,800 rounds of ammunition, 200 naval vessels, and 189 military aircraft.[15]

In Korea, the CCF policy was to turn all captured matériel against the enemy whenever possible, and the CCF depended in part on captured matériel for the success of its offensives. Arms and equipment which could not be used directly and immediately were dispatched to higher echelons for use or transport to Manchuria for study.[16] The principal means of obtaining food stocks for the CCF was by requisition from the rear or by local procurement; however, both in the civil war and in Korea it was not unknown for the Chinese Communists to launch offensives primarily for the purpose of capturing food supplies.[17] At the level of the individual soldier, looting had long been a primary motivation to combat, and in Korea Communist Chinese soldiers were often encouraged to attack in expectation of capturing food, clothing, and medical supplies as well as arms and ammunition.[18]

Local Procurement

Both the NKPA and CCF relied heavily on supplies acquired in the area of operations to supplement supplies obtained through the normal military supply system. Food was the main item obtained by local procurement, but the method was also used to obtain forage, fuel, and labor. The NKPA initially planned to obtain only one third of its rations by means of local procurement in South Korea, but successful UNC air interdiction of its lines of communications quickly compelled it to depend almost entirely on local supplies of food.[19] In some cases, the required supplies were paid for in cash or with certificates redeemable at a later date.[20] In rear areas, NKPA security units often coerced village "People's Committees" to provide the necessary supplies. More often the supplies were simply stolen, and there were reports of NKPA or CCF units taking the entire food supply of some individuals or villages. The leaders of the CCF officially proscribed the outright theft of food from the civilian population, but their political instructions were frequently ignored.[21]

The maintenance of adequate stocks of rice to support the CCF in Korea was given a high priority, and inasmuch as the flow of rice from Manchuria was often interrupted, the procurement of rice from the local area of operations was highly organized by the CCF. Rice collection details of thirty to thirty-five men were organized by the Supply Section chief and the chief of the Political Section (commissar) at the regimental level. Similar foraging units were also organized at division and army levels to supply the needs of headquarters personnel. Korean farmers from whom rice was obtained were issued "rice notes," certificates printed in fixed amounts (5, 10, 100, and 250 kilograms) which could be submitted to the North Korean government in lieu of taxes or to a CCF supply section for reimbursement in cash.[22]

The other principal logistical resource obtained by the NKPA and CCF by requisition on the local population was labor. Both armies used large numbers of impressed civilians for carrying supplies in forward areas and for incidental labor throughout the theater of operations. Civilian carts and animals were also frequently impressed wherever they were available. Apparently labor services were obtained by coercion and were not reimbursed; they were considered a form of taxation on the captured populace of South Korea or a required public service in the North.[23]

Soviet Support

Given the age and poor condition of most captured Japanese and American equipment as well as the inability of North Korea and Communist China to manufacture heavy weapons and equipment, the Communist forces in Korea were almost entirely dependent on the Soviet Union for their heavy weapons, ammunition, vehicles, and other military supplies during the Korean War. This was particularly true with respect to aircraft and aircraft parts, artillery and artillery ammunition, tanks, motor vehicles, communications equipment, and other specialized matériel. It is readily apparent that the Soviet Union went to great lengths to supply the NKPA and later the CCF in Korea with war matériel, and as the Korean War progressed the proportion of modern Soviet weapons was substantially increased and some CCF units were entirely reequipped with new Soviet equipment. Most of the Soviet-supplied arms and equipment was of World War II vintage, but it was rugged, simply designed, and easy to maintain.

From its beginnings, the NKPA was the creature of the Soviet Army with respect to supply. Beginning in December 1946, the newly created North Korean Communist army was provided with arms and equipment transferred from the departing Soviet occupation forces, which also turned over quantities of matériel surrendered by the Japanese Kwantung Army at the end of World War II in return for food shipments from North Korea to the Soviet Union.[24] Thereafter the growing logistical demands of the expanding NKPA were met almost entirely by Soviet-supplied matériel, and by June 1947 the bulk of even the small arms and small arms ammunition of the NKPA had been obtained by direct shipment from the USSR.[25] In 1948, the North Koreans began a major drive to stockpile Soviet equipment, including tanks, artillery, large caliber ammunition, vehicles, engineer equipment, petroleum products, medical supplies, and uniform material. The amounts obtained dwarfed the quantities produced locally.[26]

The military build-up of the NKPA was further augmented by the return to North Korea of Korean units which had been part of the Chinese Communist Eighth Route Army.[27] These units brought with them all of their arms and equipment, most of which was of Japanese or American manufacture. Some of these units were reequipped with Soviet equipment and others received supplementary issues of heavier Soviet weapons to upgrade their firepower. Otherwise the direct supply of arms and equipment to the NKPA by the Chinese Communists before October 1950 seems to have been negligible with the NKPA receiving only a few 62-mm mortars and some submachine guns manufactured in Manchuria.

Although the Soviets admitted to supplying arms and equipment to the newly formed NKPA before and at the time of the departure of their occupation forces from North Korea in December 1948, they later consistently denied supplying war matériel to North Korea after that time, a claim that was patently false.[28] In April and May 1950, the North Koreans began to receive large shipments of heavy artillery, trucks, tanks, automatic weapons, and aircraft from the USSR.[29] Much of this matériel, which included T-34 tanks, 76-mm and 122-mm howitzers, 122-mm guns, 76-mm self-propelled guns, 45-mm antitank guns, mortars, small arms, and ammunition of all types as well as trucks, jeeps, radios, and fire control, signal, and medical equipment, consisted of older models either reconditioned or newly manufactured.[30] Preliminary planning for the invasion of South Korea most likely began before March 1949 with direct Soviet participation and the conclusion of a secret military agreement to supply sufficient equipment for six infantry divisions, three mechanized units, and eight battalions of border constabulary troops as well as combat aircraft.[31]

The Soviet Army also provided advisors and instructors to assist the North Koreans in learning to operate and maintain the equipment provided.[32] At first instructors were provided from nearby Soviet occupation force garrisons, but by December 1946 NKPA training units had regularly assigned Soviet advisors. Soviet occupation units scheduled to turn over their equipment to the NKPA upon their withdrawal from Korea also provided instructors to train the North Koreans. Technical advisors were also available after June 1950 to assist in the receipt, maintenance, and operation of Soviet-supplied arms and equipment.[33]

The CCF in Korea was also largely dependent on Soviet support for the supply of heavy weapons, vehicles, and artillery ammunition as well as a variety of other war matériel, although the Soviet Union provided very little military support to the Chinese Communists until after the CCF was deployed in Korea. In 1945, Soviet forces in Manchuria did facilitate the takeover by the Chinese Communists of military depots of the Japanese Kwantung Army.[34] However, there was little or no contact, much less military aid, between the Soviets and the Chinese Communists until the signing of a defensive pact in February 1950.[35] Subsequently, the pace of Chinese military rearmament and modernization hinged on the relationship with the Russians.[36] Although 3,000 Russian advisors and technicians arrived in China in April 1950, Sino-Soviet relations remained cool until mid-1951.[37] CCF participation in the Korean War and improvement in Sino-Soviet relations after the spring of 1951 led to massive Soviet military aid. The first major shipments of Russian matériel arrived in China in August 1951, and both the PLA and the CCF in Korea were subsequently reorganized and reequipped with modern Soviet equipment.[38] There is much to suggest that the flow of Soviet arms and equipment and the granting of loans to the Chinese for the purchase of war matériel were viewed by Soviet leaders as means of manipulating the Chinese and protecting Soviet interests.[39] In any event, the Soviets provided generally excellent equipment, and Soviet aid did much to improve the capability of the Chinese Communist air and ground forces to engage in modern warfare.[40] In some ways, the military advice provided by the Soviets to the Chinese and the organizational and doctrinal model of the Soviet Army itself were more important than the actual war matériel supplied. The tactical and logistical know-how provided by the Soviets was an invaluable aid to the modernization of the PLA and, while it existed, the CCF in Korea.[41]

Other Support

Although practically insignificant, some military equipment reached both the NKPA and CCF in Korea from sources other than the Soviet Union. Until 1953, North Korean trade was limited almost entirely to the People's Republic of China and the Soviet Union, but there was some contact with other Soviet bloc countries and with the neutral countries of Asia, Europe, Africa, Latin America, and the Middle East. It is probable that countries sympathetic to the Communist cause provided support for the war against so-called "capitalist aggression" in Korea, and it is likely that the NKPA and CCF obtained some of their supplies indirectly from one or more of the United Nations allies, including the United Kingdom and the United States.[42]

REQUISITION AND ISSUE SYSTEM OF THE NKPA

Procedures for the requisitioning and issuing of supplies in the NKPA (depicted in Diagram 4.1) differed somewhat between combat units controlled by NKPA Front Headquarters and rear area units controlled directly by GHQ NKPA. In frontline units, supply requisitions were seldom necessary during active operations in that at each echelon the operational plan and the estimates of weapons and ammunition and of food, clothing, and other supplies required to support the plan were carefully coordinated by the responsible senior officers: the Chief of Staff, Chief of the Artillery Section, and Chief of the Rear Service Section (RSS).[43] Issues were made on the basis of the established plan and normally did not require a formal requisition. Food supplies were issued daily on the basis of strength figures provided by the personnel officer of the receiving unit. Major end items (weapons and vehicles, for example) and construction materials were issued as needed. The replacement of clothing, camp equipment, and other small items was usually accomplished by direct exchange of damaged or worn equipment at the servicing repair organization.[44] The fuel and lubricants section of the RSS at each echelon calculated the petroleum, oils, and lubricants (POL) allocations for subordinate units based on predetermined performance quotas set for the number of vehicles operating in each unit. POL was issued periodically in accordance with the established allocation, although special requisitions were apparently possible.[45] The ordnance section of the artillery organization at each echelon maintained a daily check on ammunition status, and when the number of rounds on hand fell below the preestablished stockage level (calculated in Units of Fire), action was initiated to requisition ammunition on a basic load replacement basis.[46]

At infantry company and battalion level, all requisitions for ammunition and other supplies were made orally and no records were kept.[47] Requests for weapons and ammunition were made by company commanders, approved by the battalion executive officer, and passed up to the ordnance section of the regimental artillery section, which either filled the requisition from stocks on hand or submitted a consolidated formal requisition to the ordnance section of the division artillery section. Requisitions for other supplies were transmitted orally from the battalion supply officer to the supply section of the regimental RSS, where they were consolidated and passed on to higher levels.

Diagram 4.1
NKPA Supply Channels[48]

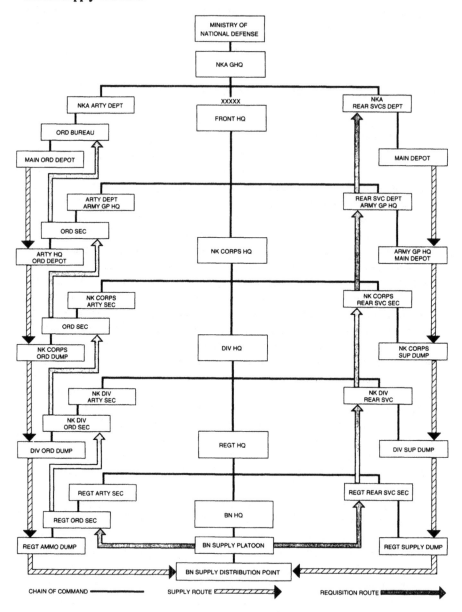

Formal written or telegraphic requisitions were normally required above the regimental level. Requisitions for weapons and ammunition were passed up the chain of command through the ordnance section of the artillery organization at each echelon.[49] Requisitions of subordinate units were either filled by the ordnance storage facility controlled by the senior echelon or were consolidated and passed to the next higher level. The procedure was much the same for other supplies; the requisitions were passed up to the appropriate section (food, fuel, clothing, etc.) of the RSS at each level until filled.

For those rear area NKPA units under the direct control of GHQ NKPA, the supply requisition procedures were somewhat different. Artillery ammunition was obtained on the basis of authorized stockage levels prescribed by the Artillery Section, GHQ NKPA, to which a daily ammunition status report was sent by radio.[50] However, in most cases the GHQ NKPA Artillery Section authorized replenishment of depleted stocks automatically and an actual requisition was not required. As was the case in combat units under the NKPA Front Headquarters, POL was issued on the basis of preestablished vehicle performance quotas.[51] Procedures for requisitioning other supplies were much the same as for units under NKPA Front control, except that rear area units generally dealt directly with the Rear Service Department (RSD) of GHQ NKPA.

The requisitioning of clothing and food constituted something of a special case in both combat units under NKPA Front Headquarters and rear area units controlled directly by GHQ NKPA. Clothing for all NKPA troops was issued twice yearly in accordance with established types and quantities for each NKPA soldier. Most food supplies for the NKPA were obtained directly from the countryside by means of "spot taxes" or payment in the form of "procurement notes" issued by the responsible food supply officer at each echelon.[52] Units attempted to maintain a certain level of food supplies on hand, usually about seven to ten days' supply below division level and thirty days' supply above division and in rear area units.[53] When stocks fell below the prescribed level, the food supply officer of the unit concerned initiated arrangements to obtain necessary foodstuffs through the local political administration—that is, the People's Committee at *myon* (district), *gun* (county), or *do* (province) level. Normally, food supplies were collected from the local area by units for their own use or for subsequent issue to their subordinate units based on their daily strength reports. The procedure followed by rear area units under direct GHQ NKPA control was typical.[54] When food was required, the unit food supply officer made out a requisition and took it to the nearest government control section, which in turn obtained approval from the 514th North Korean Army Unit, a section of the GHQ NKPA RSD. The approved requisition was returned to the unit food supply officer, who then took it to a specified *do* (Provincial) People's Committee, which then appointed a *gun* (county) People's Committee to fill the requisition. The food was collected from the farmers (usually in exchange for the requisite quantity of procurement notes or as spot taxes) and delivered directly to the requesting unit or, if delay was unavoidable, stored temporarily in a government food storage area until picked up by the requesting unit.[55]

REQUISITION AND ISSUE SYSTEM OF THE CCF IN KOREA

The system of requisitioning and issuing supplies of the CCF in Korea was similar to that of the NKPA, except that in the CCF system requisitions for weapons and ammunition were handled by an element of the Rear Services Department (RSD) at each level rather than through a separate ordnance/artillery channel. As with the North Korean system, the paperwork associated with the CCF supply system was kept to a minimum, and most requisitions were passed by messenger, telephone, radio, or telegraph.[56] As with other aspects of the CCF logistical system in Korea, there was considerable variation in requisitioning and issue procedures from unit to unit.

At the company level, NCOs tracked unit supply status, and requisitions were initiated orally and passed up the chain of command through the RSD at each echelon. At regiment, requests were either filled or consolidated and passed in written form to the appropriate section of the division RSD. There the process was repeated and so forth on up the line to the RSD of GHQ CCF in Korea.[57] Appropriate records were maintained at the regimental level and above.[58]

The small stockage levels and limited transport capability of CCF divisions meant that most requisitions were filled at the Army level or higher. Army requisitions were passed either to the RSD of its parent Army Group or directly through the Army Supply Point, located at the servicing Branch Unit Main Depot.[59] The Army Group forwarded requisitions received from its subordinate armies either to the GHQ CCF RSD or directly to the servicing Branch Unit. Requisitions from Army were filled directly by the Branch Unit Main Depots or Sub-Depots; only supplies for the Army Group headquarters or units directly attached to the Army Group headquarters were routed through the depot controlled by the Army Group RSD.[60]

As was the case with the NKPA, the CCF in Korea obtained a high proportion of its food from local sources rather than through requisitions on higher headquarters. However, procedures were in place for the requisitioning of ration items from higher headquarters on the basis of the strength reports submitted by the requesting unit.[61] The procedures for the supply of POL products were also similar to those of the NKPA. POL was allocated and issued to CCF units on the basis of pre-determined performance standards for the number and types of vehicles in each unit.[62] The requisitioning of ammunition was also on a basic load replenishment basis; the necessary records and reports were prepared by the ammunition (ordnance) supply section of the RSD at each level.[63] Generally, ammunition requisitions made by combat units and routed to the Army level or higher were filled in five to seven days.[64]

MAINTENANCE SYSTEMS OF THE NKPA AND CCF IN KOREA

Maintenance was a major deficiency of both the NKPA and CCF logistical systems in Korea. Although later standardized on Soviet models, the weapons, vehicles, and other equipment used by the NKPA and CCF were a hodgepodge of older, well-worn Japanese, American, and Soviet models. Operator maintenance was generally poor or nonexistent, and neither weapons accessories nor lubricating oils were commonly available.[65] Although repair tools were adequate, spare parts and replacement parts were always in short supply, and such items as connecting rod bearing inserts, fuel pumps, carburetors, and batteries were practically irreplaceable.[66] Cannibalization of the oldest or worst-damaged vehicles was common practice. The maintenance of motor vehicles was further compromised by the persistent shortage of trained drivers and mechanics in both armies. Trucks in North Korean paramilitary organizations (i.e., civilian trucking companies under government control) were inspected two or three times per year by government inspection teams, and NKPA standard operating procedure called for overall check-ups on vehicles every 10,000 kilometers and a general overhaul every 20,000 kilometers with tire replacement every 30,000 kilometers, but it is doubtful that these standards were met.[67]

Procedures for the repair of vehicles and other major items were cumbersome. Major repairs were often made in the unit area or at roadside by soldiers who had received some mechanical training, but damaged or broken-down vehicles were frequently abandoned in place.[68] In some cases, vehicles were evacuated to one of the few available repair installations.[69] Supply depots usually operated collection points for damaged or worn weapons and vehicles, which were subsequently evacuated to Manchuria for repair.[70]

NKPA maintenance shops at various echelons were operated by ordnance personnel assigned to tactical units or by North Korean civilians.[71] The NKPA Central Artillery Repair Center was located in 1953 at Kopyong-Myon.[72] One of the largest North Korean government-operated truck repair shops in 1953 was near Sadong and made all types of repairs, but it was able to rebuild an average of only three trucks per month.[73] The repair shop of the Ordnance Section, Artillery Section, of the NKPA corps RSS was typical of the repair facilities found in the tactical units. Apparently capable of performing a variety of minor repairs, it consisted of a small arms shop with one officer and twenty-five enlisted technicians, an artillery shop, a medical squad, and a political officer.[74] Most CCF tactical units in Korea did not have an organic maintenance capability; however, the independent truck regiments assigned to the Transportation Department of the GHQ CCF RSD each had an organic maintenance company, and each truck company had an organic maintenance squad.[75] The truck company maintenance squad of six officers and six enlisted men did not carry spare parts and performed only minor repairs. The regimental maintenance company provided tires and spare parts from salvaged vehicles.

Map 4.1
Major NKPA-CCF Logistical Installations in North Korea, July 1953

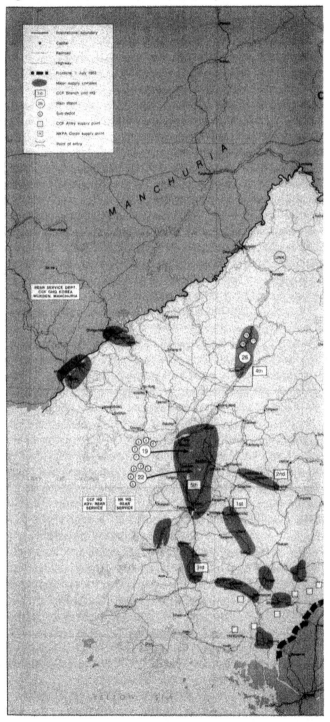

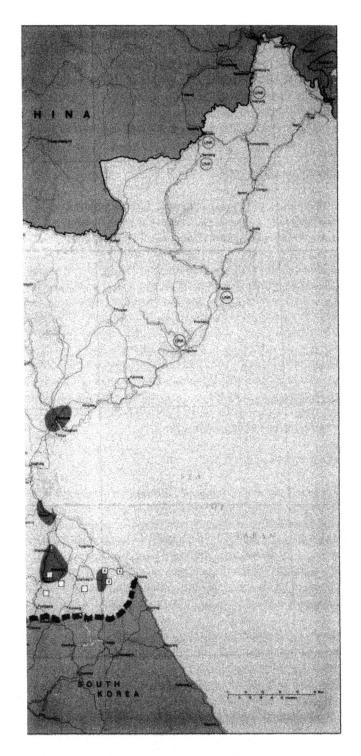

Military truck organizations generally strived for an 85 percent vehicle availability rate.[76] Priority units such as field artillery and anti-aircraft artillery batteries were generally successful but other units seldom attained the goal; at any
given time about 85 percent of CCF trucks, 65 percent of NKPA trucks, and
only 40 percent of quasi-military (North Korean) trucks were operational.[77]
Thus, of an estimated 16,500 trucks available to the Communists in North Korea
in July 1953, less than 12,200 were operational on an average day (or night).

NKPA-CCF SUPPLY INSTALLATIONS

During the Korean War, North Korea was generally divided into three zones:
a forward area, in which minimal quantities of supplies (predominantly rations
and ammunition) were stocked in numerous small, well-dispersed, and well-
camouflaged packets readily accessible by frontline troops; an intermediate
zone, in which were located the larger and more formalized supply dumps and
depots operated by divisions and NKPA corps/CCF armies; and a rear area, in
which were located the large ammunition depots and maintenance facilities operated by the GHQ NKPA Artillery Department and the various CCF Branch
Units as well as the NKPA GHQ RSD and GHQ CCF RSD supply complexes
linked by rail and highway to the enemy industrial base in North Korea and
Manchuria.[78] One might add a fourth zone in the frontier areas of Manchuria
close to the North Korean border, in which were located a number of CCF supply installations and organizations assigned to support the Communist forces in
Korea. Map 4.1 portrays the location of key NKPA-CCF supply installations in
North Korea in July 1953, the last month of the war.

Supply Installations in the Forward Area

In the forward areas (within about 30 miles of the frontline), the storage of
food (Class I) and ammunition (Class V) predominated and the numerous small
supply dumps normally handled only a single type of item.[79] Supply points at
the regimental level and below in both the NKPA and CCF were little more than
breakdown or issue points for subordinate units and normally did not stock significant quantities of supplies.[80] Small quantities of rations and ammunition
(constituting the regimental basic load) might be retained as a reserve in regimental dumps, but normally no supply reserves were carried at the battalion or
company level.

The depots operated by the artillery sections and rear services organizations
of the divisions stored minimal quantities of ammunition and other classes of
supply for limited periods in the forward areas.[81] Normally, supplies were issued to the subordinate units as soon as possible and were moved by division
transport down to the regiments and battalions and drawn directly from the divisional supply points (depots or dumps) by division troops. Personnel were not

available at the division level to maintain permanent depots, but personnel from the CCF division RSD and from the NKPA division RSS and artillery ordnance section established and operated supply points as necessary.[82] Apparently, there was no doctrine regarding the establishment of divisional supply points in either the NKPA or CCF.[83] Temporary supply dumps were set up as required by the tactical situation and were organized mostly on an ad hoc basis. Most often a divisional supply point was located in a ditch alongside a road, in a ravine, or in some other sheltered location. In the early part of the war, the NKPA divisions were known to establish their major supply point or depot in the division rear area near a major communication center and to set up forward supply points, notably an ammunition dump, in the forward echelon of the division near the regimental rear boundary, usually from 5 to 10 miles from the frontline.[84]

Supply Installations in the Intermediate Zone

The first semipermanent supply installations were encountered in the inter-mediate zone (generally 30 to 60 miles from the frontline) in the depots operated by the NKPA corps and CCF Armies.[85] Each NKPA corps RSS operated one or more corps supply depots, which carried a full range of supplies.[86] Weapons and ammunition were stocked in the NKPA corps ammunition depot run by the Ord-nance Section subordinate to the Corps Artillery Section. In the CCF Army, arms and ammunition as well as other supplies were stocked in the three depots normally operated by the Army RSD.[87] The organization and employment of the three depots operated by the CCF Army RSD were extremely flexible. They were commonly numbered (1st Depot, 2nd Depot, 3rd Depot) or designated as Forward Depot, Central Depot, and Rear Depot.[88] In some cases, each Army depot supported a specific division; in other cases, the three depots were de-ployed "two up, one back," with the rear depot supporting the two forward ones, or even with "one up, two back."[89] Such deployment of the three depots per-mitted the dispersal of Army supplies over a relatively wide area, facilitated flexibility of support by shifting the depots from place to place in accordance with the tactical situation, and enhanced tactical mobility by the leap-frogging of depots in offensive and retrograde operations.[90] Supplies were distributed among the three depots according to the expected needs of the units supported.

Supply Installations in the Rear Area

The large fixed and semipermanent supply installations controlled by the NKPA Front Headquarters and GHQ NKPA and by the CCF Army Group and GHQ CCF Supply Base were located in the rear area. The lowland area of the west coast of North Korea between Sinanju and Pyongyang, including the Chongchon River valley, the Ipsong-Sukchon area, the Sunchon area, and the Sopo-Yongsong area, contained major concentrations of NKPA and CCF logis-tical facilities.[91] In April 1952, UNC air intelligence officers knew of major

NKPA-CCF supply installations located at Sopo, Pyongyang, and Yangdok, with forward depots located at Mulgae-ri, Koksan, Singosan, Sepo-ri, and Hoey-ang.[92] By 1953, major NKPA supply installations were known to be located in or near most of the major towns of North Korea.[93] In addition to military supply depots, the North Korean government maintained government food storage areas throughout its territory, the most extensive of which was reported to have been in Hwanghae province in southwestern North Korea.[94]

The ordnance section subordinate to the Artillery Department of the NKPA Front Headquarters operated ammunition depots and ordnance repair facilities in the rear area, and the NKPA Front Headquarters RSD operated other major supply installations. Also found in the rear area were the ordnance depots and maintenance facilities controlled by the Ordnance Bureau of the GHQ NKPA Artillery Department and the supply depots operated by the GHQ NKPA RSD, as well as a wide variety of large and small industrial facilities and storage areas that constituted the North Korean industrial base.[95]

The rear area also contained the depots and supply points controlled by the CCF army group RSDs as well as the main depots and subdepots of the GHQ CCF Supply Base. The logistical functions of the CCF army group are still not clearly understood, but it seems that, as a minimum, each of the CCF army groups in Korea operated a supply point co-located with the servicing Branch Unit, which received supplies and forwarded them to the depots of its subordinate armies.[96] The army group RSDs also operated supply depots in the rear area, which serviced the troops of the army group headquarters and units directly controlled by headquarters as well as transients. However, the normal flow of supplies seems to have been direct from the main depots and subdepots of the Branch Units of the CCF Supply Base to the CCF Army depots.[97] In addition to its three to six main depots and their subdepots, each Branch Unit controlled by the GHQ CCF Supply Base also directly controlled a supply receiving point staffed by personnel from the various sections of the Branch Unit.[98] The Branch Unit supply receiving point was usually located at a railhead and road terminal, and its principal function was to receive supplies and route them through the main depots down to the subdepots. The supply receiving points normally retained supplies less than twenty-four hours. Labor for the supply receiving points was provided by Chinese civilians assigned to the Branch Unit labor organization.

Each main depot controlled three to six subdepots. The subdepots were semipermanent installations capable of supporting a division of 13,000 men as well as transients passing through their assigned area of responsibility.[99] The main depot controlled the type and amount of supplies to be stored in each subdepot based on the needs of the tactical units being supported.[100] The subdepots were inventoried and reported monthly to the main depot, and when necessary an officer was sent from the subdepot to the main depot to arrange the replenishment of subdepot stocks.[101] As a general rule, different categories of supply were stored in different subdepots and temporary dumps due to their different storage requirements.[102]

NKPA-CCF Support Facilities in Manchuria

The logistical system of the NKPA and CCF in Korea extended back across the border into Manchuria and China itself. The CCF maintained a number of supply installations in Manchuria close to the North Korean border which equipped troops enroute to Korea, reequipped combat units withdrawn from the Korean front for reorganization, and generally supported the NKPA-CCF logistical structure in Korea. The most extensive of these reequipment and training centers were in or near Suping-chieh, Mukden, Suchian-tan, Penchi-hu, and Anshan in southeastern Manchuria.[103] The movement of supplies from these Manchurian bases into Korea was the responsibility of the RSD of the PLA North East Military Area Headquarters located in Mukden. According to some reports, the CCF 6th and 7th Branch Units operated CCF supply depots on the Manchurian side of the border and were responsible for the movement of supplies into Korea.[104] Military storage sites were located throughout China along main lines of communications and often near industrial facilities. The most important concentrations of logistical installations involved in supporting Communist forces in Korea were located along the Peking-Mukden-Hunchun axis and on the Yalu River boundary in a region embracing the Chinese provinces of Hopeh, Shansi, Jehol, Liaoshi, Liaotung, and Chilin (Kirin).[105] A number of the CCF armies deployed to Korea were staged and reequipped in these regions.[106]

Siting of Supply Installations

NKPA and CCF units were usually serviced by the same railheads and supply installations although the supplies of the two armies were maintained and managed separately.[107] NKPA and CCF supply installations in all three zones were located adjacent to main supply routes (MSR) on natural avenues of approach.[108] All major supply installations, with one exception, were served by major railroad and highway routes, and their size was proportionate to the amount of traffic the servicing routes were capable of handling.[109] The location of supply installations at intervals along the main north-south arteries leading to the front reduced the flexibility of the enemy logistical system by limiting the ease with which supplies could be shifted laterally along the front to support short-notice operations.[110] Consequently, in forward areas near the 38th Parallel, where there were inadequate lateral routes of communication, the enemy committed large amounts of supplies to all terrain compartments leading to the front.[111]

In general, NKPA and CCF supply and ammunition depots were well dispersed, made maximum use of underground storage, and practiced strict camouflage discipline.[112] Extensive use was made of caves, tunnels, revetments, ditches, holes, ravines, and houses, particularly in forward areas, and even major supply complexes consisted of numerous small supply dumps dispersed over a wide area.[113] The NKPA and CCF even adopted the World War II Soviet practice of burying equipment and ammunition before a withdrawal in anticipation of its retrieval during a subsequent advance.[114] Before June 1951, both the NKPA and CCF maintained rather large supply dumps at the division and army/corps level, but the increasing pressure of UNC air and artillery activity forced the enemy to reduce the size of its supply complexes and to disperse them more widely.[115] The layout of a typical small NKPA-CCF storage area is depicted in Sketch 4.1.

Sketch 4.1
Typical Small NKPA-CCF Storage Area[116]

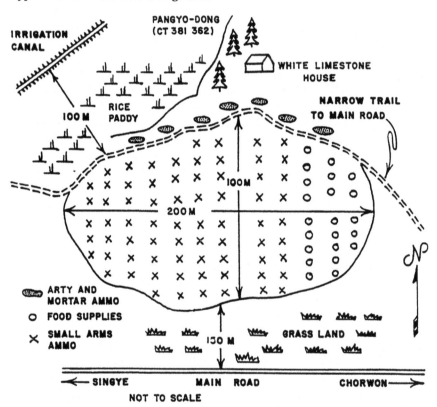

Basic Loads and Stockage Levels

Only limited amounts of reserve supplies were maintained below the division level by NKPA or CCF units. The quantities of food and ammunition constituting unit basic loads and the amount of supplies of all types constituting the authorized stockage level of depots at all echelons in the NKPA and CCF logistical system varied widely, and the exact amounts cannot be determined with any certainty.[117] We do have some idea, however, of the prescribed amounts of food, ammunition, and POL stocked at various echelons.

For the most part, rations for the NKPA and CCF in Korea were gathered from the local area and issued daily for immediate consumption. However, an emergency supply of five days of rations was maintained in all frontline NKPA units and was carried individually by each soldier.[118] Until May 1953, NKPA ration depots above division level generally maintained a three-month supply of rations for supported units, regimental supply points maintained three to five days of supply, and battalion supply points kept two to four days of supply.[119] Thus, most NKPA combat units were capable of sustaining themselves in the line for about seven to ten days without resupply of rations. After May 1953, there was a trend to stock larger amounts of rations at lower units of the NKPA, perhaps as much as sixty days of supply at the regimental level and below.[120] Depots controlled by GHQ NKPA generally aimed to keep a ninty-day supply of rations on hand at all times.[121] CCF units usually maintained at least a fifteen-day supply of rations in forward areas.[122] Normally, no food supplies were maintained by the CCF Branch Units, and all food was distributed immediately to supported units. However, the RSD of GHQ CCF in Korea apparently did maintain a reserve (probably located in the depots of the Branch Units) of flour paste (a mixture of oil and flour to which water was added before consumption) and biscuits sufficient to provide at least 13.3 pounds to each CCF soldier in Korea.[123]

Combat units of both the NKPA and CCF always maintained a reserve of ammunition on hand. Early in the war, the NKPA infantry regiment's normal basic load of ammunition was reported to consist of one Unit of Fire (UOF), which in offensive operations was distributed with 0.4 UOF with the weapons, 0.3 UOF in the battalion trains, and the remaining 0.3 UOF in the regimental trains.[124] Generally, another 0.5 UOF was carried in the division trains.[125] Later (in 1953), NKPA frontline combat units were reported to keep as much as four UOF on hand for infantry weapons and two to four UOF for artillery weapons.[126] Late in the war, all CCF units also maintained relatively large quantities of ammunition in forward areas and in the hands of the troops, amounting to about eight UOF in the early months of 1953 and as much as 20 UOF by May 1953 in anticipation of the disruption of supply lines by the coming rainy season.[127] The ammunition depots controlled by the GHQ CCF RSD generally maintained sufficient ammunition on hand to meet immediate requirements for an attack in division strength.[128]

Large stocks of POL were not maintained in forward areas.[129] Line-haul trucks were normally refueled at the northern end of their route, and each truck normally carried two 55-gallon drums of fuel in the bed behind the cab, although sometimes the last vehicle in a convoy carried all of the fuel for the convoy.[130]

In 1953, POL supplies were stocked farther forward and in greater quantities at the extreme eastern end of the front to support both the NKPA units stationed in that area (which generally had more motor vehicles than CCF units) and the vehicles hauling supplies to the depots of the NKPA Front Headquarters RSD, which was served extensively by truck rather than rail.[131] Significant supplies of POL were also maintained in the vicinity of Kaesong in western North Korea, an area with heavy truck traffic.[132] Major fuel storage areas in North Korea, reported at Kusong and Usan in 1953, may have been resupplied with fuel barged up the Yalu River to enter Korea just below the Suiho Dam.[133]

CONCLUSION

Although incapable of producing heavy war matériel and technical items such as radios and only marginally able to manufacture sufficient clothing, small arms, and small arms ammunition for their forces, the NKPA and CCF in Korea were adequately supplied with food, clothing, arms, and ammunition of all kinds captured from the enemy, requisitioned from the civilian population, or supplied by the Soviet Union. The requisition and issue systems utilized by both the NKPA and the CCF in Korea were relatively simple but served their purpose effectively. Maintenance and the supply of spare parts were problem areas for both armies and certainly increased their requirements for weapon and vehicle replacements, but the generally low level of technological sophistication of the Communist forces served to minimize complex maintenance requirements in any event. Nor was the storage of supplies a major problem for either the NKPA or the CCF in Korea. Adequate storage facilities were available, including areas free from UNC attack in Manchuria, and the Communist soldiers proved adept at hiding forward supply installations from UNC observation. Although the Communist supply, maintenance, and storage systems appeared lean and relatively simple as compared to those of the UNC forces, they were adequate to the demands placed on them. Local shortages of food, clothing, weapons, and ammunition did occur, but such shortages were usually only temporary and resulted from the effects of UNC air interdiction rather than any inherent defect in the NKPA or CCF supply, maintenance, and storage systems.

NOTES

1. "Chinese Communist Army and North Korean Army Logistics and Class Supply," *USAFFE Intelligence Digest*, VI, no. 4 (April 1956), 49. NKPA and CCF supply installations were often co-located but were operated independently.

2. Unless otherwise noted, the following description of North Korean industry is based on material included in Headquarters, Department of the Army, *Area Handbook for Korea* (DA Pamphlet No. 550-41; Washington: USGPO, November 1964).

3. General Headquarters, Far East Command, Military Intelligence Section, Allied Translator and Interpreter Service, "Interrogation Reports—North Korean Forces: North Korean Logistics," *ATIS Research Supplement*, Issue No. 1 (19 October 1950), 19.

4. Robert Frank Futrell, *The United States Air Force in Korea, 1950-1953* (rev. ed., Washington: Office of Air Force History, 1983), 183–184.

5. *Area Handbook*, 46 and 363–364; "Food Supply in the Communist Far East," *USAFFE Intelligence Digest*, VI, no. 1 (January 1956), 13–14.

6. Robert B. Rigg, *Red China's Fighting Hordes* (rev. ed., Harrisburg, PA: The Military Service Publishing Company, 1952), 296–297.

7. Rigg, 297–298.

8. James A. Huston, *Guns and Butter, Powder and Rice: U.S. Army Logistics in the Korean War* (Selinsgrove, PA: Susquehanna University Press, 1989), 37.

9. Rigg, 298.

10. "Interrogation Reports—North Korean Forces: North Korean Logistics," 20.

11. T. R. Fehrenbach, *This Kind of War: A Study in Unpreparedness* (rev. ed., New York: Bantam Books, 1991), 651.

12. Fehrenbach, 64.

13. "Interrogation Reports—North Korean Forces: North Korean Logistics," 20.

14. Samuel B. Griffith, II, *The Chinese People's Liberation Army* (New York: McGraw-Hill Book Company for the Council on Foreign Relations, 1967), 344–345, note 43, based on a U.S. embassy report of early November 1948.

15. Rigg, 255, citing *The People's Liberation Army* (Peking: Foreign Language Press, 1950).

16. Headquarters, Eighth United States Army, Assistant Chief of Staff G-2/Headquarters, United States Fifth Air Force, Assistant Chief of Staff A-2, *Supply and Transportation System of the Chinese Communist and North Korean Forces in Korea* ([Tokyo]: Headquarters, Eighth United States Army, Assistant Chief of Staff G-2/Headquarters, United States Fifth Air Force, Assistant Chief of Staff A-2, 23 September 1951), 43.

17. *Supply and Transportation System of the Chinese Communist and North Korean Forces in Korea*, 29; Rigg, 216–217.

18. Alexander L. George, *The Chinese Communist Army in Action: The Korean War and Its Aftermath* (New York: Columbia University Press, 1967), 146–147.

19. "Interrogation Reports—North Korean Forces: North Korean Logistics," 20.

20. The NKPA frequently paid for requisitioned goods in inflated ROK currency. The finance section of the NKPA 73rd Independent Regiment was reported to have crossed the 38th Parallel with 20 million *won* to be used for local procurement. See "Interrogation Reports—North Korean Forces: North Korean Logistics," 20.

21. Headquarters, United States IX Corps, G-2 Section, *Enemy Tactics, Techniques and Doctrine* ([Korea]: Headquarters, United States IX Corps, September 1951), 41–42.

22. *Supply and Transportation System of the Chinese Communist and North Korean Forces in Korea*, 27–29. The "rice note" system was established by the CCF Rear Service Department in Mukden at the end of October or beginning of November 1950. The system for issuing and accounting for rice notes was fairly complex. Combat units unable to forage for their own supplies were issued rice by higher headquarters in exchange for rice notes.

23. E. L. Atkins, H. P. Griggs, and Roy T. Sessums, *North Korean Logistics and Methods of Accomplishment* (ORO Technical Memorandum ORO-T-8 [EUSAK];

[Chevy Chase, MD]: Operations Research Office, The Johns Hopkins University, 1951), 78.

24. General Headquarters, Far East Command, Military Intelligence Section, General Staff, *History of the North Korean Army* ([Tokyo]: General Headquarters, Far East Command, Military Intelligence Section, General Staff, 31 July 1952), 14.

25. *History of the North Korean Army*, 14.

26. *History of the North Korean Army*, 4.

27. "Interrogation Reports—North Korean Forces: North Korean Logistics," 19.

28. "Soviet Assistance to North Korean Forces Subsequent to 1948," *USAFFE Intelligence Digest*, I, no. 11 (2 June 1953), 23–28. See also Fourth Report of the CINCUNC, 17 September 1950, in United States Senate, Committee on Armed Services, *Military Situation in the Far East: Hearings before the Committee on Armed Services and the Committee on Foreign Relations, United States Senate, Eighty-second Congress, First Session, to Conduct an Inquiry into the Military Situation in the Far East and the Facts Surrounding the Relief of General of the Army MacArthur from His Assignments in That Area* (Washington: USGPO, 1951), V, 3402. Analysis of matériel captured by UN forces early in the Korean War definitely establishes that the NKPA was equipped with Soviet matériel manufactured as late as 1950.

29. *History of the North Korean Army*, 24; Roy E. Appleman, *South to the Naktong, North to the Yalu* (Washington: Office of the Chief of Military History, Department of the Army, 1961), 12.

30. "Interrogation Reports—North Korean Forces: North Korean Logistics," 18; Appleman, 11-12.

31. Griffith, 105. Allen S. Whiting in *China Crosses the Yalu: The Decision to Enter the Korean War* (New York: Macmillan, 1960), 42–43, suggests that the secret military aid pact was concluded at the same time as the Soviet–North Korean ten-year economic and cultural cooperation agreement of 17 March 1949.

32. *History of the North Korean Army*, 14.

33. There were approximately 10,000 Soviet and Soviet-Bloc anti-aircraft artillerymen, advisors, and technicians in North Korea in 1953. See Walter G. Hermes, *Truce Tent and Fighting Front* (Washington: Office of the Chief of Military History, Department of the Army, 1966), 283–284.

34. Rigg, 248.

35. Edgar O'Ballance, *The Red Army of China: A Short History* (New York: Frederick A. Praeger, 1963), 191–192.

36. John Gittings, *The Role of the Chinese Army* (New York: Oxford University Press, 1967), 121.

37. O'Ballance, 192.

38. O'Ballance, 197–198.

39. Gittings, 126–127.

40. Griffith, 178.

41. Rigg, 209.

42. There is little overt evidence to support this contention, but the UK is known to have pushed hard for trade with Communist China even during active hostilities in Korea. The post-Korean War record of U.S. arms manufacturers also raises suspicions that some arms and equipment reached the Communist forces in Korea from the United States. For example, a large proportion of NKPA medical supplies were U.S. produced (see Huston,

363), and perhaps not all of it was obtained from former Nationalist Chinese stocks or by capture on the battlefield in Korea.

43. "The Enemy Supply System in North Korea," *USAFFE Intelligence Digest*, II, no. 4 (2 September 1953), 21.

44. "The Enemy Supply System in North Korea," 21–22.

45. "Chinese Communist Army and North Korean Army Logistics and Class Supply," 58; "The Enemy Supply System in North Korea," 23; "Interrogation Reports—North Korean Forces: Typical North Korean Infantry Division," *ATIS Research Supplement*, Issue No. 1 (19 October 1950), 13.

46. "Chinese Communist Army and North Korean Army Logistics and Class Supply," 58; "The Enemy Supply System in North Korea," 22.

47. *Supply and Transportation System of the Chinese Communist and North Korean Forces in Korea*, 63.

48. "Chinese Communist Army and North Korean Army Logistics and Class Supply," 56.

49. See Diagram 4.1: NKPA Supply Channels.

50. "The Enemy Supply System in North Korea," 22.

51. "The Enemy Supply System in North Korea," 22.

52. *Supply and Transportation System of the Chinese Communist and North Korean Forces in Korea*, 62; "Chinese Communist Army and North Korean Army Logistics and Class Supply," 57–58. The amount of food collected/paid for was based on the food allowance for each man supported.

53. "Chinese Communist Army and North Korean Army Logistics and Class Supply," 55.

54. "The Enemy Supply System in North Korea," 22.

55. "The Enemy Supply System in North Korea," 22.

56. *Handbook on the Chinese Communist Army*, 67–68; *Supply and Transportation System of the Chinese Communist and North Korean Forces in Korea*, 37–38 and 41. Usually supply requests were transmitted from company to battalion orally or by a runner bearing a written request authenticated by the company commander, political officer, or supply officer; from battalion to regiment by telephone call from the battalion supply officer to the appropriate section in the regimental RSS; from the appropriate section of the regimental RSS to its counterpart section in the division RSD in writing; from division to Army and from Army to Army Group/Branch Unit by telephone or radio; and from Branch Unit to GHQ CCF RSD in Manchuria by radio and telegram.

57. *Handbook on the Chinese Communist Army*, 67–68; "Chinese Communist Army Supply System," *USAFFE Intelligence Digest*, IV, no. 4 (June 1954), 32.

58. *Supply and Transportation System of the Chinese Communist and North Korean Forces in Korea*, 38–39. The actual issue of supplies was acknowledged at all levels by means of supply receipts taking the form of a simple memorandum. Receipts were forwarded and consolidated at each level ending up at the RSD in Mukden, Manchuria, where supply records for all CCF units in Korea were maintained (see *Supply and Transportation System of the Chinese Communist and North Korean Forces in Korea*, 27). The forms utilized by CCF units in Korea are reproduced and discussed in *Supply and Transportation System of the Chinese Communist and North Korean Forces in Korea*, 42–43 and Charts 11–18.

59. *Supply and Transportation System of the Chinese Communist and North Korean Forces in Korea*, 26. The Army Supply Point was a liaison element drawn from the

Army RSD and co-located with the servicing Branch Unit. Its functions included the processing of Army requisitions, coordination with the Branch Unit, acting as a receiving and distributing point for Army supplies received through the Branch Unit and as a receiving and forwarding point for inoperative arms and equipment which the Army sent to the rear for repair or replacement, and as a medical clearing station for sick and wounded Army personnel enroute to rear area base hospitals. The Branch Unit was a command and administrative element responsible for processing requisitions and for controlling a number of subordinate Main Depots and Sub-Depots, which actually handled supplies (see *Supply and Transportation System of the Chinese Communist and North Korean Forces in Korea*, 5 and 8).

60. *Supply and Transportation System of the Chinese Communist and North Korean Forces in Korea*, 15–19.

61. "Chinese Communist Army and North Korean Army Logistics and Class Supply," 55.

62. "Chinese Communist Army and North Korean Army Logistics and Class Supply," 55.

63. "Chinese Communist Army and North Korean Army Logistics and Class Supply," 55; *Supply and Transportation System of the Chinese Communist and North Korean Forces in Korea*, 33–34.

64. *Supply and Transportation System of the Chinese Communist and North Korean Forces in Korea*, 42. However, more time was required if, as often happened, the Army RSD had to pass the requisition higher.

65. *Supply and Transportation System of the Chinese Communist and North Korean Forces in Korea*, 43 and 93. Vegetable oils were frequently used as lubricants, but due to their high water content, the weapons had to be cleaned frequently to reduce rust. Many replacement weapons were received already in a rusted condition. CCF soldiers generally maintained their individual weapons in excellent condition, but motor vehicles were apparently beyond many of them. Chinese soldiers were reported to have filled radiators with *kaoliang* wine in lieu of antifreeze and to have lit bonfires under the engine compartments of their trucks to thaw the engine. See Rigg, 112.

66. "Enemy Motor Transport in North Korea," *USAFFE Intelligence Digest*, I, no. 9 (2 May 1953), 37.

67. "Enemy Motor Transport in North Korea," 37.

68. *Supply and Transportation System of the Chinese Communist and North Korean Forces in Korea*, 93.

69. "Enemy Motor Transport in North Korea," 36.

70. *Supply and Transportation System of the Chinese Communist and North Korean Forces in Korea*, 43.

71. "Enemy Motor Transport in North Korea," 37.

72. "The Enemy Supply System in North Korea," 22.

73. "Enemy Motor Transport in North Korea," 37.

74. *Supply and Transportation System of the Chinese Communist and North Korean Forces in Korea*, 43.

75. *Supply and Transportation System of the Chinese Communist and North Korean Forces in Korea*, 11.

76. "Enemy Motor Transport in North Korea," 37.

77. "Railroads and Highway Transport in North Korea and Their Impact on Enemy Logistics," *USAFFE Intelligence Digest*, I, no. 13 (2 July 1953), 39; "Military Supply in North Korea," *USAFFE Intelligence Digest*, V, no. 10 (October 1955), 41.

78. "The Enemy Supply System in North Korea," 25; "Military Supply in North Korea," 40.

79. "The Enemy Supply System in North Korea," 24 and 26.

80. "Chinese Communist Army and North Korean Army Logistics and Class Supply," 54; *Supply and Transportation System of the Chinese Communist and North Korean Forces in Korea*, 61–62.

81. *Supply and Transportation System of the Chinese Communist and North Korean Forces in Korea*, 33.

82. *Supply and Transportation System of the Chinese Communist and North Korean Forces in Korea*, 32.

83. *Supply and Transportation System of the Chinese Communist and North Korean Forces in Korea*, 13, 32, and 44.

84. "Interrogation Reports—North Korean Forces: North Korean Logistics," 23.

85. Some NKPA or CCF divisional supply installations were also located in the intermediate zone when the terrain or tactical situation required.

86. *Supply and Transportation System of the Chinese Communist and North Korean Forces in Korea*, 58–59. The larger supply complexes in the intermediate zone and rear area generally handled all classes of supplies in a single installation, although normally the major classes of supply were physically separated.

87. *Handbook on the Chinese Communist Army*, 66; *Supply and Transportation System of the Chinese Communist and North Korean Forces in Korea*, 24–25.

88. *Supply and Transportation System of the Chinese Communist and North Korean Forces in Korea*, 24.

89. *Handbook on the Chinese Communist Army*, 66; *Supply and Transportation System of the Chinese Communist and North Korean Forces in Korea*, 24–25.

90. *Supply and Transportation System of the Chinese Communist and North Korean Forces in Korea*, 24.

91. Inclosure 8 to Headquarters, Eighth United States Army in Korea, Office of the Assistant Chief of Staff G-2, *Periodic Intelligence Report No. 878*, 6 December 1952.

92. Futrell, 471.

93. "The Enemy Supply System in North Korea," 20. See Map 4.1.

94. "The Enemy Supply System in North Korea," 23.

95. "Chinese Communist Army and North Korean Army Logistics and Class Supply," 55.

96. *Supply and Transportation System of the Chinese Communist and North Korean Forces in Korea*, 15–17.

97. *Supply and Transportation System of the Chinese Communist and North Korean Forces in Korea*, 19.

98. *Supply and Transportation System of the Chinese Communist and North Korean Forces in Korea*, 8–9.

99. *Supply and Transportation System of the Chinese Communist and North Korean Forces in Korea*, 10.

100. *Supply and Transportation System of the Chinese Communist and North Korean Forces in Korea*, 9–10.

101. "Chinese Communist Army and North Korean Army Logistics and Class Supply," 55. Main Depots were inventoried and reported to Branch Unit every two months, and a consolidated report of all supply stock was submitted by each Branch Unit to the RSD of CCF GHQ every five months.

102. "Chinese Communist Army and North Korean Army Logistics and Class Supply," 53.

103. General Headquarters, Far East Command, Military Intelligence Section, Intelligence Division, *Order of Battle Information, Chinese Communist Regular Ground Forces (China, Manchuria, and Korea)* ([Tokyo]: General Headquarters, Far East Command, Military Intelligence Section, Intelligence Division, 9 December 1951), 13–14.

104. "The Enemy Supply System in North Korea," 16.

105. "Chinese Communist Army Supply System," 37.

106. "Chinese Communist Army Supply System," 37–38. The 1st and 15th Chinese Communist Armies (CCA) staged at Tunghua; the 12th at Shihchianchuang; the 16th at Mukden; the 20th at Meihokou; the 39th at Liaoyuan; the 42nd at Tiehling; the 54th at Penchi; the 47th and 66th at Tientsin; and the 23rd, 46th, 50th, 60th, 63rd, and 64th at Antung.

107. "Chinese Communist Army and North Korean Army Logistics and Class Supply," 49; "Effect of the Armistice on Enemy Logistics in North Korea, Part II: Enemy Supply System and Logistics Requirements in North Korea," *USAFFE Intelligence Digest*, IV, no. 8 (October 1954), 25.

108. "The Enemy Supply System in North Korea," 26.

109. "The Enemy Supply System in North Korea," 24. The exception was the NKPA supply complex in the Sinanjung/Marhwi-ri area, which supported the far eastern sector of the front. It was served exclusively by truck.

110. "Military Supply in North Korea," 38.

111. "The Enemy Supply System in North Korea," 26.

112. "Chinese Communist Army and North Korean Army Logistics and Class Supply," 53.

113. "The Enemy Supply System in North Korea," 23. One reported regulation prohibited more than 7 tons of supplies in an individual shelter.

114. *Enemy Tactics, Techniques and Doctrine*, 41.

115. *Enemy Tactics, Techniques and Doctrine*, 52.

116. *Enemy Tactics, Techniques and Doctrine*, Sketch No. 8.

117. *Supply and Transportation System of the Chinese Communist and North Korean Forces in Korea*, 41.

118. "The Enemy Supply System in North Korea," 21; "Chinese Communist Army and North Korean Army Logistics and Class Supply," 57.

119. "The Enemy Supply System in North Korea," 21.

120. "The Enemy Supply System in North Korea," 21.

121. "The Enemy Supply System in North Korea," 21.

122. "Chinese Communist Army and North Korean Army Logistics and Class Supply," 55.

123. *Supply and Transportation System of the Chinese Communist and North Korean Forces in Korea*, 40–41.

124. "Interrogation Reports—North Korean Forces: Typical North Korean Infantry Division," 12. The concepts of "basic load" and "Unit of Fire" are discussed in Chapter 5.

125. "Interrogation Reports—North Korean Forces: Typical North Korean Infantry Division," 11.

126. "The Enemy Supply System in North Korea," 22.

127. "The Enemy Supply System in North Korea," 19.

128. *Supply and Transportation System of the Chinese Communist and North Korean Forces in Korea*, 40. This would have amounted to about one to three UOF for a CCF infantry division.

129. "Chinese Communist Army and North Korean Army Logistics and Class Supply," 55; "The Enemy Supply System in North Korea," 24.

130. "Chinese Communist Army and North Korean Army Logistics and Class Supply," 55; *Supply and Transportation System of the Chinese Communist and North Korean Forces in Korea*, 66 and 94.

131. "The Enemy Supply System in North Korea," 24–25.

132. "The Enemy Supply System in North Korea," 25.

133. "The Enemy Supply System in North Korea," 24–25.

5

NKPA and CCF Supply Requirements

One of the more persistent myths of the Korean War is that North Korean and Chinese Communist soldiers were able to subsist on a mere handful of rice per day, obtained all their arms and ammunition from their enemies, and moved all supplies by animal cart or human porters. Although the supply requirements of the NKPA and CCF in Korea were amazingly low when compared to the requirements for equivalent UNC units, the Communist forces did generate substantial requirements for formal supply and transport forward of tremendous quantities of food, petroleum products, weapons, and ammunition. The size of the Communist forces in Korea alone was sufficiently great to preclude living off the land and to require an established line of communications. Although technologically primitive by Western military standards, both the NKPA and CCF were equipped with a significant number of motor vehicles requiring resupply of POL, and both armies possessed towed and self-propelled artillery capable of a high rate of fire. It is only in comparison with UNC forces that the Communist requirements seem very low.

SIZE OF FORCES SUPPORTED

The supply requirements of any force are determined primarily by the size of the force in terms of the number of soldiers and animals, the number of weapons of different types, and the number of combat and logistical vehicles supported. Supply requirements are also influenced by the mode of combat (attack, defense, pursuit, withdrawal), and in a dynamic combat situation supply requirements change over time as casualties are sustained, reinforcements arrive, and the tempo of operations changes. This was certainly true of the supply requirements of the NKPA and CCF in Korea; strengths, types and amounts of equipment, and the tempo of combat operations fluctuated significantly between June 1950 and July 1953, and as a consequence the supply requirements of the Communist forces in Korea varied somewhat at different times during the war.

Reliable information about the strength and equipment of the NKPA and CCF in Korea was not easy to obtain, and as a result UNC intelligence estimates were somewhat unreliable. However, a careful collation of the available historical data makes possible the depiction of estimated NKPA and CCF strength at various times during the Korean War (Table 5.1).

The North Korean army which invaded South Korea on 25 June 1950 was composed of some 135,000 men in two corps comprising eight full-strength infantry divisions, two half-strength infantry divisions, an armored brigade, an independent infantry regiment, a motorcycle reconnaissance regiment, and five brigades of the *Bo An Dae*, or Border Constabulary.[1] By the time the attacking NKPA forces had reached the Pusan Perimeter and launched their major attack across the Naktong River on 4-5 August 1950, they had been reduced to probably no more than 70,000 effectives in the eleven committed divisions (ten infantry and one armored) and retained less than 75 percent of their original equipment.[2] Almost the entire NKPA was subsequently destroyed during the advance of UNC forces to the Yalu River in late 1950 and was subsequently reformed under CCF auspices in Manchuria and reequipped on a slightly different pattern. By 1 July 1951, the rebuilt NKPA included 213,600 men in twenty-three infantry divisions, one mechanized division, one armored division, and two independent infantry brigades controlled by seven corps headquarters. NKPA strength peaked in October 1952 at around 266,600 men in eighteen divisions and six independent brigades.

Elements of the Chinese Communist XIIIth Army Group of the Fourth Field Army began to enter Korea around the middle of October 1950 and were followed in early November by elements of the IXth Army Group of the Third Field Army. By late November some 300,000 Chinese Communist troops were in Korea: 180,000 in the six armies (eighteen divisions) of the XIIIth Army Group facing the U.S. Eighth Army in western Korea and 120,000 in the three armies (twelve divisions) of the IXth Army Group facing the U.S. X Corps near the Chosin Reservoir.[3] The total of 300,000 men also included two artillery divisions and part of a third, a cavalry regiment, and two truck regiments as well as other support troops.

By the time the CCF launched the second "pulse" of the spring offensive in mid-May 1951, the total strength of the CCF in Korea had grown to about 542,000 men.[4] The Chinese suffered serious casualties during their spring offensives, but when armistice talks began at Kaesong on 1 July 1951 they still had about 282,100 men in some forty divisions in Korea. One year later, on 1 July 1952, fifty-one CCF divisions with some 540,200 men manned the line across Korea from the west coast to the central Taebaek Range and were supported by about 10,000 Soviet and Soviet-bloc advisors and technicians. The Chinese had some 732,300 men in the field at the beginning of October 1952,

Table 5.1
Estimated Strength of Communist Ground Forces in Korea, 25 June 1950–27 July 1953[3]

Date	NKPA		CCF		Soviet and Satellite	Total	
	Div/Brigade	Personnel	Divisions	Personnel	Personnel	Div/Brigade	Personnel
25 June 1950	10/6+	135,000	-	-		10/6+	135,000
5 August 1950	11+	70,000	-	-	?	11+	70,000
1 September 1950	14+	97,850	-	-	?	14+	97,850
28 December 1950	23/3	173,297	34	278,579	?	57/3	451,876
7 January 1951	25/4	200,949	35	299,579	?	60/4	500,528
19 June 1951	24/3	181,489	41	274,479	?	65/3	455,968
1 July 1951	25/2	213,600	40	282,100	?	65/2	495,700
14 July 1951	24/3	227,721	42	264,854	?	66/3	492,575
1 October 1951	24/3	208,900	49	412,200	?	73/3	621,100
1 January 1952	21/4	204,600	52	513,100	?	73/4	717,700
1 April 1952	20/4	223,800	52	544,300	?	72/4	768,100
1 July 1952	19/4	221,400	51	540,200	10,000	70/4	771,600
1 October 1952	18/6	266,600	51	732,300	10,000	69/6	1,008,900
7 December 1952	17/7	263,500	53	752,900	10,000	70/7	1,026,400
21 December 1952	17/7	262,800	53	752,600	10,000	70/7	1,025,400
1 January 1953	18/7	263,400	51	751,300	10,000	69/7	1,024,700
1 April 1953	18/7	263,400	54	793,200	10,000	72/7	1,066,600
1 July 1953	18/7	262,200	54	818,700	10,000	72/7	1,090,900
12 July 1953	18/7	262,900	58	836,500	10,000	76/7	1,109,400
27 July 1953	18/7	263,800	58	783,300	10,000	76/7	1,057,100

but they lost heavily in the fighting in October 1952; on 1 November 1952, seven CCF armies (166,000 men) were on the frontlines and another ten CCF armies (over 350,000 men) were in reserve.[6] Beginning in January 1953, three CCF armies and one NKPA corps were replaced on line by newly trained and equipped units, and the other divisions on the front were reinforced by men from reserve elements so that by 12 July 1953 the total of NKPA-CCF manpower in the field peaked at 1,109,400 men.[7]

At the time of the armistice on 27 July 1953, the Communist ground forces in Korea totaled about 1,057,100 men: 783,300 Chinese in fifty-eight CCF infantry divisions and supporting units; 263,800 North Koreans in eighteen NKPA infantry divisions and supporting units; and some 10,000 Soviet and Satellite troops, mostly anti-aircraft artillerymen and some advisors and medical technicians.[8] These forces were equipped with some 4,186 artillery pieces, 174 self-propelled guns, 692 antitank guns, 72 multiple-rocket launchers, 474 medium tanks, and 16 heavy tanks.

Inasmuch as supply requirements are often discussed in terms of the quantities required to support a combat division, it is important to have some idea of the size and equipment of both the NKPA and CCF division. The strength and organization of both the NKPA and CCF infantry division changed significantly during the course of the war, and there was little standardization among divisions. Furthermore, no division was ever at 100 percent of authorized allowances; indeed some divisions operated for extended periods considerably understrength. Nevertheless, snapshots of the "average" NKPA and CCF infantry division can be useful.[9]

The June 1950 NKPA infantry division was based on the Soviet model, was comparatively mechanized, and at full-strength consisted of 709 officers, 8 nurses, and 10,218 enlisted men distributed in a division headquarters, three rifle regiments, an artillery regiment, a self-propelled artillery battalion, an antitank gun battalion, an engineer battalion, a signal battalion, a training battalion, a medical battalion, a reconnaissance troop, and a division rear services section.[10] The NKPA infantry division underwent several reorganizations during the course of the war. In April 1953, the "standard" NKPA infantry division had a strength of 855 officers, 18 nurses, and 9,737 enlisted men distributed among a headquarters, three rifle regiments, an artillery regiment, an antitank battalion, an anti-aircraft battalion, an engineer battalion, a reconnaissance battalion, a signal battalion, a submachinegun company, a medical battalion, and a rear services section.[11] The weapons densities of both the 1950 and 1953 variants of the NKPA infantry division are depicted in Table 5.2.

The CCF infantry divisions which entered Korea in October and November 1950 were relatively "light" and much less mechanized than their NKPA counterparts, factors which contributed to the serious underestimation of their combat potential by UNC intelligence agencies.[12] CCF commanders also exercised much greater latitude in the organization of their commands, and thus there was wide variance in the size and armament of various CCF divisions. However, two main types were encountered: Type I, with an organic artillery battalion, and Type II, with an organic artillery regiment.[13] At full strength, the Type I CCF infantry division had 1,414 officers and 10,990 men distributed in a head-quarters (command section, staff section, and political section), three infantry regiments, an artillery battalion (sixty officers and 558 enlisted men), a recon-naissance company, an engineer company, a signal company, a transportation company, a security company, and a rear services section.[14] The Type II CCF infantry division was identical except that the 718-man artillery battalion was replaced by a 1,778-man artillery regiment, thus bringing the division total to 1,580 officers and 11,984 enlisted men.[15] The CCF infantry division also con-

Table 5.2
Authorized Weapons Density of NKPA and CCF Infantry Division[16]

Weapon	1950 NKPA Div	Apr 1953 NKPA Div	1950 CCF Div Type I/II	Apr 1953 CCF Div Type II
Pistols	1,298	1,441		959
Rifles and Carbines	6,089	5,746		6,608
Submachineguns	3,198	3,445		3,613
Light Machineguns	385	399	204/213	225
Heavy Machineguns	162	162	54	54
12.7-mm AA Machineguns	24	30	27/39	39
37-mm Anti-Aircraft Guns		8	0/12	12
3.5-in Rocket Launchers			57	54
14.5-mm Antitank Rifles	66	66		
45-mm Antitank Guns	54	30		
57-mm Recoilless Rifles			18	27
60-mm Mortars			57	87
82-mm Mortars	81	108	45	45*
120-mm Mortars	18	24	12	
70-mm Howitzers			12	12
75-mm Pack Howitzers			12	12
76-mm Guns	24	24		
76-mm Self-Propelled Guns	16			
76-mm Howitzers	12			24**
76.2-mm Guns			0/12	
122-mm Howitzers	12	12		
Trucks	ca. 194	ca. 100	< 30/ca. 23	ca. 23

* 82-mm and 120-mm mortars ** 75-mm and 76-mm guns and howitzers

tinued to evolve throughout the war, generally in the direction of more firepower and greater mechanization. By April 1953, the "normal" (Type II) full-strength CCF infantry division comprised 1,430 officers and 12,619 enlisted men.[17] The weapons densities of the 1950 Type I and Type II and of the April 1953 Type II variants of the CCF infantry division are depicted in Table 5.2.

RATIONS

The quantity and quality of food (Class I supplies) required by the soldiers of the NKPA and CCF in Korea was substantially less than that required by U.S., ROK, and other UNC troops. Although the "official" ration was adequate, it was seldom available in full due to UNC interdiction and routine inefficiencies of the Communist supply distribution system. Consequently, Communist troops were normally required to supplement their meager issue rations by foraging. Nevertheless, throughout the Korean War the troops of the NKPA and CCF remained sufficiently well-fed to permit them to operate with a fair degree of efficiency.[18]

The normal diet of the NKPA soldier consisted principally of rice and millet supplemented with issues of soy sauce, salt, potatoes, fresh vegetables, fish, kelp, and corn.[19] The official peacetime NKPA ration (i.e., daily issue) had a total weight of about four pounds: 1,000 grams of rice, 400 grams of vegetables, 150 grams of meat, 150 grams of fish, and 150 grams of condiments (spices, soy sauce, bean curd, salt, oils, etc.).[20] The official ration was designed to provide the NKPA soldier two or three meals a day. Of course, the official peacetime ration was not available after hostilities began, and UNC intelligence agencies usually estimated the amount of food issued to the NKPA soldier at about three pounds per day.[21] The combat ration sometimes consisted of baked rice or millet and rice in the form of flour or biscuits.

Under normal conditions, the Chinese Communist soldier in Korea received two meals per day, consisting principally of a mixture of *kaoliang* (sorghum), millet, corn, and beans.[22] Rice was also provided, but less frequently than other grains (e.g., millet for northern Chinese). This basic ration was sometimes supplemented by salt, soy sauce, oil, pickled vegetables, peanuts, mushrooms, powdered eggs, and/or canned meat or fish. Considerable variation existed in western estimates of the total weight of the CCF ration. Apparently, the normal "peacetime" standard was 2.66 lb/man/day comprised of 1.95 lb of rice (or millet), .63 lb of vegetables, and .09 lb of meat plus small quantities of tea and condiments.[23] Estimates of the CCF ration in Korea range from 2.2 to 4.05 lb.[24] The best evidence seems to be that the "standard" CCF ration in 1951 was 2.96 lb/man/day (1.75 lb of rice or other cereal, 1.1 lb of vegetables, and .11 lb of oil, salt, and meat).[25]

The actual amounts issued to the CCF soldier each day usually differed significantly from the established standards. In the summer of 1951, CCF soldiers in Korea received mainly rice or millet with salt, often in insufficient quantities, but by the end of 1951, the CCF supply situation had improved enough to provide about 2.2 lb of cereal with salt and small amounts of meat, vegetables, and oils daily. By the end of 1952, most CCF soldiers were receiving 3.5 lb of food per day: 1.98 lb of cereal, 1.48 lb of meats, vegetables, and oils, and .04 lb of condiments.[26] Technicians, doctors, senior officers, and individuals singled out for special treatment by political officers received small additional quantities of meat and slightly more of other ration elements.

FORAGE

The number and types of animals used for transport and other military purposes by the NKPA and CCF in Korea varied widely from time to time. In general, the NKPA was somewhat more mechanized and used slightly fewer animals than did the CCF. In both cases, most of the animal transport was utilized at division level and below. UNC intelligence agencies usually estimated the number of animals in the NKPA division slice at 500 and in a CCF division slice at 600.[27] The daily forage ration for "Communist" animals (horse, mules, and oxen) was about 12 lb/day.[28] In all armies employing animals, forage constitutes a major supply and transport problem given the enormous quantities required and the high volume per unit of weight of most forage.

CLOTHING, WEAPONS, VEHICLES, AND OTHER EQUIPMENT

Supply requirements for individual clothing and equipment were substantially less for the NKPA and CCF in Korea than for UNC forces. NKPA soldiers were issued one uniform at a time and seldom carried extra clothing.[29] Under normal circumstances, soldiers of the CCF received two issues of clothing per year (two summer uniforms in February or March and one winter uniform in September or October) plus a pair of rubber-soled canvas "tennis" shoes every two months.[30] There was no salvage or replacement system for individual clothing and equipment in either army. Uniforms were made of cotton cloth, which came in a variety of colors. Khaki, mustard, brown, green, olive-drab, and gray uniforms were common. The Chinese soldier's winter uniform was constructed of the quilted cotton material frequently seen in Korean War-era photographs. Both NKPA and CCF soldiers were usually equipped with a pint-sized canteen, mess kit (rice bowl, chop sticks, and cup), first-aid kit, cloth bandoleers for ammunition and provisions, and often a small cloth utility pouch for carrying these items.[31]

The wide variety of weapons, vehicles, and other heavy equipment utilized by the NKPA and CCF as well as the varied distribution and sources of such matériel (issue or capture) and the lack of reliable consumption data generally preclude any independent calculation of NKPA and CCF supply requirements for such items. In any event, individual and crew-served weapons, artillery pieces, and vehicles were issued only irregularly to replace items lost or damaged in combat or otherwise rendered unserviceable.

Under the definitions used by the U.S. Army during the Korean War, Class II supplies included individual clothing and equipment, general Quartermaster supplies (for example, stoves, cleaning supplies, and tentage), most medical supplies and equipment, and various Chemical, Engineer, Signal, and Ordnance Corps items. Class IV supplies included individual and crew-served weapons, tracked and wheeled vehicles, repair parts, radios and radar sets, Quartermaster sales store (PX) items, and construction materials. Reliable consumption data for Class II and Class IV supplies for the NKPA and CCF in Korea are not available, but UNC intelligence agencies generally estimated Communist requirements for such items to be between 5 and 20 percent of the U.S. requirement.[32] The contemporary U.S. planning figures were 4.67 lb/man/day for Class II supplies and 17 lb/man/day for Class IV supplies when calculated on a theater-wide basis.[33] Calculated solely for the infantry division in the defense, the requirement was 5.63 lb/man/day.[34] Thus, if we assume that NKPA-CCF requirements averaged 15 percent of U.S. requirements, Communist forces in Korea probably required about 2.824 lb/man/day of Class II and IV supplies when calculated on a theater-wide basis, or about .85 lb/man/day when calculated solely on the basis of the infantry division in the defense.[35]

PETROLEUM, OILS, AND LUBRICANTS

NKPA and CCF units in Korea were generally less mechanized than comparable UNC units and generally did not use petroleum products for other than vehicle fuel (i. e., for heating or cooking purposes). Thus, the requirements of the NKPA and CCF in Korea for petroleum, oils, and lubricants (Class III supplies) were substantially less than for equivalent size UNC units, and such products were utilized mainly above division level. In 1950, NKPA fuel consumption was probably about 1.3 lb/man/day versus a U.S. planning requirement of 10.8 lb/man/ day.[36]

In practice, fuel was issued to both NKPA and CCF units on the basis of preestablished vehicle performance standards (i.e., a certain number of miles per gallon) and anticipated utilization.[37] Following the Soviet Army method, NKPA-CCF fuel resupply requirements were usually calculated on the basis of the number of refills required for various types of combat.[38] For example, the 1950 NKPA infantry division had 194 trucks and sixteen SU-76 self-propelled guns. The usual NKPA divisional truck was the GAZ-51, which had a 27-gallon tank, and the SU-76 fuel tank held 116 gallons.[39] Thus 5,238 gallons would be required to refill the 194 GAZ-51s, and 1,856 gallons would be required to refill the sixteen SU-76s. Gasoline weighs 6 lb per gallon; thus, 21.28 short tons of fuel would be required to refill the vehicles of the 1950 NKPA infantry division. In addition, allowance was made for lubricants and wastage. The usual Soviet practice was to allow 10 percent for lubricants and 10 percent for wastage.[40] However, the NKPA (and presumedly the CCF) acknowledged the age and inferior maintenance of their vehicles by allowing 20 percent for lubricants.[41] Thus, 30 percent (6.38 short tons) for lubricants and wastage must be added to 21.28 short tons of fuel required for the 1950 NKPA infantry division, thereby yielding a requirement of 27.66 short tons per division refill. Table 5.3 displays the daily fuel consumption factors (refills) required for various types of operations and the resulting theoretical daily resupply requirement in short tons for the 1950 NKPA division. Estimates of actual requirements at various times during the war, as shown for example in Tables 5.6 and 5.7, were quite different from these theoretical calculations due to fluctuations in the number and types of vehicles authorized and on hand, the actual combat situation, the different methods of calculating requirements used at various times by UNC intelligence analysts, and other factors, which generally served to reduce the actual POL supply requirements of NKPA (and CCF) units significantly.

Table 5.3
1950 NKPA Infantry Division Fuel Resupply Requirements by Type of Combat[42]

Type of Operation	Daily Refills Required	Daily Resupply Requirement (ST)
Long-Term Operations	.25	6.92
Attack	.75	20.75
Pursuit	1.00	27.66
Covering Action	.60	16.60
Defense	.50	13.83
Withdrawal	.70	19.36
Average for All Types of Combat	.63	17.43

Most of the motor vehicles used by the NKPA and CCF were located in rear area support units rather than in the forward divisions.[43] UNC intelligence agencies estimated the fuel requirements for NKPA-CCF logistical and combat vehicles in general to be 7 gallons (gasoline) per truck per day, 14 gallons (diesel) per tank per day, and 11.5 gallons (gasoline) per self-propelled gun per day.[44]

AMMUNITION

The resupply of ammunition (Class V supplies) was perhaps the most difficult logistical problem for both the NKPA and the CCF in Korea. The wide
variety of weapons in use and the small indigenous production of ammunition
was compounded by UNC air interdiction. Captured ammunition met only
minimal short-term requirements. Nevertheless, by 1953 the Communists were
apparently well supplied with ammunition of all types and were even able to
stockpile significant quantities in forward areas.

Both the NKPA and CCF calculated ammunition requirements using the concept of the *Unit of Fire* (UOF). The UOF represented a specific number of
rounds per type weapon and could be translated into tonnage factors using standard weights for various types of ammunition. Table 5.4 displays the calculation of the ammunition requirements (one UOF) for a full-strength June 1950
NKPA division.

Table 5.4
Calculation of One Unit of Fire for a June 1950 NKPA Infantry Division[45]

Type of Weapon	Rounds per UOF	Weight (lb) of UOF per Weapon	Number of Weapons in Division*	Total Weight of UOF (ST)
Pistol	22	.5**	1,298	.33**
Rifle or Carbine, 7.62-mm	100	7.7	6,089	23.44
Submachinegun, 7.62-mm	300	8.8	3,198	14.07
Light Machinegun, 7.62-mm	800	54.6	385	10.51
Hvy Machinegun, 7.62-mm	2,500	205.2	162	16.62
AA Machinegun, 12.7-mm	6,000	2,257.2	24	27.09
Antitank Rifle, 14.5-mm	120	34.5	66	1.14
Antitank Gun, 45-mm	200	1,408.0	54	38.02
Mortar, 82-mm	120	1,071.4	81	43.39
Mortar, 120-mm	80	4,400.0	18	39.60
Gun or Howitzer, 76-mm	140	3,592.6	52	93.41
Howitzer, 122-mm	120**	4840.0**	12	29.04
Hand Grenade	2 per man	4.8	***	26.24
Antitank Grenade	500/inf regt	1,870.0	3 inf regts	2.81
TOTAL				366 ST

* At full strength   ** Estimated; no data available   *** 10,935 men

Ammunition expenditure rates vary with the type of operation, but once the total weight of one UOF for a type division is known, the required resupply tonnages can be calculated easily using standard expenditure factors. Table 5.5 displays the expenditure factors for various modes of combat and the resulting daily resupply requirements for a June 1950 NKPA infantry division.

Table 5.5
Estimated Daily Expenditure in UOF and Resulting Required Resupply Tonnages—
June 1950 NKPA Infantry Division[46]

Type of Combat	Estimated Daily Expenditure (UOF)	Required Resupply Tonnage*
Deliberate Attack—First Day	.75	272.25
Deliberate Attack—Succeeding Days	.30	108.9
Hasty Attack	.50	181.5
Pursuit	.30	108.9
Defense—First Day	1.50	544.5
Defense—Succeeding Days	.75	272.25
Delaying Action	.50	181.5
Average for All Types of Combat	.51	185.13

* Division at full strength

As was the case with POL requirements, there were several alternate methods of calculating ammunition requirements. Theater-wide gross requirements, for example, could be calculated on the basis of lb/man/day. The authors of *North Korean Logistics and Methods of Accomplishment* proposed an ammunition resupply planning factor for the NKPA of 5.14 lb/man/day, the same factor used to calculate U.S. requirements at that time.[47]

DIVISIONAL REQUIREMENTS

As has been noted, the structure of both the NKPA and the CCF infantry division changed substantially during the course of the war, and Communist divisions in Korea were seldom at 100 percent of authorized strength in men or weapons. Consequently, a precise estimate of the daily tonnage of various classes of supply required to sustain the NKPA or CCF division at various times during the Korean War is difficult to compile. However, Table 5.6 presents an estimate of NKPA and CCF divisional supply requirements based on the consumption factors discussed earlier in this chapter.[48]

Table 5.6

Estimate of NKPA-CCF Divisional Supply Requirements in Short Tons per Day[49]

Class of Supply	Factors (lb/man /day)	NKPA Infantry Division		CCF Infantry Division		
		June 1950	April 1953	October 1950	April 1953	Average
I (Rations)	3	16.41	15.92	18.61	21.08	18.01
I (Forage)	12	3.00	3.00	3.60	3.60	3.30
II & IV (Eqp)	.85	4.65	4.51	5.28	5.98	5.11
III (POL)	-	17.43	5.10	1.17	1.17	3.14
V (Ammo)	5.14	28.11	27.28	31.88	36.11	30.85
TOTAL		69.60 ST	55.81 ST	60.54 ST	67.94 ST	60.41 ST

In some respects, a more accurate assessment of supply requirements is obtained by considering the requirements for a division slice rather than for the division alone. The division slice is a planning concept, usually expressed as a number of individuals, and represents the number of individuals in a type division plus a proportionate share of the individuals at higher echelons (corps, army, and theater) providing support to the division. In May 1953, UNC intelligence officers calculated the daily requirements for NKPA and CCF division slices of 10,180 and 12,170 men, respectively, as of 9 April 1952.[50] Their calculations are presented in Table 5.7.

Table 5.7

Estimated NKPA-CCF Daily Supply Requirements in Short Tons per Division Slice, 9 April 1952[51]

Class of Supply	NKPA (ST/day)	CCF (ST/day)
I (Rations)	18.21	16.33
II & IV (Equipment)	8.20	7.72
III (POL)	3.33	3.33
V (Ammunition)	9.59	6.48
TOTAL	39.33 ST	33.86 ST

OVERALL THEATER REQUIREMENTS

Throughout the Korean War, UNC intelligence agencies attempted to maintain up-to-date estimates of the supply requirements of the North Korean and Chinese Communist forces in Korea. Those estimates were based on detailed analysis of the number of personnel, weapons, and vehicles supported and thus were probably far more accurate than estimates of gross requirements obtained by the lb/man/day, POL refill, or ammunition Unit of Fire methods. Indeed, the UNC intelligence estimates provided a fairly accurate picture of overall Communist logistical requirements, particularly during the last year of the war. Table 5.8 presents UNC intelligence estimates of average theater-wide daily Communist supply requirements in Korea at various times in 1952 and 1953.

Table 5.8
NKPA-CCF Theater Logistical Requirements, 1952–1953[52]

Class of Supply	Total NKPA and CCF Supply Expenditures (ST/day)				
	1 Jan 1952	9 Apr 1952	1 Jan 1953	Jan-Mar 1953	Apr-Jun 1953
I (Rats & Forage)	1,508	1,392	2,062	2,102	2,143
II & IV (Equip)	884	650	1,080	1,177	1,291
III (POL)	292	276	408	486	515
V (Ammunition)	72	603	276	253	416
TOTAL	2,756	2,921	3,826	4,018	4,365

CONCLUSION

On a lb/man/day basis, NKPA and CCF resupply requirements for food, equipment, and fuel were much lower than for the UNC forces in Korea. NKPA-CCF ration requirements, for example, were only about 75 percent of the daily requirement for U.S. troops. NKPA-CCF requirements for equipment (Class II and IV supplies) and petroleum products (Class III supplies) were even lower, roughly 15 percent and 10 percent of U.S. requirements, respectively. On the other hand, ammunition requirements were approximately the same on a lb/man/day basis and, due to the greater number of animals employed by the NKPA and CCF, forage requirements were much higher. However, as the foregoing calculations demonstrate, in terms of the tonnages that had to be obtained and transported to the forward areas, the daily supply requirements of the Communist forces in Korea were substantial. After October 1952, the Communist forces in Korea numbered over one million men, and even given relatively low lb/man/day resupply rates the total requirements far exceeded any reasonable expectation of what could be captured from the enemy, foraged from the countryside, or transported exclusively on the backs of men and animals. Contrary to the popular myth, the NKPA-CCF required, and in fact possessed, both a fairly sophisticated supply system to acquire and manage the enormous amounts of supplies needed and a relatively efficient system of mechanized transport, which relied heavily on railroads and trucks to move those supplies forward.

NOTES

1. Roy E. Appleman, *South to the Naktong, North to the Yalu* (Washington: Office of the Chief of Military History, Department of the Army, 1961), 11.

2. Appleman, 263; James L. Stokesbury, *A Short History of the Korean War* (New York: Quill/William Morrow, 1988), 73. The NKPA 105th Tank Brigade was redesignated the 105th Tank Division in late July 1950.

3. Billy C. Mossman, *Ebb and Flow, November 1950–July 1951* (Washington: Center of Military History, United States Army, 1990), 53–54; Appleman, 768–769.

4. James F. Schnabel, *Policy and Direction: The First Year* (United States Army in the Korean War; Washington: Office of the Chief of Military History, Department of the Army, 1972), 387.

5. Data abstracted from Eighth United States Army in Korea, G-2, *Periodic Intelligence Reports* and *Weekly Intelligence Summaries*; United States Far East Command, G-2, *Daily Intelligence Summaries*; Appleman, 11 and 263.

6. Walter G. Hermes, *Truce Tent and Fighting Front* (Washington: Office of the Chief of Military History, Department of the Army, 1966), 367–368 and note 5.

7. Hermes, 389. See Table 5.1.

8. Headquarters, Eighth United States Army, Office of the Assistant Chief of Staff, G-2, *Intelligence Estimate, 27 July 1953* (APO 301: Headquarters, Eighth United States Army, Office of the Assistant Chief of Staff, G-2, 27 July 1953), 5.

9. Organizational diagrams for variants of both the NKPA and CCF infantry division can be found in Chapter 3.

10. "Interrogation Reports—North Korean Forces: Typical North Korean Infantry Division," *ATIS Research Supplement*, Issue No. 1 (19 October 1950), 3–15 and Charts 1 and 2; Headquarters, Department of the Army, Assistant Chief of Staff G-2, *North Korean Order of Battle* (Intelligence Research Project No. 5942; Washington: Headquarters, Department of the Army, Office of the Assistant Chief of Staff, G-2, 1 September 1950). See Diagram 3.4.

11. Headquarters, United States X Corps, *Organization Charts, Strength of Units, Weapons Tables, Korea, April 1953* (APO 909: Headquarters, United States X Corps, April 1953). See Diagram 3.5.

12. Eliot A. Cohen and John Gooch, *Military Misfortunes: The Anatomy of Failure in War* (New York: Vintage Books, 1991), 176–177. Cohen and Gooch note that "Intelligence, therefore, came to view Chinese forces as a kind of inferior version of the North Koreans."

13. See Diagram 3.13.

14. Headquarters, United States Army Forces Far East (Advance), Office of the Assistant Chief of Staff, G-2, *Chinese Communist Ground Forces in Korea: Tables of Organization and Equipment* (APO 500: 1953), Chart 6.

15. *Chinese Communist Ground Forces in Korea: Tables of Organization and Equipment*, Chart 21.

16. "Interrogation Reports—North Korean Forces: Typical North Korean Infantry Division," 3–15 and Charts 1 and 2; *North Korean Order of Battle, Organization Charts, Strength of Units, Weapons Tables, Korea, April 1953*; *Chinese Communist Ground Forces in Korea: Tables of Organization and Equipment*, Charts 6 and 21.

17. *Organization Charts, Strength of Units, Weapons Tables, Korea, April 1953*.

18. Most NKPA prisoners of war (PWs) claimed their rations had been inadequate. Local shortages did occur, but PWs were seldom emaciated and NKPA troops continued to march long, dig deep, and fight hard. There was some indication that night blindness induced by vitamin deficiencies was prevalent among NKPA troops (see Headquarters, Eighth United States Army, Assistant Chief of Staff G-2/Headquarters, United States Fifth Air Force, Assistant Chief of Staff A-2, *Supply and Transportation System of the Chinese Communist and North Korean Forces in Korea* {[Tokyo]: Headquarters, Eighth United States Army, Assistant Chief of Staff G-2/Headquarters, United States Fifth Air Force, Assistant Chief of Staff A-2, 23 September 1951}, 65).

19. *Supply and Transportation System of the Chinese Communist and North Korean Forces in Korea*, 65. Issue of meat was rare.

20. E. L. Atkins, H. P. Griggs, and Roy T. Sessums, *North Korean Logistics and Methods of Accomplishment* (ORO Technical Memorandum ORO-T-8 [EUSAK]; [Chevy Chase, MD]: Operations Research Office, The Johns Hopkins University, 1951), 8–9. By comparison, the ROK Army ration, developed with U.S. assistance in September 1950, provided 3,210 calories, weighed 2.3 pounds, and included rice starch, biscuits, rice cake, peas, kelp, fish, chewing gum, and condiments and was packed in a water-proofed bag (see Appleman, 115–116).

21. *North Korean Logistics and Methods of Accomplishment*, 10–11 (Tables II and III), estimates three lbs/man/day. United States Far East Command *Intelligence Summary (FEC INTSUM) No. 3544*, dated 23 May 1952 (p. M-2), a generally more accurate source, yields 2.99 lb/man/day.

22. *Supply and Transportation System of the Chinese Communist and North Korean Forces in Korea*, 64.

23. Robert B. Rigg, *Red China's Fighting Hordes* (rev. ed., Harrisburg, PA: The Military Service Publishing Company, 1952), 123; James A. Huston, *Guns and Butter, Powder and Rice: U. S. Army Logistics in the Korean War* (Selinsgrove, PA: Susquehanna University Press, 1989), 357. One CCF PW reported that the daily ration issued in China was 3.5 lb (2.4 lb of rice, 0.4 lb of meat, and 0.7 lbs. of vegetables). See *Supply and Transportation System of the Chinese Communist and North Korean Forces in Korea*, 64.

24. Headquarters, Department of the Army, *Handbook on the Chinese Communist Army* (DA Pamphlet No. 30-51; Washington: USGPO, 1952), 68 (2.2 lb); *FEC INTSUM No. 3544*, M-2 (2.5 lb); *Supply and Transportation System of the Chinese Communist and North Korean Forces in Korea*, 32 (4.05 lb); and Headquarters, United States I Corps, G-2 Section, *CCF Logistical Capabilities: A Study of the Enemy Vehicular Effort on I Corps Front* ([Korea]: Headquarters, United States I Corps, G-2 Section, 28 June 1952), 4 (4.05 lb).

25. Inclosure 7 (CCF Rations) to Eighth United States Army Korea, Office of the Assistant Chief of Staff, G-2, *Periodic Intelligence Report (EUSAK PIR) No. 899*, 262400-272400 December 1952; *FEC INTSUM No. 3544*, 23 May 1952, M-2.

26. Inclosure 7 (CCF Rations) to *EUSAK PIR No. 899*, 262400-272400 December 1952. This ration provided about 3,700 calories per day compared to the 4,200 calories per day of the U.S. ration.

27. *FEC INTSUM No. 3544*, 23 May 1952, M-2.

28. *FEC INTSUM No. 3544*, 23 May 1952, M-2. A Far East Command intelligence study in February 1953 (Headquarters, Far East Command, Office of the Assistant Chief of Staff, J-2, *Logistical Capability of Communist Forces in Korea to Support a Major*

Offensive [APO 500: Headquarters, Far East Command, Office of the Assistant Chief of Staff, J-2, 28 February 1953], 1) estimated the Communist forage requirements at only 5 lb/animal/day based on an average of 500 animals per NKPA/CCF infantry division. Contemporary U.S. planning data estimated forage requirements at 10 lb of grain, 14 lb of hay, and 0.125 lb of salt per horse/mule per day (see Headquarters, Department of the Army, *Field Manual 101-10: Staff Officers' Field Manual—Organization, Technical, and Logistical Data* [Washington: Headquarters, Department of the Army, August 1949], 224).

29. *North Korean Logistics and Methods of Accomplishment*, 8.

30. "Chinese Communist Army Supply System," *USAFFE Intelligence Digest*, IV, no. 4 (June 1954), 33.

31. *Handbook on the Chinese Communist Army*, 78–79.

32. The authors of *North Korean Logistics and Methods of Accomplishment* (pp. 10–11, Tables II and III) estimated NKPA-CCF requirements for Class II and IV supplies at 5 to 10 percent of the U.S. requirement. The authors of *FEC INTSUM No. 3544*, 23 May 1952 (p. M-2) estimated NKPA-CCF requirements as 10 percent of the U.S. requirement (for the infantry division in the covering force and security role). The authors of *Logistical Capability of Communist Forces in Korea to Support a Major Offensive* (p. 2) estimated the NKPA-CCF requirement at 20 percent of the U.S. requirement (on a division basis).

33. *FM 101-10*, August 1949, 304. These planning data were derived from the experience of U.S. forces in the Pacific in World War II and do not include Air Force requirements.

34. *FM 101-10*, August 1949, 313.

35. The great difference between the theater-wide and infantry division in the defense estimates is due primarily to the large quantities of construction materials required in rear areas. The authors of *North Korean Logistics and Methods of Accomplishment* (pp. 10–11, Tables II and III) estimated the NKPA Class II and IV requirement at 0.8 lb/man/day. The estimate in *FEC INTSUM No. 3544*, 23 May 1952 (pp. M-1 and M-2) was 0.48 lb/man/day, and that in *Logistical Capability of Communist Forces in Korea to Support a Major Offensive* (p. 2) was 1.5 lb/man/day (at division level) plus a proportionate share of combat losses in intermediate and rear areas. These estimates all seem too low in view of the extensive enemy use of construction materials from mid-1951 onward. Twenty percent of the 1949 U.S. planning figure for construction materials alone (11.9 lb/man/day; *FM 101-10*, August 1949, 304) would have been 2.38 lb/man/day.

36. *FM 101-10*, August 1949, 304. The U.S. planning factor was for Pacific theater-wide usage, exclusive of Air Force and nonvehicle uses. The 1950 NKPA infantry division had about 12 percent of the number of motor vehicles of the U.S. infantry division. The lb/man/day method, using the concept of the division slice, was useful for calculating overall theater requirements, especially since much of the NKPA and CCF motorized transport was located above division level and was employed in combat service support tasks rather than direct combat tasks. Reverse calculation of the data on Class III consumption given in *FEC INTSUM No. 3544* yields planning factors of 0.55 lb/man/day for NKPA forces and 0.65 lb/man/day for CCF (see *FEC INTSUM No. 3544*, 23 May 1952, M-1). A slightly higher planning factor, 1.08 lb/man/day, was proposed in *North Korean Logistics and Methods of Accomplishment*, 10–11 (Tables II and III).

37. "Interrogation Reports—North Korean Forces: Typical North Korean Infantry Division, 13; "Chinese Communist Army Supply System," 35; "Chinese Communist

Army and North Korean Army Logistics and Class Supply," *USAFFE Intelligence Digest*, VI, no. 4 (April 1956), 55 and 58.

38. There were several alternative methods of calculating fuel requirements. When the distances to be driven were known (for example, for a specific convoy or for operations over a set route on a repetitive basis), the amount of required POL could be calculated using the factors of 1.0 gallon per mile for tracked vehicles and 0.125 gallons per mile for wheeled vehicles (see "Petroleum, Oils and Lubricants Requirements for Communist Ground Forces, Far East," *USAFFE Intelligence Digest*, V, no. 4 [April 1955], 67–68).

39. "Interrogation Reports—North Korean Forces: Typical North Korean Infantry Division," 14. *FEC INTSUM No. 3544*, 23 May 1952, M-3, indicated that the GAZ-51 tank held only 21 gallons. The higher figure is used here.

40. *FEC INTSUM No. 3544*, 23 May 1952, M-3. The Soviets also multiplied fuel consumption estimates by a factor of 1.3 during winter weather to account for warm-up time, etc.

41. "Interrogation Reports—North Korean Forces: Typical North Korean Infantry Division," 14.

42. "Interrogation Reports—North Korean Forces: Typical North Korean Infantry Division," 14. The refill factors are based on Soviet data. A 30 percent allowance has been made for lubricants, spoilage, and wastage. Similar tables could be constructed for variants in the structure of NKPA and CCF division encountered at later dates.

43. *Logistical Capability of Communist Forces in Korea to Support a Major Offensive*, 2–3. In early 1953, UNC intelligence agencies estimated that the Communists had about 16,000 wheeled motor vehicles in Korea, of which only about 12,000 to 13,000 were operational each day (night) and only about 300 of which operated exclusively in forward areas. The Communists also had approximately 530 tracked combat vehicles (tanks and self-propelled guns) operational in May 1953 (see *FEC INTSUM No. 3544*, 23 May 1952, M-3).

44. *Logistical Capability of Communist Forces in Korea to Support a Major Offensive*, 2. These estimates include an allowance of only 20 percent for lubricants, spoilage, and wastage.

45. "Interrogation Reports—North Korean Forces: Typical North Korean Infantry Division," 11–12. The weight of one June 1950 NKPA infantry division UOF given in the reference is slightly lower than that calculated in Table 5.4 (345.75 ST in reference vs. 363 ST in Table 5.4). Table 5.4 reflects a full-strength division. As is pointed out in *FEC INTSUM No. 3544*, 23 May 1952 (pp. M-3 and M-4), NKPA and CCF units were seldom at 100 percent of authorized TOE in personnel and weapons. The authors of *FEC INTSUM No. 3544* (p. M-4) estimated the actual weight of a UOF for various type enemy units (based on their estimated strength in May 1953) as NKPA infantry division = 291 ST; CCF infantry division = 164 ST; CCF artillery division = 104 ST. NKPA-CCF units in 1953 were generally smaller than their 1950 counterparts.

46. "Interrogation Reports—North Korean Forces: Typical North Korean Infantry Division," 13. The expenditure factors are derived from the experience of Soviet divisions in World War II. The expenditure rates encountered in Korea were probably somewhat lower, but in the absence of good historical expenditure data the Soviet figures should be used. During their initial drive into South Korea, NKPA combat units probably expended between 0.1 and 0.5 UOF per day (see "Interrogation Reports—North Korean Forces: Typical North Korean Infantry Division," 12). The authors of *FEC INTSUM No.*

3544, 23 May 1952 (p. M-4) indicated that as of 23 May 1952 no reliable expenditure factors for the NKPA and CCF were available but that they used a factor of 0.08 UOF/day for an infantry division in contact and 0.03 UOF/day for an infantry division in forward reserve.

47. *North Korean Logistics and Methods of Accomplishment*, 10–11 (Tables II and III). *FM 101-10*, August 1949 (p. 304) provided an ammunition planning factor of 5.14 lb/man/day for the Pacific theater less Air Force requirements.

48. The estimates presented by various authorities vary widely, ranging from 40 to 60 ST/division/day. Some discrepancies arise from the use by UNC intelligence agencies of various estimates of the authorized strength of NKPA and CCF divisions. Generally, the figures used were June 1950 NKPA infantry division = 10,970 officers and men; 1953 NKPA infantry division = 10,650 officers and men; 1950 CCF infantry division, Type I = 12,404 officers and men; 1950 CCF infantry division, Type II = 13,654 officers and men; and April 1953 CCF infantry division, Type II = 14,049 officers and men. The authors of *North Korean Logistics and Methods of Accomplishment* (pp. 10–11, Tables II and III) opt for 56.96 ST/day for an NKPA infantry division of 10,970 men. The authors of *Supply and Transportation System of the Chinese Communist and North Korean Forces in Korea* (p. iv) put the daily requirement at 48 ST (10 ST of Class I, eight ST of Class III, and 30 ST of Class V) for an NKPA or CCF division of 10,000 men. Huston (p. 354) estimates the daily supply consumption of a Communist division in the attack as ca. 60 ST/day (20 tons of Class I, four ST of Class II and IV, six ST of Class III, and 30 ST of Class V). Griffith (p. 157) states the daily requirements of a CCF frontline division as 40 ST (19.2 ST of Class I, 8.8 ST of Class II, 4.0 ST of Class III, and 8.0 ST of Class V). An interesting comparison is provided by the estimated daily supply requirement of 63.5 ST for a 16,000-man Japanese infantry division in China, Manchuria, or Korea in 1944 contained in Headquarters, Army Service Forces, Office of the Director of Plans and Operations, Planning Division, Strategic Logistics Branch, *Ability of the Japanese to Maintain Themselves in China, Manchuria, and Korea* (Report 13: *Economic Study*, Part 9; [Washington]: Headquarters, Army Service Forces, 21 October 1944), 4.

49. All quantities are notional and are based on a division at 100 percent strength. The June 1950 NKPA infantry division had 10,935 men. The April 1953 division was somewhat smaller at 10,610 men. The October 1950 Type I CCF infantry division had 12,404; the April 1953 Type II CCF infantry division had 14,049. It has been assumed that both types of NKPA division employed 500 draft animals, and both types of CCF division employed 600 draft animals. Class II and IV calculations are based on 15 percent of the contemporary U.S. requirement of 5.63 lb/man/day (division in the defense). Class III calculations are based on 0.63 refills per day (all types of combat) for sixteen SU-76 SP guns and 194 GAZ-51 trucks in the June 1950 NKPA division; 100 GAZ-51 trucks in the April 1953 NKPA division; and twenty-three GAZ-51 trucks in both the October 1950 and April 1953 CCF divisions. The Class III average is based on April 1953 NKPA and CCF divisions only; the high requirement of the well-motorized 1950 NKPA division unduly skews a straight average of the four figures. For Class V calculations, it is assumed that the same factor applied to all four types of division. Much larger estimates would result from using the Unit of Fire method (division in the defense): about 272 ST/day for the 1950 NKPA division; about 218 ST/day for the 1953 NKPA division; about 153 ST/day for the 1950 CCF division; and about 191 ST/day for the 1953 CCF division. Any discrepancy between calculations using the UOF method and the lb/man/day method can be explained by the higher concentration of heavy weapons in

forward combat divisions. The lb/man/day method is useful for calculating gross overall theater or division slice requirements, but the UOF method is more precise for determining the requirements of frontline combat units.

50. *FEC INTSUM No. 3544*, 23 May 1952, M-1.

51. *FEC INTSUM No. 3544*, 23 May 1952, M-1. The FEC intelligence staff based their estimates on a total NKPA strength of 243,386 men in twenty divisions and a total CCF strength of 641,471 men in sixty-three divisions as well as a total of 7,500 motor vehicles and 536 armored vehicles. Forage requirements were included with rations and were estimated for 500 animals in the NKPA division and 600 animals in the CCF division. The division slice was based on estimates of actual strength rather than the authorized strength per division. Thus the number of men in a division slice can be less than the authorized strength of the division itself, as in the current example.

52. *Logistical Capability of Communist Forces in Korea to Support a Major Offensive*, *FEC INTSUM No. 3544* , 23 May 1952; "Effect of the Armistice on Enemy Logistics in North Korea, Part II: Enemy Supply System and Logistics Requirements in North Korea," *USAFFE Intelligence Digest*, IV, no. 8 (October 1954), 25–32; "Railroads and Highway Transport in North Korea and Their Impact on Enemy Logistics," *USAFFE Intelligence Digest*, I, no. 13 (2 July 1953), 25. Total NKPA-CCF supply requirements for other dates in 1952 were as follows: 1 April 1952 = 2,893 ST/day; 1 July 1952 = 3,150 ST/day; and 1 October 1952 = 3,888 ST/day.

6

NKPA-CCF Distribution Systems

The critical segment of the NKPA-CCF logistical system in Korea was the distribution network. Given abundant Soviet support and secure production and storage facilities in Manchuria off limits to UNC attack, the principal logistical problem for the Communist forces was the movement of men and supplies from base areas in Manchuria and North Korea to the frontlines. Except for limited quantities of captured matériel and locally procured foodstuffs, all Communist supplies were subjected to the hazards of a distribution system under constant UNC interdiction, which compounded the difficulties posed by unfavorable terrain and weather, a comparative shortage of transport facilities and equipment, poor communications, and a minimally adequate management structure.

The NKPA and CCF in Korea maintained two separate but coordinated distribution systems, each of which employed a variety of transport means ranging from railroads and motor vehicles to ox carts and manpack operations. Both armies relied on railroads as the principal means of moving supplies from bases in Manchuria and North Korea as far forward as possible. After mid-1951, the area served by rail extended from the Manchurian border south approximately 100 miles to a line running generally from Pyongyang to Wonsan.[1] Trucks as well as animal transport and porters were frequently employed to shuttle around breaks in the rail system, and trucks were also used to supplement the railroads and to move supplies between rear area depots. From the rear area depots, supplies were moved forward by truck to supply points in the Army Group and Army/Corps rear areas and, in some cases, on down to division level or below. Rail and highway motor transport were very vulnerable to UNC air interdiction and the NKPA and CCF were thus forced to limit most of their supply and troop movements to the hours of darkness and to use less vulnerable, but also less effective, animal and human transport.

Motor transport in the NKPA, and to an even greater extent in the CCF in Korea, was limited at division level and practically nonexistent at lower echelons. At division level, distribution was effected primarily by animal and human transport, although trucks were used to the maximum extent possible whenever they were available. At regimental level and below, primary reliance was placed on animal transport and porters to deliver supplies to the frontline soldier. The practical effect of the lack of sufficient motor transport at lower echelons was to limit Communist tactical mobility and flexibility as well as the ability of the NKPA and CCF to maintain high levels of supply consumption over extended periods unless tell-tale stockpiles were created in advance in the area of operations.

NKPA-CCF LINES OF COMMUNICATIONS

The normal civilian lines of communications in Korea in 1950 have been described in Chapter 2.[2] Rail and highway routes were constantly improved and extended by both sides during the Korean War and provided the base facilities upon which the military lines of communications (LOCs) and main supply routes (MSRs) were established. From the end of June to mid-September 1950, the NKPA had access to nearly the entire rail and highway system of North and South Korea. After mid-1951, the Communist LOC and MSR were restricted to the northern portion of Korea from the Manchurian border to just north of the 38th Parallel along the frontline trace. In general, the rail lines and highways available to the NKPA and CCF were more than adequate to meet their requirements for the movements of troops and supplies.[3] Throughout the war, the Communists were able to maintain the six principal rail lines in North Korea in a partially serviceable and operating condition and by mid-1953 were using railroads at their reduced wartime capacity.[4] The capacity of the fifteen major highway routes in North Korea did not restrict enemy supply movements, and under average trafficability conditions the combined capacity of enemy MSRs in forward areas exceeded supply requirements there, even disregarding rail usage in forward areas and secondary routes supporting animal and human transport.[5]

In the first phase of the war, from 25 June to 15 September 1950, the major NKPA supply depots were located at Pyongyang and Wonsan, and the movement of almost all military supplies to the front in South Korea began there. Three major supply routes connected these depot centers with the frontlines.[6] Initially, the most important of the three was the western route, which originated in Seoul and provided the major channel of support for the NKPA 2nd, 3rd, 5th, 6th, 7th, 9th, and 10th Divisions operating in the western and southern portions of South Korea. Most supplies were transported across the Han River at Seoul by boat and barge (the railroad bridge was destroyed by the retreating ROK forces) and then moved by rail to the major railroad hub at Taejon. Some cargoes moved by truck along the highway paralleling the railroad. From Taejon, goods destined for the southern front continued by rail through Chonju to the principal supply center of Chinju. Cargo for the central front was shipped by rail or road to Kumchon via Okchon and Yondong. Kumchon was the distribution point for NKPA units in the Waegwan area, and the supply dumps of several NKPA divisions were reported to be located there. Okchon was also a major supply depot and transfer station at which cargoes were transferred to trucks, animal transport, or porters for movement via Muju and Kochang to divisions on the south-central front.

The second, or central, route was of little direct value until after Seoul was retaken by UNC forces, when it became the main supply artery for NKPA forces remaining south of the 38th Parallel. The city of Wonju was the focal point, receiving cargo by truck from Chorwon and Kumhwa destined for forces on the northern and north-central fronts. From Wonju, goods were moved by rail through Tanyang to the railhead at Yongju and by truck to Andong, a major supply depot and regulating station. From Andong, supplies for the NKPA 12th Division (and probably elements of the NKPA 5th Division) were directed through Chongsong and through Uisong for combat units on the north-central front, including the 1st, 8th, and 15th NKPA Divisions. The supply depots of the 1st, 8th, and 15th Divisions were at Kunwi, Uisong, and 5 miles north of Yongsong, respectively. The NKPA 13th Division was supplied by a line supplementary and parallel to the central supply line, which branched off at Chunchon and ran through Yoju, Changhowon-ni, Umsong, Mungyong, Sangju, and Naktong-ni.

The third, and least important, of the three MSRs was focused on the railhead at Yangyang just north of the 38th Parallel on the east coast. From the railhead at Yangyang, supplies were trucked southward along the coastal road to the NKPA 5th Division at Samchok, Utchin, and Yongdok. This eastern route was never considered a major supply artery due to the difficult terrain along the eastern coast of South Korea and due to its vulnerability to UNC interdiction by naval gunfire and raids as well as aircraft. Apparently its capacity was inadequate to support the single division (the NKPA 5th Division) it was designed to support.

While NKPA forces were operating south of the 38th Parallel, the focal point of their distribution system was at Seoul, through which approximately two thirds of all NKPA supplies for its forces in the south moved. The loss of Seoul subsequent to the UNC landings at Inchon on 15 September 1950 compelled the North Koreans to abandon the western route and to reroute traffic over the less advantageous central and eastern routes, thereby severely crippling their distribution system. Of course, the entire system collapsed with the ensuing rout of NKPA forces in South Korea. Communist forces never again penetrated so deeply into South Korea, and consequently their LOCs and MSRs were mostly confined to the area north of the 38th Parallel.

The NKPA-CCF had two main supply corridors from Manchuria into North Korea.[7] These two corridors included three major rail and five major highway entry routes supplemented by limited water transport. The Eastern corridor routes entered North Korea from the USSR and Manchuria at Namyang, Hoery-ang, and Musan, and supplies were then moved by rail and motor transport along the east coast to Hamhung, Wonsan, Kumsong, and Pyonggang. The Western corridor routes entered North Korea from Manchuria at Manpojin, Namsan-ni, and Sinuiju, and supplies were subsequently moved by rail and motor transport to facilities in or near Sinanju, Pyongyang, Sariwon, Haegu, and Kaesong. The fact that the enemy's main north-south supply routes were fun-neled through the Sinanju-Kaechon area in the West and the Hamhung area in the East made the enemy's principal LOCs extremely vulnerable to UNC inter-diction.[8] As a consequence, inland routes assumed greater importance as the war progressed. The major shortcoming was the existence of only one main route in all of North Korea which permitted speedy access from one coast to the other, and a great deal of effort was expended to improve lateral communica-tions routes, especially those in the immediate rear of the front.[9]

The bulk of supplies for both the NKPA and CCF entered North Korea over the routes of entry through Sinuiju, Sakchu, Manpojin, Linchiang, Hyesajin, Namyang, and Hongui and were moved to the major depots in the enemy rear areas by rail and motor transport. Most major NKPA-CCF supply installations were located in the western part of North Korea to take advantage of shorter supply routes to Manchuria and the better transportation facilities in western North Korea.[10] Supplies were moved from these major rear area bases through the communications centers of Pyongyang in the west and Wonsan in the east to forward supply complexes dispersed along major traffic arteries north of the 38th Parallel.[11]

In general, the physical condition of NKPA-CCF LOC remained poor throughout most of the war due to constant UNC air attack and limited quanti-ties of repair parts and reconstruction supplies. However, through the use of massive manpower and determined attention to the problem of repairing facili-ties and providing alternate routes, the enemy was able to maintain most of these routes in serviceable condition throughout the conflict and the actual usage of both rail and highway LOCs seldom approached their capacity.

WATER MOVEMENTS

Korean international maritime traffic, coastal shipping, and inland waterway transport before 1950 were limited, and for the most part the NKPA and CCF were denied use of all types of water-borne transportation almost immediately after the Korean War began. The UNC naval blockade of North Korea was par-ticularly effective, and UNC air interdiction made the use of coastal and river navigation hazardous and uncertain. Nevertheless, some military cargo contin-ued to arrive in North Korea by sea and was moved forward by small coastal vessels and even smaller river boats.[12]   However, the amounts of such cargo were almost certainly insignificant.

RAIL MOVEMENTS

Both the NKPA and CCF in Korea relied primarily on rail transport for the importation of military supplies from Manchuria and delivery to depots in the rear areas and as far forward as possible.   In July 1953, the Communist forces in Korea were served by five principal north-south rail lines, four of which connected with lines in Manchuria and one which traversed the Korean peninsula. The characteristics and capacities of these lines are shown in Table 6.1 and on Map 6.1.

Table 6.1
Major Railroad Lines in North Korea as of July 1953[13]

Line No.	Terminals	Length (miles)	Train Density*	Avg Daily Tonnage**
1n	Sinuiju-Sinanju	92	4	1,000
47a	Namsan-Chongju	77	1	250
47b	Namsan-Sinpyong	127	3	750
29	Manpojin-Kaechon	186	5	1,250
17	Namyang-Wonsan	406	1	250
28	Sunchon-Kowon	85	8	2,400

  * Trains/day forward, 12-hour operation
 ** ST/day forward, 12-hour operation

The railroad capacities cited for July 1953 bear little proportionate relationship to the previous peacetime capacity.[14] For example, UNC interdiction of the east coast line (Line 17) caused its July 1953 capacity to be rather low, something on the order of one freight train per night in the Wonsan area. On the other hand, in July 1953, Line 29 (inland from Manpojin to Kaechon) was more important and exceeded its prewar capacity. The wartime capacity was utilized almost exclusively for military cargo, and UNC intelligence agencies estimated the overall capacity of the North Korean railroad system in July 1953 to be thirty-seven trains of ten cars each during a twelve-hour period.[15]

Map 6.1
North Korean Railroad System, 27 July 1953

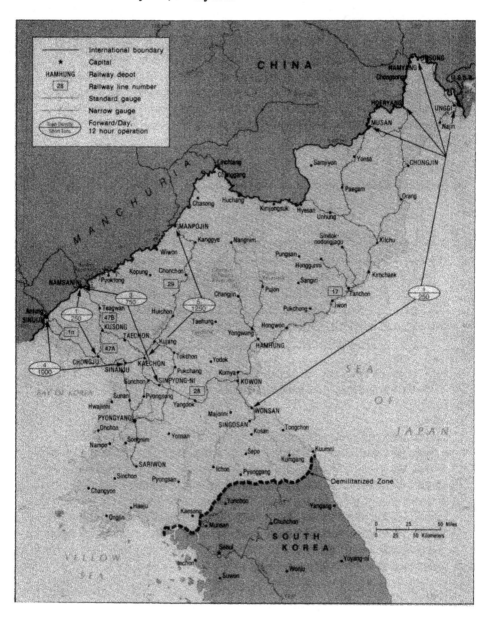

Chart 6.1
Serviceability of Major North Korean Rail Lines, 1952–1953[16]

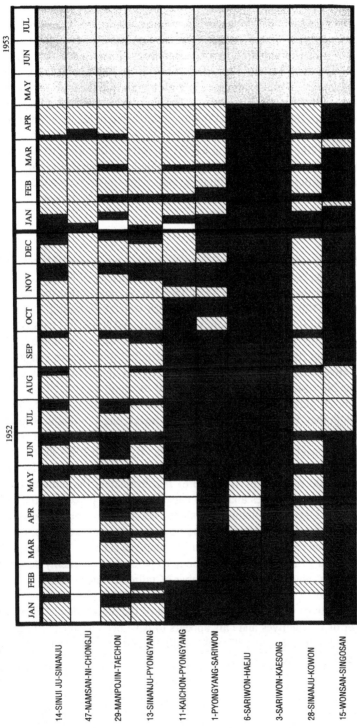

NOTE:
KOWON-HOERYONG LINE UNDER CONSTANT NAVAL
INTERDICTION, EXACT DATA NOT AVAILABLE

From mid-1952 onward, there was marked improvement in the serviceability of the main railroad lines in North Korea coincident with the shift of the UNC air effort from railroad interdiction to other missions. Chart 6.1 portrays the status of major North Korean rail lines in 1952–1953. In late March 1953, the Communists succeeded in constructing an additional rail line (Line 47b) to by-pass the vulnerable Chongchon River bridge complex and to connect Lines 47a and 29. The entire seventy-five miles of track were installed in less than seventy days.[17] Although it utilized an existing point of entry into North Korea, the construction of the new line more than doubled the capacity of the old Line 47a by avoiding bottlenecks at Sinanju and Pyongyang, being less vulnerable to carrier-based UNC air interdiction, and providing an outlet for traffic across the new (March 1953) railroad bridge, which crossed the Yalu River at Namsan-ni.

Motive Power and Rolling Stock

The number of locomotives and rail cars of various types available to the NKPA-CCF in Korea remained sufficient to match the capacity of North Korean rail lines throughout the war. In June 1950, the UNC estimated that the North Koreans had some 700 locomotives (half of which were serviceable), 15,000 freight cars (about 12,000 of which were serviceable), and some 700 passenger cars.[18] The advancing North Korean forces seized a considerable number of locomotives and cars from the South Koreans, including thirty steam and four electric locomotives in July 1950 alone. However, by the time UNC forces took Pyongyang, the North Koreans had lost about 350 locomotives to UNC air attacks and about 20 percent of their freight cars had been destroyed.[19] Subsequently, although they were under constant UNC attack, the Communists were able to maintain the number of their serviceable locomotives and rolling stock at a level adequate to meet their railroad requirements. By March 1953, they were reported to have available and operating on North Korean lines at least 228 locomotives and 5,500 railcars; by the time of the Armistice, the number had grown to about 260 locomotives and 6,600 cars.[20] About 20 percent of the locomotives were assigned to switching and shuttle service and about 30 percent were deadlined for repairs, maintenance, and inspection at any given time, with a required operational reserve factor of seven locomotives per line.[21] At the time of the Armistice on 27 July 1953, when about 73 percent of all enemy supply imports were being moved by rail, the number of railroad cars available to the NKPA-CCF was about 95 percent of the prewar level (of 6,930 cars), but the number of locomotives was only about 32 percent of the prewar stock.[22] Even so, the number of locomotives and cars appears to have been adequate to meet and even to expand the then current level of railroad service in North Korea although it never reached prewar levels.

Planning Factors

The planning factors for standard-gauge NKPA-CCF rail operations at the time of the Armistice on 27 July 1953 are shown in Table 6.2.

Table 6.2
NKPA-CCF Rail Transport Planning Factors[23]

Train Distance per Hour (Average Speed)	6 mph
Hours of Operation per Day	12 hours
Train Distance per 12-Hour Day	72 miles
Locomotive Distance per Day	72 miles
Average Freight Car Distance per Day	15 miles
Average Train Size	10 cars
Average Car Capacity	25 ST
Average Net Payload per Train	250 ST

In some cases, the average performance was exceeded by a significant factor. Locomotives occasionally attained speeds of up to 45 miles per hour where track conditions permitted, and thirty-car trains were occasionally reported on the Manpojin line.[24] On the other hand, the average capacity of cars operating in North Korea was generally lower than the rated capacity due to poor maintenance, route limitations, and other factors. Table 6.3 displays the general characteristics of the freight cars used in North Korea.

Table 6.3
Characteristics of NKPA-CCF Freight Cars[25]

Type	Length (feet)	Volume (cubic feet)	Average Rated Capacity (metric tons)
Boxcar	33	2,154	30
Boxcar	43	3,566	50
Gondola	34	2,687	30
Flatcar	34	-	30
Flatcar	41	-	50 or 60

Railroad Management

Operation of the railroad system in North Korea was formally a responsibility of the North Korean government until early 1953. At the beginning of the war, all roads and railroads were under the jurisdiction of the North Korean Ministry of Transportation and Communications.[26] With the collapse of the NKPA in late 1950, most of the remaining North Korean railway equipment was evacuated to Manchuria and remote areas of North Korea, and in early 1951 the CCF assumed responsibility for operating most of the North Korean rail lines.[27] A joint NKPA-CCF military railroad bureau was formed at Manpojin to act as an advisory and liaison agency under the joint NKPA-CCF Supreme Command, while "civilian" aspects of the North Korean railway system remained in the hands of the North Korean Ministry of Transportation and Communications. In March 1951, the joint NKPA-CCF railroad bureau moved to Anju, and as the reorganized North Korean forces resumed a greater share of the fighting, a greater share of the railway system was returned to North Korean control. By the late summer of 1951, most of the CCF railroad personnel had been withdrawn, and the North Koreans were operating most of the railway system. However, in February 1953, the CCF again assumed control over all North Korean railroads, except for the east coast line south of Tanchon. Maintenance and reconstruction, however, remained a joint responsibility. In practice, the operation of trains was determined by the ownership of the rolling stock. Initially all of the available rolling stock was North Korean owned and thus North Korean operated, but combat losses, poor maintenance and replacement facilities, and normal deterioration necessitated the importation of considerable CCF equipment. By July 1953, about 80 percent of the available rolling stock in North Korea was Chinese owned and thus Chinese operated.[28]

Diagram 6.1
Organization of the North Korean Railroad Command[29]

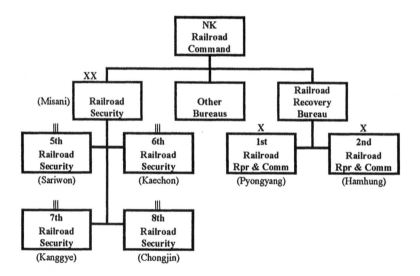

Even before the general militarization of North Korean government agencies in the spring of 1952, the Railroad Bureau of the Ministry of Transportation and Communications was given ministerial status and placed under the control of GHQ NKPA for the duration of the war.[30] Subsequently known as the North Korean Railroad Command, the new ministry was directed by the North Korean Railroad Minister Pak I Wan, a Soviet citizen who was given assimilated military rank. Supervision and operation of the North Korean railway system was exercised through 21 subordinate bureaus and four regional administrative bureaus. Some of these bureaus existed only on paper, but the two most important (outlined in Diagram 6.1) were the Railroad Recovery (Maintenance) Bureau and the Railroad Security Division.

Railroad Maintenance

The Railroad Recovery Bureau played a major role in keeping the North Korean railroad system in operation under intense UNC air, naval gunfire, and guerrilla interdiction. Two railroad repair and communication brigades were formed, each consisting of about 7,000 men in six battalions: a bridge repair and construction battalion, a heavy equipment and construction battalion, a railroad repair battalion, an engineer battalion, a security battalion, and a communications battalion.[31] The 1st Brigade had its headquarters in Pyongyang and was responsible for the west coast railroad network from Manpojin to Sinuiju and from Sinuiju to Kaesong. The 2nd Brigade had its headquarters in Hamhung and was responsible for the east coast railroad network from Chongjin through Wonsan to the Pyonggang area. Elements of the brigades were deployed in small groups at some fifty major railway stations and in ten-man crews positioned every 4 miles along the track.[32] From these locations, they could move quickly to repair rail facilities damaged by weather and UNC air attack.

Elements of the PLA Railway Corps were deployed to Korea soon after the intervention of CCF and assisted the North Koreans in the operation, maintenance, and construction of rail lines. Subordinate to the PRC Ministry of Railways for technical matters, the PLA Railway Corps was controlled by PLA headquarters and included at least two Railroad Divisions organized along military lines with three to four regiments and supporting units, and by July 1953 as many as 40,000 Chinese railway workers were reported in North Korea.[33]

Railroad Security

The security of the North Korean railway system was the responsibility of the North Korean Railroad Security Division commanded by General Kang Pyong Hak.[34] This subordinate element of the North Korean Railroad Command was formed from remnants of the NKPA 38th Security Unit, which was deployed in Hwangae Province prior to the start of the war. In October 1950, the 38th Security Unit retreated to Manpojin, and about 21 January 1951 it was reorganized as the Railroad Security Division and assigned the mission of guarding all railroad lines and railroad installations in North Korea.

The Railroad Security Division, which reached a total strength of 8,000 personnel in January 1953, was organized with four infantry-type regiments and several independent units operating under direction of the division headquarters. Each regiment was assigned to a specific geographical area and consisted of a regimental headquarters; three infantry-type battalions; submachinegun, signal, and anti-aircraft machinegun companies; reconnaissance, guard, and supply platoons; and medical, personnel, and administration sections. The regiments of the Railroad Security Division were equipped with small arms and automatic weapons but did not have organic artillery. Table 6.4 lists the regiments of the Railroad Security Division and their areas of assignment as of January 1953.

Table 6.4
North Korean Railroad Security Division[35]

Unit	Commander	Location	Area of Responsibility
Division HQ	Kang Pyong Hak	Misani	Pyongyang vicinity
5th Regiment	Hon Song Kwan	Sariwon	Southwest NK
6th Regiment	Hong Soon Bo	Kaechon	Northwest NK
7th Regiment	?	Kanggye	North Central NK
8th Regiment	Pak Chung Song	Chongjin	Northeast NK

The battalions of the Railroad Security Division regiments were seldom deployed as a unit but were dispersed to provide guard elements for critical areas such as railheads, marshaling yards, bridges, tunnels, and crossings. Personnel of the Railroad Security Division frequently performed a variety of other missions as well. Until November 1952, elements of the 5th and 6th Regiments were assigned to harvest crops in the summer and fall in the western coastal provinces of North Korea. Railroad security troops were also used to guard supply dumps, act as aircraft spotters and air-warning guards, protect railroad maintenance and reconstruction personnel, and, on occasion, provide replacements for NKPA combat units.

North Korean railway security personnel were supplemented by a number of CCF independent security divisions assigned to protect the main supply routes in North Korea. Two such units were firmly identified: the 17th Independent Security Division and the 18th Independent Security Division.[36] The latter was organized in Liaotung Province, Manchuria, in July 1950 from an independent CCF infantry division and was subordinate to the Northeast Military District. It crossed the Yalu at Antung in late January 1951.

HIGHWAY MOVEMENTS

Both the NKPA and the CCF in Korea used motor vehicles extensively to supplement the railroads in the importation of military cargo from Manchuria and its movement to rear area depots, to carry out interdepot movements, and to move supplies from depots to using units. However, NKPA-CCF motor transport did not match that of UNC forces in either quantity or performance, particularly during the first two years of the war. Moreover, the lack of motor transport at lower echelons was a major shortcoming and required the frequent use of less efficient animal transport and porters to supplement the few trucks available. Nevertheless, both the NKPA and the CCF made effective use of the trucks they did have, and despite UNC interdiction efforts they operated a limited but adequate highway transport system throughout the war.

Routes and Highway Capacities

There were at least nine highway entry points from Manchuria and the Soviet Union into North Korea, but most of the traffic was routed along the five major supply routes indicated on Map 6.2 (Highway Routes 1 through 5). Route 1 (Sinuiju to Pyongyang) and Route 5 (Hoeryang to Wonsan) were extremely vulnerable to UNC interdiction, and alternate routes located further inland were used extensively during the war. Route 5 on the east coast was particularly vulnerable, and consequently much of the traffic entering on Route 3 through Manpojin was destined for the east coast and was routed via lateral roads and Route 4.[37]

All highways entering North Korea crossed either the Yalu River or the Tumen River, both of which were unfordable. The four principal crossings of the Yalu were at Sinuiju, Chongsongjin, Manpojin, and Linchiang.[38] The main bridge at Sinuiju was originally a double-track railroad bridge, but the easternmost track was taken up and that span was used as a highway bridge.[39] The Sinuiju bridge was 3,100 feet long and was constructed of steel and reinforced concrete. The steel and concrete highway bridge at Chongsongjin was badly damaged by UNC air attacks early in the war and was supplemented by a pontoon bridge upstream, which was subject to flood waters. There were two railroad bridges across the Yalu at Manpojin. One was approximately 950 feet long and was a temporary structure constructed between 8 May and 6 July 1951. The other was a single-track railroad bridge 1,980 feet long constructed of steel and reinforced concrete. It was used by both trains and motor vehicles. The steel and concrete highway bridge at Linchiang was 1,850 feet long. Several bridges crossed the Tumen River in northeastern Korea, and numerous ferries supplemented the bridges across both rivers.

Map 6.2
Principal North Korean Highways, 27 July 1953

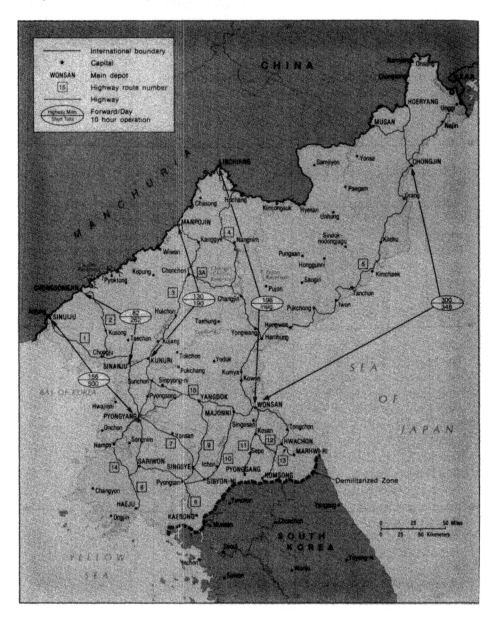

North of the 39th Parallel, the quantities of supplies moved by rail and by highway were approximately equal.[40] However, south of the line Pyongyang-Wonsan most transport was accomplished with trucks, and the amount of rail-transported supply decreased progressively as the distance to the front diminished.[41] In this area, the NKPA and CCF relied on one major east-west road and nine north-south roads leading to the main battle area. These routes were passable in all weather except during the rainy season, when certain points became impassable due to floods and washouts. Perhaps the most critical route was Route 15 from Pyongyang to Wonsan, the only major east-west highway available to the NKPA and CCF near the front. This route was a one-and-one-half- to two-lane gravel road with some paved stretches but had many steep grades, sharp curves, and frequent defiles, particularly in mountain areas. As a result of intensive NKPA-CCF maintenance efforts, in July 1953 Route 15 was capable of handling more traffic in relation to its original peacetime capacity than any other route in North Korea.[42] The capacity of Communist Main Supply Routes (MSRs) in forward areas appears not to have been a restricting factor under average trafficability conditions.[43]

Table 6.5
Average Daily Tonnage Capacity of North Korean Highways, May–July 1953[44]

| Rte No. | Terminals | Restricted Capacity | | Average Daily ST Forward, May–Jul 53 |
		Normal (ST/day fwd)	Maximum (ST/day fwd)	
1	Sinuiju-Pyongyang	525	630	500
2	Chongsongjin-Sinanju	500	600	262
3	Manpojin-Kunu-ri	375	450	190
4	Linchiang-Wonsan	380	455	Insignificant
5	Chongjin-Wonsan	500	600	348
6	Pyongyang-Kaesong	460	550	406
7	Pyongyang-Sibyon-ni	365	435	340
8	Sariwon-Haeju	Unknown	Unknown	155
9	Yangdok-Singye	225	270	225
10	Majon-ni-Sibyon-ni	225	270	225
11	Wonsan-Pyonggang	330	395	300
12	Wonsan-Kumsong	237	295	237
13	Hwachon-ni-Marhwi-ri	145	175	145
14	Pyongyang-Haeju	Unknown	Unknown	155
15	Pyongyang-Wonsan	1,000	1,200	1,000
	System Total	**5,267+**	**6,325+**	**4,488+**

As was the case with rail capacity, the wartime capacity of the various highway routes in North Korea was not directly proportionate to the peacetime rating.[45] For example, the peacetime capacity of Route 3 was 7,000 to 8,400 ST/day, but in July 1953 Route 3 could support a daily forward movement of only about 375 to 450 ST. On the other hand, in July 1953 Route 15 was handling 1,000 ST/day versus a peacetime capacity of 5,000 to 6,000 ST/day. Overall, the five main highway entry routes (Routes 1–5) were not being used to their full capacity in July 1953. Apparently capable of handling 2,280 to 2,735 ST/day, they were carrying only about 1,300 ST/day and thus retained a significant surge capacity of some 980 to 1,435 ST/day. The wartime capacity and average daily tonnage moved over the principal highways in North Korea in May to July 1953 is shown in Table 6.5.

Highway Maintenance and Repair

The North Korean Military Highway Administration Bureau (MHAB), subordinate to the Rear Services Department of GHQ NKPA, was responsible for the maintenance and repair of roads and bridges.[46] The MHAB was organized along military lines, as shown in Diagram 6.2, with up to twelve regiments, each consisting of approximately 1,700 men organized in a headquarters, three 550-man military road maintenance battalions, a signal company, a medical platoon, and a supply section.[47] Each battalion was composed of a headquarters, three road repair companies of about 184 men each, a medical section, a signal platoon, and a supply platoon. Each company had three road repair platoons. The equipment of these battalions was rather primitive and consisted primarily of hand tools such as shovels, picks, and axes. Apparently, none of the MHAB units were equipped with bulldozers, road graders, or other heavy equipment.

Each MHAB battalion was assigned to one of the twenty to thirty-six critical geographical areas in North Korea which included a major road network. For example, the 622nd Military Highway Administration Battalion was assigned to the Wonsan area and was responsible for the maintenance of all roads into and out of Wonsan. In some cases, more than one battalion was assigned to a particularly critical or heavily attacked area. Platoons of the road repair battalions were stationed every 2.5 to 3 kilometers along important routes. When a route was damaged or blocked, the nearest road repair element was dispatched to make the necessary repairs with the assistance of civilian laborers impressed locally. Using nothing but hand tools, road repair crews typically cleared a road break overnight. Within its assigned area, each battalion was responsible for traffic control as well as road repair and maintenance. Foot patrols reported on the condition of routes within the assigned areas, and fixed posts directed traffic, warned convoys of approaching UNC aircraft, and informed convoy leaders about road conditions.

Diagram 6.2
North Korean Military Highway Administration Bureau[48]

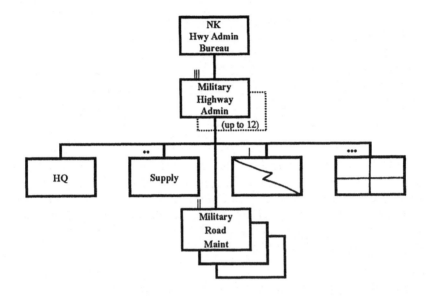

NKPA-CCF Motor Transport Assets

The actual strength of NKPA-CCF motor transport organizations, and consequently the number of vehicles operating at various levels at different times during the war, has proven all but impossible to determine with any degree of accuracy. There was not only considerable variation in authorizations among types of units of the NKPA and CCF, but many organizations supplemented their authorized motor transport with vehicles captured from UNC forces or requisitioned from civilians in the area of operations. Of course, the effectiveness of UNC air operations, maintenance factors, and an uncertain replacement stream also caused considerable variation in the number of trucks available at any given time. In general, however, the number of motor vehicles, particularly those organic to CCF combat units, increased steadily during the course of the war as additional vehicles were supplied by the Soviet Union and CCF units were reorganized with a greater vehicular authorization.

UNC intelligence agencies estimated that in January 1953 the NKPA-CCF had approximately 16,000 trucks available in North Korea. They were distributed as shown in Table 6.6. By 1 May 1953, the number of trucks, including quasi-military North Korean vehicles, available to the NKPA-CCF had grown to approximately 19,200 trucks; and by the Armistice on 27 July 1953, the Communists had over 21,000 trucks available in Korea.[49]

Table 6.6
Distribution of NKPA-CCF Trucks, January 1953[50]

Location	Trucks
Administrative Vehicles and NK Quasi-Military Truck Fleet	4,000
Undergoing Maintenance and Repair	3,000
Operational in Rear Areas (Line Haul)	3,300
Operational in Rear Areas (Local Haul)	3,000
Operational in Forward Areas	2,700
Total	**16,000**

Tables 6.7 and 6.8 present some estimates of the number of motor vehicles authorized for the military motor transport organizations supporting various echelons of the NKPA and CCF. Of course, the number of trucks available on any given day was less than the number of trucks authorized. UNC planners and intelligence analysts usually estimated the number of vehicles actually in operation at 85 percent of the authorized number.

Table 6.7
Organizational Distribution of NKPA Trucks, 2 May 1953[51]

Type Unit	No. Units	Trks/Unit	Total
GHQ and Miscellaneous Units	2*	120**	240**
GHQ RSD Truck Battalion	9	120	1,110***
Corps Truck Battalion	6	120	720
Division Truck Company	18	40	720
Independent Brigade Truck Company	7	40	280
Division Artillery Regiment (organic)	18	40	720
Regimental Artillery Battery (organic)	53	4	212
76-mm SP Gun Battalion (organic)	10	16	160
AAA Regiment (RSS and Miscellaneous)	5	8	40
AAA Automatic Weapons Bn (organic)	36	12	432
Independent Artillery Regiment (organic)	2	40	80
Independent Mortar Regiment (organic)	2	40	80
Tank Regiment (organic)	6	20**	120**
Engineer Regiment (organic)	2	18	36
Total Authorized NKPA Trucks		**4,950**	

*Battalion (Bn) equivalents   **Estimated   ***Includes 30 nontask trucks

Table 6.8
Organizational Distribution of CCF Trucks, 2 May 1953[52]

Type Unit	No. Units	Trks/Unit	Total
GHQ Truck Regiment	1	318*	318*
GHQ RSD Independent Truck Regiment	7	318	2,226
Army Group Truck Regiment	5	409	2,045
Infantry Division (organic; less AA Bn)	54	15*	810*
Army Artillery Regt (organic to Bns)	36	23	828
AA Gun Battalion (organic)	44	16	704
AA Automatic Weapons Bn (organic)**	20	21	420
Motorized Arty Div Trk Co (+ organic)	4	446	1,784
Horse-Drawn Artillery Division (organic)	1	58	58
Motorized Antitank Division (organic)	2	184	368
Rocket Division (organic)	1	200*	200*
Engineer Regiment Truck Platoon	4	15	60
Horse-Drawn Arty Regt (in AA Bn)	2	23	46
Motorized Arty Regt Trk Co (+ organic)	2	125	250
Tank Regiment Truck Company	3	45	135
Total Authorized CCF Trucks	**10,272**		

* Estimated   ** Less anti-aircraft automatic weapons battalions otherwise accounted for in artillery divisions and horse-drawn artillery regiments
AA = Anti-aircraft; Arty = Artillery; Bn(s) = Battalion(s); Co = Company; Div = Division; Regt = Regiment; Trk = Truck

Quasi-Military Truck Transport in North Korea

In addition to the military motor transport assigned to elements of the NKPA and CCF in Korea, a number of trucks belonging to quasi-military private trucking organizations in North Korea were utilized to supplement military highway operations and carry normal civilian cargo. Civilian trucking firms such as the National Trucking Corporation and *Choso Haeun Kongsa* (North Korean and USSR Sea Transportation Company) were taken over by the North Korean government at the beginning of the war and trucking companies in each North Korean province were subsequently controlled by the Bureau of Special Transportation of the North Korean Transportation Bureau (which was commanded by a Major General) through the Ministry of Home Affairs.[53] There were estimated to be about 4,000 such trucks in May 1953.[54] Perhaps 25 percent of the quasi-military North Korean truck assets were used to supplement railroads and military truck units in the importation of supplies from Manchuria and the Soviet Union.[55] Apparently, most of these quasi-military trucks were used to meet normal civilian requirements, but they constituted a significant surge capability for military movements during stress periods.[56]

Drivers

Qualified drivers were apparently available in adequate numbers. In most cases, the normal truck crew consisted of a driver and an assistant driver (who acted as mechanic and handyman), although a third man was sometimes added as a guard.[57] In some cases, a transportation officer was assigned to each truck to insure the security and expeditious delivery of its cargo.[58] Most drivers had a civilian background as a driver or mechanic, and the average NKPA driver received about six months of formal schooling whereas the CCF driver had from three to six months of training.[59] Drivers and assistant drivers were frequently given special privileges such as increased rations, cigarettes, or the designation of "Transportation Hero."[60] It appears that drivers were assigned to a given section of a MSR and drove only specified routes, thus insuring that they were familiar with their particular route and able to operate more effectively under poor weather and road conditions and in periods of reduced visibility.[61]

NKPA Highway Distribution System

Overall, the NKPA highway distribution system was simple and straightforward even though the control of motor transport assets in the NKPA was somewhat more decentralized than in the CCF.[62] While the impetus of supply in the NKPA was from rear to front, from higher echelon to lower echelon, NKPA truck movements were frequently effected using transport assets from the supported (lower echelon) units.

The nine independent truck battalions controlled by the Transportation Bureau of the Rear Services Department of GHQ NKPA were normally used to supplement the railroads in the movement of military supplies from points of entry on the Manchuria border to NKPA rear area supply installations, to move supplies from railheads to depots, and to carry out interdepot movements.[63] The tasking and geographical assignment of the NKPA independent truck battalions, each of which had 120 task vehicles, changed frequently, but in July 1953 two of the independent truck battalions were being used routinely to supplement the railroads, five battalions were employed in railhead-to-depot and depot-to-depot movements, and the remaining two battalions (the 3rd and 8th) were attached directly to NKPA Frontline Headquarters and were employed in the movement of supplies from railheads and depots to the forward depots operated by the NKPA Frontline Headquarters at Yongdok and Kowon.[64]

Highway movements from the forward Frontline Headquarters depots to corps supply dumps were accomplished by trucks from the corps truck battalions assisted, as required, by the GHQ NKPA RSD Transportation Bureau truck battalions under Frontline Headquarters control.[65] Theoretically, the NKPA corps was responsible for moving supplies from railheads and corps depots down to division dumps, utilizing motor transport from the organic corps truck battalion.[66] On occasion, corps truck assets were also used to move supplies down to regimental and battalion supply points as well. In practice, when road conditions were unfavorable or the corps motor transport assets were otherwise engaged, trucks from the divisional truck companies were used to pick up supplies from the corps supply dumps and move them down to divisional or even regimental supply points.[67]

The NKPA divisional motor transport company was normally responsible for the movement of supplies from division supply dumps to regimental supply points, and, in the case of artillery ammunition, to the actual firing positions.[68] The twenty-three trucks controlled by the (1950) NKPA regiment, supplemented by animal transport and porters, were then used to distribute supplies down to the battalions and directly to the firing positions of the heavier supporting weapons. However, to maintain a rapid and uninterrupted flow of supplies to the front, this system was sometimes modified. Regimental transport vehicles might be used to haul all classes of supply from division dumps to regimental or battalion supply points, or the divisional truck company might be charged with the delivery of ammunition and fuel to units below the regimental level while all other classes of supply were moved by regimental trucks and battalion animal transport and porters.[69]

CCF Highway Distribution System

Most CCF motor transport movements in Korea were carried out by the independent truck regiments assigned to the GHQ CCF in Korea. The initial movement of the CCF into Korea in October 1950 was supported by deployment of the two best-equipped independent motor transport regiments of the PLA: the 42nd Truck Regiment, initially subordinate to the Northeast Military District, crossed into Korea in October 1950 via Antung, Manchuria, and assumed responsibility for the support of the CCF XIIIth Army Group in western Korea; the 5th Truck Regiment, subordinate to the Fourth Field Army, crossed the Yalu at Manpojin on or about 26 October 1950 and subsequently supported the operations of the CCF IXth Army Group in eastern Korea.[70] By mid-March 1951, concurrent with the reorganization and creation of the seven Branch Units with geographical support responsibilities, the number of independent CCF truck regiments in Korea increased to fourteen.[71] By the time of the Armistice in July 1953, eighteen such regiments were accepted in Korea by UNC intelligence agencies, ten of which were being used to supplement the railroads in the movement of military supplies from Manchuria to CCF rear area depots in North Korea.[72] The remaining regiments were normally attached to the various Branch Units but could be attached directly to the subordinate Army Groups or Armies,

Diagram 6.3
CCF Independent Truck Regiment (Type I)[73]

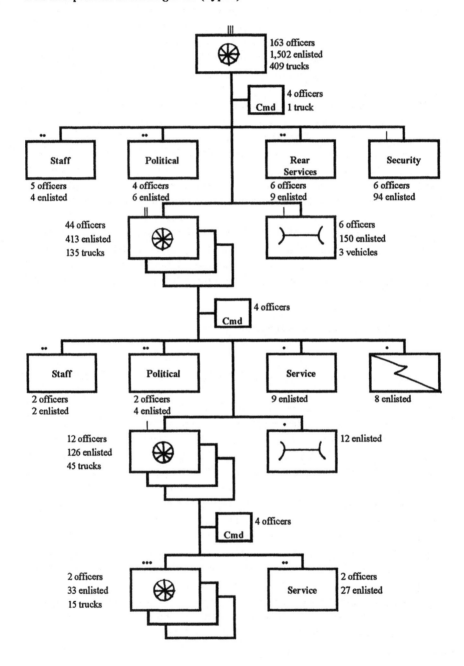

163 officers
1,502 enlisted
409 trucks

Cmd
4 officers
1 truck

Staff
5 officers
4 enlisted

Political
4 officers
6 enlisted

Rear Services
6 officers
9 enlisted

Security
6 officers
94 enlisted

44 officers
413 enlisted
135 trucks

6 officers
150 enlisted
3 vehicles

Cmd
4 officers

Staff
2 officers
2 enlisted

Political
2 officers
4 enlisted

Service
9 enlisted

8 enlisted

12 officers
126 enlisted
45 trucks

12 enlisted

Cmd
4 officers

2 officers
33 enlisted
15 trucks

Service
2 officers
27 enlisted

depending on tactical requirements.[74] Occasionally they were used to deliver supplies directly to echelons below Army level.

The independent CCF truck regiments were of two types as shown in Diagrams 6.3 and 6.4.[75] The Type I CCF truck regiment was authorized 163 officers, 1,502 enlisted men, and 409 trucks organized in three truck battalions (135 trucks each) of three companies (forty-five trucks each). The Type II regiment (111 officers, 1,206 enlisted men, and 318 trucks) was normally organized with six to nine truck companies (forty-five trucks each) directly subordinate to the

Diagram 6.4
CCF Independent Truck Regiment (Type II)[76]

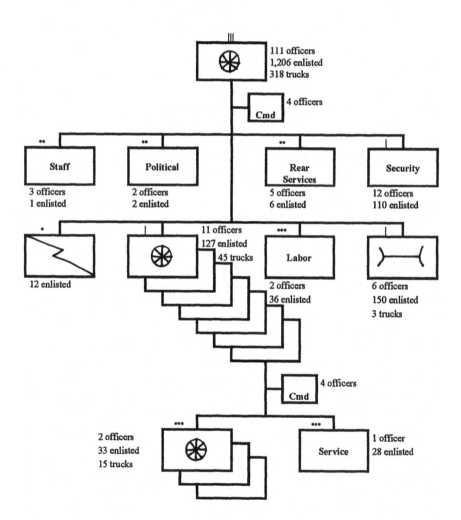

regimental headquarters. The Type I regiment was a latter development that appeared in mid-January 1951 in response to heavy truck losses to UNC air operations, the CCF decision to commit six new armies to the 1951 spring offensives, and the expansion and reorganization of the CCF supply system.[77]

Supplies reached the main depots controlled by the CCF Branch Units in the immediate rear and forward areas either by rail or highway directly from the points of entry or by truck from supply installations in the rear area.[78] Each of the CCF Branch Units was supported by one or more truck regiments attached from the Rear Services Department of the GHQ CCF.[79] These regiments were employed in the movement of supplies from railheads to depots and from the main depots down to the subdepots. Although in general the control of CCF motor transport was centralized above CCF Army level to the greatest degree possible, the operational control of the independent CCF truck regiments attached to the Branch Units was very flexible.[80] At times, companies from the regiments supporting a Branch Unit were attached directly to the supported Army, in which case they were used to transport supplies from the Branch Unit subdepots to either the rear or forward depots of the Army or directly to its subordinate divisions. This flexible approach to the utilization of motor transport assets enabled units needing supplies and lacking necessary transportation to draw on the truck assets controlled by higher echelons. The truck units so utilized returned to Branch Unit control at the end of the mission.

The ultimate responsibility for transporting supplies from Branch Unit supply installations down to the depots of the Army Group/Army apparently lay with the supporting Branch Unit, but in practice such movements were usually accomplished by the trucks of the Army Groups and Armies.[81] The organic and attached trucks of the Army Groups and Armies (and, on occasion, those supporting the Branch Unit main depots and subdepots) were used to move supplies to the forward depots and supply points of the supported Army Groups and Armies, while artillery and mortar ammunition were commonly delivered directly to the firing units.[82] In some cases, the truck regiments supporting the Army Groups picked up supplies at the Branch Unit depots and moved them down to Army supply installations.[83]

The CCF Army was theoretically responsible for the movement of supplies from the forward Army depots down to the division supply points using its two truck companies (forty-five trucks each), but subordinate units with organic trucks normally hauled their supplies from Army supply points and occasionally even supplemented the Army Group truck regiments by picking up supplies directly at the Branch Unit depots.[84] The truck assets of the CCF Army were usually under the operational control of one of the three Army depots and were routinely employed in shuttling supplies from the rear supply depot to the central and forward supply depots. During build-ups before offensives, the Army truck assets might also be used to move supplies from the Branch Unit, Army Group, and Army depots to division or even regimental level.[85] Army trucks were also used to move the Army command post, relocate Army supply depots, and evacuate wounded from division aid stations back to Army branch hospitals and from Army branch hospitals back to Branch Unit depots, where the wounded were then evacuated to base hospitals in Korea or Manchuria by Branch Unit transport.[86]

The CCF division shared responsibility with the CCF Army for transporting supplies from the Army depots down to divisional, regimental, and battalion supply points.[87] Weather, road conditions, and the level of UNC air activity dictated how far down the division supply trucks might go. On return trips, division trucks evacuated wounded and were occasionally used to evacuate damaged or captured ordnance and equipment. During build-ups, or at any time that divisional transports were engaged in other duties, the responsibility for moving supplies down to regiment and battalion supply points was shifted to the regiment and battalion.

One of the well-recognized weaknesses of the CCF distribution system was the lack of adequate motor transport at lower echelons. Until the last six months of the war, CCF infantry divisions were authorized little or no organic motor transport. However, each division probably had a number of trucks captured from UNC forces or requisitioned locally, although the number varied widely from division to division and probably did not exceed thirty trucks per division.[88] The CCF began to receive additional trucks from the Soviet Union in late 1952 and early 1953, and although priority in the distribution of these vehicles went to artillery and anti-aircraft artillery units for use as prime movers, sufficient trucks were available by July 1953 to provide all of the CCF infantry divisions in Korea with an organic truck company of forty-five trucks, small detachments of which were used to support the subordinate infantry regiments.[89] The increased availability of trucks and improvements in rail capabilities resulted in an increase in the number of trucks in forward areas in the last months of the war, which was manifested in more efficient and timely resupply of dumps in the forward areas and consequent improved combat performance in the CCF offensives in June and July 1953 immediately before the cease fire.[90]

NKPA-CCF Highway Operations

From the beginning of the war, UNC air operations obliged the NKPA-CCF to keep the size of motor convoys small (less than twenty-five trucks) and to restrict most of their highway movements to the hours of darkness or inclement weather. About 85 percent of all NKPA-CCF motor transport operations conformed to this pattern.[91] Truck regiments or battalions were seldom employed as a unit, and the usual procedure was to operate the companies of the regiment/battalion individually with each assigned a zone of responsibility and a specific number of depots, subdepots, or units to service.[92] Company-sized convoys were rare, and companies usually operated their vehicles in platoon-sized groups since large convoys were easy prey to UNC air interdiction. For the most part NKPA-CCF trucks operated at night, singly or in small convoys with about 50 meters between vehicles and without lights.[93] Vehicles usually emerged from their daylight hiding places about an hour before dark to load and prepare for the evening movement; actual travel began soon after dusk and ended one to two hours before dawn.[94] During the nights of the dark of the moon, trucks used either their blackout lights (turning headlights on only on dangerous stretches) or left headlights on at all times. During moonlit nights, all lights were extinguished or were used only by the lead vehicle in a convoy.[95] Convoy speed was controlled by the lead vehicle, and no standard interval was prescribed. However, insofar as possible, vehicles in the same convoy remained in sight of one another.

Permanent and semipermanent stopover and rest areas were established where vehicles might be hidden during the day and receive necessary services. These rest areas were often located in areas such as tunnels, which offered maximum cover and concealment. An elaborate air warning system was in place, with air warning posts every 1 or 2 kilometers along MSRs in North Korea. Numerous traffic control checkpoints were established to check trip tickets and manifests, driver identification, and other matters.[96] Guides were posted at all important intersections, in villages, at bridges, and at other choke points, and rifle shots, whistles, and flags were commonly used to warn drivers of approaching UNC aircraft or to transmit other signals.[97] Despite numerous control measures, there were frequent accidents due to blackouts and poor road and weather conditions.[98]

Table 6.9
NKPA-CCF Motor Transport Planning Factors[99]

Average Distance Traveled Each Night	
In rear areas	75 miles
In intermediate areas	70 miles
In forward areas	65 miles
Average Round Trip Distance from Entry Points to Major Supply Complexes	270 miles
Average Speed	
Night	10–15 mph
Day	25–30 mph
Average Hours of Operation per Day	10–12
Average Length of Convoy	ca. 25 trks
Average Truck Load	2.2 ST
Average Gasoline Consumption	
GAZ trucks	8.1 mpg
ZIS trucks	4.7 mpg

Most of our knowledge of NKPA-CCF highway operating methods as well as of the number of motor vehicles in use by the NKPA-CCF at any given time is derived from UNC aerial observation and traffic analysis. Such analysis was useful for determining the principal routes in use, choke points, terminal areas, the relative intensity of the enemy logistical effort, a general idea of the enemy's logistical readiness, and indications of the probable sectors in which enemy offensives might occur.[100] On the other hand, traffic analysis based on vehicle sightings depended on natural phenomena, such as the phases of the moon and the weather, and were subject to duplication and counting errors on the part of aerial observers and thus tended to produce uncertain and sometimes erroneous conclusions.[101] Table 6.9 provides an outline of NKPA-CCF motor transport planning factors derived primarily from analysis of UNC aerial observation of enemy highway operations.

ANIMAL AND HUMAN TRANSPORT

Regimental and battalion supply points were little more than breakdown or distribution points for subordinate units, and below division level the NKPA and CCF in Korea relied heavily on animal transport and the use of porters to move supplies to troops in the frontlines. Animal and human transport was also used to supplement motor transport at all levels and to effect the transfer of supplies around disrupted rail and highway facilities. Theoretically, the NKPA or CCF regiment was responsible for moving supplies to battalion and company distribution points, although such movements were often accomplished by carrying parties furnished by the lower units, particularly those not heavily engaged in combat.[102] At battalion level, supplies were broken down and moved to companies by animal carts, pushcarts, pack animals, or porters.[103] Some lower echelon units did have some organic motor transport, which was used both to bring supplies, particularly artillery and heavy mortar ammunition, forward from division or even higher level supply dumps located 60 or more miles to the rear and to deliver supplies to subordinate units.[104]

The number of animals, carts, and human porters available at each echelon of the NKPA and CCF varied widely depending on the unit's success in requisitioning animals, carts, and men from the local civilian population. The NKPA infantry regimental animal transport platoon consisted of one officer, twenty-three enlisted men, and about eight ox carts.[105] The CCF were generally more dependent on animal and human transport, and the CCF Branch Units were each authorized an animal transport regiment consisting of 100 carts.[106] The CCF Army Groups were authorized an animal transport unit with fourteen officers, 164 enlisted men, thirty carts, and ninty animals, and the RSD of each CCF Army and of each CCF infantry division was authorized an animal transport company with a similar complement.[107] The CCF infantry regiment was authorized ten pack animals.[108] The usual cart drawn by two oxen or two horses had a load capacity of about 1,000 to 2,000 lb and could move that load over a distance of about 8 to 12 miles per night.[109] Pack animals could carry a load of about 130 to 200 lb, or about four to six cases of 60-mm mortar ammunition.[110]

NKPA-CCF units at all levels used large numbers of porters, mostly local civilians impressed for service on the spot, to move military supplies, particularly in close proximity to the frontlines.[111] Both North Korean and Chinese soldiers and civilians were accustomed to bearing heavy loads and could carry on their back 300 to 400 rounds of small arms ammunition wrapped in a waterproof cloth or two to four heavy artillery shells with a rope sling.[112] A seasoned Korean porter could carry an 80 to 150 lb load a distance of 10 to 15 miles per night using either the familiar "chogie stick" or an "A-frame."[113] The "chogie stick" was a wooden pole about 1.5 meters long, 2 centimeters thick, and about 6 centimeters wide with a hook on both ends, to which baskets or packages could be attached with hemp or straw ropes.[114] Such carrying tools were used on level terrain, could easily be made on the spot, and would support a load of about 80 lbs.[115] The ubiquitous Korean "A-frame," particularly useful in mountainous terrain, could also be manufactured on the spot and was capable of supporting loads of 65 to 80 lb.[116] The Chinese commander in Korea, General Peng Teh-huai, was famous for himself taking up a porter's "chogie stick" or "A-frame" and trotting off for a mile or so to encourage the other bearers.[117]

The carts, animals, and porters available to the NKPA-CCF were terribly inefficient means of transports when improved roads were available, but they offered great flexibility, particularly in the difficult mountainous terrain which comprised most of Korea.[118] However, they were not as significant a factor in the net forward movement of supplies as were railroads and motor vehicles.[119] Moreover, the carts and animals of the NKPA and CCF divisions posed serious problems when the long-distance rail or motor movement of the unit was planned.[120] When the division moved by motor march, the carts and animals had to be shipped by rail or water, sent ahead to forward assembly areas, or, as a last resort, moved by truck. In any case, the division was likely to be separated from its main, immediate means of transport for some time, often at the critical moment.

UNIT MOVEMENTS

Given their comparative lack of motor transport and near total UNC air superiority, the NKPA and CCF became masters of the art of the foot march. Of course, Chinese armies had long been adept at moving large numbers of men, animals, and equipment overland under their own power, but the perceived ability of the Communist forces to march on foot rapidly and undetected reached almost mythic proportions in Korea. Indeed, the persistent myth of NKPA-CCF reliance on animal and human transport, and the endurance of that transport, stems principally from accounts of Communist unit movements rather than the normal resupply activities of the NKPA-CCF, which were carried out mainly by rail and truck.[121] Most of the CCF units which entered or left Korea during the war did so by unit foot marches. Chart 6.2 portrays the movement of CCF units into and out of Korea between October 1950 and October 1954.

The soldiers of the NKPA and CCF during the Korean War actually marched at about the same rate as U.S. troops; their spectacular forced marches were accomplished simply by marching longer hours.[122] Major NKPA and CCF unit movements in Korea were mostly night marches of six to seven hours duration, but forced marches of 31 to 37 miles in a 24-hour period were noted.[123] Table 6.10 compares the normal rates of march of U.S. and NKPA-CCF infantry.

Table 6.10
Infantry Rates of March[124]

Division	On Road		Cross Country		Average
	Day (mph)	Night (mph)	Day (mph)	Night (mph)	Distance (Miles/Day)
U.S.	2.5	2.0	1.5	1.0	Division: 12–15 Smaller units: 15–20
NKPA-CCF	3.0	1.9	2.0	1.0	21.7–24.8

The ability of NKPA and CCF units in Korea to conduct long, rapid foot movements was influenced by the weight carried by the individual soldier and by the weight of the normal basic load of supplies maintained by each unit. Table 6.11 compares the average load carried by the U.S. soldier with that carried by the NKPA-CCF soldier. In terms of his individual load, the NKPA-CCF infantryman was obviously more foot-mobile than his U.S. counterpart.

Table 6.11
Average Weight Carried by the Rifleman in Pounds[125]

Item	U.S.	NKPA-CCF
Full Field Equipment	56.0	14.0
Rations	6.6	6.0
Weapons and Basic Load of Ammunition	13.9	19.0
Gas Mask	3.5	0
Water in Canteen	2.0	2.0
TOTAL	**82 lb**	**41 lb**

Chart 6.2
CCF Movement Into and Out of Korea, October 1950–October 1954[126]

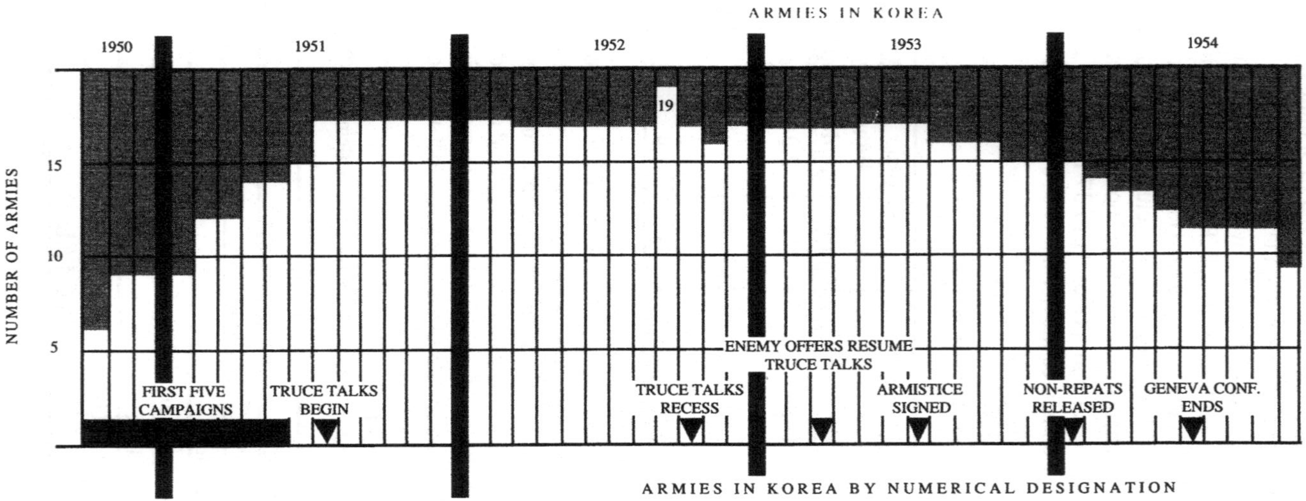

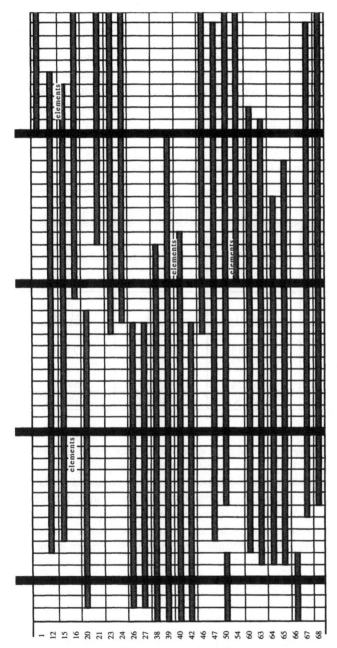

ARMY NUMERICAL DESIGNATION

139

The mobility of a division depends on more than just the mobility of the individual infantryman. The total weight of division personnel and equipment, the division's supply requirements, and the degree to which the division is motorized are also important factors. On balance, the Korean War-era U.S. infantry division was much "heavier" than either the NKPA or the CCF infantry division and thus required more trucks and/or rail cars if it were to be moved by highway or railroad.[127] Table 6.12 shows the total weight of the "basic load" of various classes of supply and of the individual soldiers and their equipment for the 1956 U.S., NKPA, and CCF divisions.

Table 6.12
Weight of Division Basic Loads and Personnel in Short Tons[128]

Item	1956 U.S. Division	1956 NKPA Division	1956 CCF Division
Class I (Rations & Forage)	265.27	247.00	392.34
Class II & IV (Equipment)	17,039.00	1,713.00	2,836.00
Class III (POL)	514.00	40.00	94.38
Class V (Ammunition)	1,785.85	130.00	224.20
Personnel with equipment	2,059.24	902.00	1,548.11
TOTAL (rounded)	**21,660 ST**	**3,030 ST**	**5,090 ST**

The mobility of the division's principal weapons systems was also an important factor, and Table 6.13 provides mobility data for the principal U.S. and NKPA-CCF weapons used during the Korean War. Over improved roads, during daylight, and under normal march conditions without tanks, the rate of march for a motorized NKPA-CCF infantry division was about 15 mph versus 21 mph for a U.S. infantry division, while the average day's motor march for a NKPA-CCF division was about 120 miles and for a U.S. division about 150 miles.[129]

Table 6.13
Mobility of Major Korean War Era Weapons Systems[130]

Weapon	Maximum Travel Speed (mph)		Time Required to Emplace		Cruising Range (miles)	
	U.S.	NKPA-CCF	U,S.	NKPA-CCF	U.S.	NKPA-CCF
76-mm Howitzer (Towed)		22	1 min			
76-mm Howitzer (SP)		28	< 1 min			224
105-mm.Howitzer (Towed)	30–58		3 mins			
122-mm Howitzer (Towed)		31	1 min			
155-mm Howitzer (Towed)	35–40		5 mins			
60-mm Mortar			< 75 secs			
81-mm Mortar			< 90 secs			
82-mm Mortar				30 secs		
4.2-inch Mortar			< 2.5 mins			
120-mm Mortar				1–3 mins		
Armored Car	32	35–50	0		120	272
76-mm Tank Gun	40		0		150	
85-mm Tank Gun		34	0			155
90-mm Tank Gun	30		0		90–100	
45-mm Antitank Gun (Towed)		37	1 min			
57-mm Antitank Gun (Towed)		28	1 min			
57-mm Recoil-less Rifle			1 min			
75-mm Recoil-less Rifle			1.5 mins			

The 1956 U.S. division, with 2,588 authorized vehicles and 17,452 personnel, had a ratio of vehicles to personnel of 1:6.8 and was about 66 percent mobile with organic transport.[131] The 1956 CCF division had 18,213 men (considerably more than during the Korean War), was authorized 372 vehicles, and thus had a ratio of vehicles to personnel of 1:49.1. It was only about 28 percent mobile with organic transport. The 1956 NKPA division had 10,608 men and 204 authorized vehicles for a ratio of 1:52 and was thus about 14 percent mobile with organic transport. Although no exact direct comparison of the organic lift capability of the U.S., NKPA, and CCF infantry divisions is possible due to the many variables involved, Table 6.14 gives a rough comparison.

Inasmuch as none of the three types of divisions (U.S., NKPA, and CCF) had sufficient organic transport to upload the entire division at one time, additional transport was required to make the divisions 100 percent mobile. The estimated number of additional, nonorganic vehicles required for each type of division is shown in Table 6.15.

Table 6.14
Organic Lift Capability of 1956 U.S., NKPA, and CCF Infantry Divisions[132]

Unit	Type of Vehicle		Number of Trucks	Total Lift (ST)
		3/4 ton	316	237
	Truck	2 1/2 tons	743	1,858
		4 tons	9	36
U.S.		1/4 ton	607	152
Infantry		3/4 ton	158	119
Division	Trailer	1 1/2 tons	525	788
		10 tons	3	30
		20 tons	14	280
		45 tons	2	90
	U.S. Division Total		2,377	3,590 ST
NKPA	Truck	GAZ-63	183	549
Infantry	Cart	1 ton (avg)	231	231
Division	NKPA Division Total		414	780 ST
CCA	Truck	ZIS-150	116	371
Infantry		ZIS-151	226	839
Division	Cart	1 ton (avg)	292	292
	CCA Division Total		634	1,502 ST

Table 6.15
Nonorganic Transport Requirements[133]

Category	U.S. Div	NKPA Div	CCF Div
Number of Personnel Who Normally Walk	5,850	9,125	13,045
Number of Vehicles Required to Carry Personnel	270	305	435
Subtotal	270	305	435
Number of Organic Animal Carts	0	231	292
Vehicles Required to Carry Organic Animals	0	177	213
Subtotal	0	177	213
Total	270	482	648

Most of the CCF divisions which entered Korea from Manchuria moved by foot march, but some unit movements as well as most of the supply movements of the NKPA and CCF were carried out on the railroads. In mid-1953, it was estimated that to move a CCF Army by rail, without its organic vehicles, would require at least forty-eight trains of twenty-five cars each, or 1,467 trucks.[134] Organizational changes in the CCF after the Armistice in Korea resulted in significant increases in personnel and equipment, which in turn increased the number of rail cars or trucks needed to move a CCF unit. The 1956 CCF Army, with its organic vehicles, required a minimum of 114 trains of twenty-five cars each, or 2,314 trucks.[135] At the same time, sixty standard-gauge, forty-car trains were required to move a U.S. infantry division, fourteen to move an NKPA infantry division, and twenty-eight to move a CCF infantry division.[136] More detailed rolling stock requirements for the Type A (no organic tank or artillery regiment) CCF Armies found in Korea or nearby in Manchuria in 1956 are outlined in Table 6.16.

Table 6.16
Rolling Stock Requirements for One Type A CCF Army ca. 1956[137]

Items	No.	Usual Load	Rolling Stock Required		
			Boxcars	Flatcars	Gondolas
Personnel	58,327	48 men per boxcar	1,216		
Animals	2,556	9 per gondola			284
Loaded Carts	876	12 per flatcar		73	
Loaded Cargo Trucks	1,180	1 per flatcar		1,180	
GAZ-67b Trucks	89	3 per flatcar		30	
122-mm Howitzers	36	2 per flatcar		18	
76-mm Division Guns	36	3 per flatcar		12	
120-mm Mortars	36	6 per gondola			6
75-mm Guns	36	3 per flatcar		12	
37-mm AA Guns	36	2 per flatcar		18	
Total (100% of Authorized)		2,849 cars	1,216	1,343	290

The procedures employed by the NKPA and CCF for unit movements by rail, highway, and foot march were derived from Soviet Army doctrine, which emphasized that railroads should be the primary method for effecting unit movements over 100 kilometers in distance and which stressed the difficulties and vulnerabilities of large-scale troop movements by truck.[138] The advantages of the foot march were noted as being the speed and simplicity with which foot marches could be organized and controlled; the relatively low impact on foot movements of weather, time of day, and road conditions; the mobility, flexibility, and readiness for combat retained by the troops enroute; the ability to conceal even large numbers of troops during foot marches; and the relative invulnerability of marching troops to enemy air and armored attack.[139] The disadvantage of the relatively slow rate of foot marches was well recognized, but Soviet doctrine also noted that rail transport saved time only when the distance to be moved was greater than a three-day infantry march and that motor transport saved time only when troops without equipment were to be moved more than 75 kilometers, and then only if more than two routes were available.[140] The accepted Soviet (and thus CCF and NKPA) doctrine was that the foot march remained the preferred method for moving troops within the Army/Corps area.

NKPA-CCF troop movements during the Korean War were almost invariably conducted at night due to the dominance of UNC airpower. Movements usually ended about an hour before dawn in order to provide sufficient time to construct or occupy the daytime bivouac and insure its camouflage and other security measures.[141] Unit marches were generally conducted on secondary roads or trails, especially if they were more direct and offered greater protection from UNC air observation. Local guides and a variety of route marking methods, including rocks painted with luminous materials, were utilized. Troops usually marched single file or in double columns on either side of a road with three to five paces between men, 8 to 10 yards between platoons, and 10 to 15 yards between companies. The normal rate of foot march for NKPA and CCF troops, including a five- to ten-minute rest stop every hour, was 3 to 4 mph on good roads and level terrain, about 3 mph on secondary roads and trails, and about 1.5 mph on difficult terrain or when entering or leaving assembly areas. Under emergency conditions, CCF troops could sustain a pace of 5.5 mph for several hours without rest stops.

Both the NKPA and the CCF in Korea stressed both passive and active defense of moving troops against air attack. Aircraft spotters were stationed along the route of march and provided warning of approaching UNC aircraft, usually by means of warning rifle shots.[142] However, CCF march security was otherwise surprisingly lax. Flank or rear guards were seldom employed, and the small advance guards were often not far enough ahead of the main body to prevent a surprise attack.[143]

Bivouac and rest areas were chosen with great care to provide maximum cover and concealment, and security measures in bivouac were strictly enforced. Most CCF bivouacs were provided with squad-sized entrenchments, often with overhead cover, and camouflage discipline was usually excellent and innovative. However, the CCF also had a tendency to congregate in houses and other buildings and thus frequently suffered heavy casualties from UNC air attacks.[144]

CONCLUSION

Although the NKPA and CCF frequently conducted unit tactical and administrative movements using only their organic manpower and animal transport, NKPA-CCF logistical (supply) movements, by their very volume, required extensive use of rail and motor transport. Although the North Korean railroad system (and its Manchurian connecting system) was more than adequate, motor transport remained inadequate throughout the war. The NKPA-CCF distribution system in Korea was plagued in particular by the lack of motor transport at lower levels. The practical effect of this deficiency during the first phase of the war was to limit the Communist offensives in 1951 to only six to eight days, the period representing the time required to exhaust existing stockpiles in the forward areas. Unable to press the attack, the NKPA and CCF failed to crush the battered UNC forces, and the war soon evolved into a defensive battle along fixed fortified lines reminiscent of the World War I trenches. Although Communist tactical mobility and flexibility were limited, the largely static nature of combat operations in the last two years of the war and the failure of UNC forces to maintain constant pressure on frontline Communist units made it possible for the NKPA and CCF to improve their distribution systems continually and to overcome the shortage of lower echelon transport by extensive and elaborate stockpiling efforts, which allowed them to amass sufficient supplies for defensive operations and limited offensives.[145]

The severe distribution problems faced by the NKPA and CCF during the extended, fast-moving operations down the length of the Korean peninsula in the first phase of the war were eased by the more static conditions which later prevailed. Subsequent to the stabilization of the frontlines just north of the 38th Parallel in mid-1951, the Communist forces were able to establish an effective distribution system employing all modes of transport which proved capable, despite determined UNC attack, of supporting large numbers of combat troops on the frontlines. At the time of the Armistice in July 1953, the enemy railroad and highway transport systems were more than adequate to meet enemy logistics requirements, and indeed the Communists appeared to be moving supplies forward at a rate approximately 10 percent greater than that required to meet current consumption.[146]

NOTES

1. James A. Huston, *Guns and Butter, Powder and Rice: U.S. Army Logistics in the Korean War* (Selinsgrove, PA: Susquehanna University Press, 1989), 360; Headquarters, United States IX Corps, G-2 Section, *Enemy Tactics, Techniques and Doctrine* ([Korea]: Headquarters, United States IX Corps, September 1951), 40.

2. See Map 2.1 and Tables 2.1 through 2.4 in Chapter 2.

3. "Railroads and Highway Transport in North Korea and Their Impact on Enemy Logistics," *USAFFE Intelligence Digest*, I, no. 13 (2 July 1953), 44.

4. "Railroads and Highway Transport in North Korea and Their Impact on Enemy Logistics," 44. However, North Korean railroad capacity was reduced to about 20 percent of its prewar level by UNC interdiction efforts (see Headquarters, Eighth United States Army, Assistant Chief of Staff G-2/Headquarters, United States Fifth Air Force, Assistant Chief of Staff A-2, *Supply and Transportation System of the Chinese Communist and North Korean Forces in Korea* {[Tokyo]: Headquarters, Eighth United States

Army, Assistant Chief of Staff G-2/Headquarters, United States Fifth Air Force, Assistant Chief of Staff A-2, 23 September 1951}, 104–105).

5. "Railroads and Highway Transport in North Korea and Their Impact on Enemy Logistics," 44.

6. General Headquarters, Far East Command, Military Intelligence Section, Allied Translator and Interpreter Service, "Interrogation Reports—North Korean Forces: North Korean Logistics," *ATIS Research Supplement*, Issue No. 1 (19 October 1950), 21–23.

7. "Military Supply in North Korea," *USAFFE Intelligence Digest*, V, no. 10 (October 1955), 43–44.

8. "Railroads and Highway Transport in North Korea and Their Impact on Enemy Logistics," 44.

9. "Chinese Communist Army and North Korean Army Logistics and Class Supply," *USAFFE Intelligence Digest*, VI, no. 4 (April 1956), 50.

10. "Military Supply in North Korea," 44.

11. "Military Supply in North Korea," 36.

12. *Supply and Transportation System of the Chinese Communist and North Korean Forces in Korea*, 91–92. For example, in March 1951 UNC intelligence agencies reported the movement of supplies by diesel-powered motor launches from Port Arthur and Darien to Antung, Manchuria, for subsequent delivery to North Korea.

13. "Effect of the Armistice on Enemy Logistics in North Korea, Part I: Enemy Transport Facilities," *USAFFE Intelligence Digest*, IV, no. 6 (August 1954), 5. See also Map 2.1 and Table 2.3 in Chapter 2.

14. "Railroads and Highway Transport in North Korea and Their Impact on Enemy Logistics," 27. In general, UNC interdiction efforts reduced the North Korean railroad system to about 20 percent of its peacetime capacity (see *Supply and Transportation System of the Chinese Communist and North Korean Forces in Korea*, 104–105).

15. Headquarters, Eighth United States Army, Office of the Assistant Chief of Staff, G-2, *Intelligence Estimate, 27 July 1953* (APO 301: Headquarters, Eighth United States Army, Office of the Assistant Chief of Staff, G-2, 27 July 1953), 15.

16. "Railroads and Highway Transport in North Korea and Their Impact on Enemy Logistics," 31.

17. "Military Supply in North Korea," 30.

18. E. L. Atkins, H. P. Griggs, and Roy T. Sessums, *North Korean Logistics and Methods of Accomplishment* (ORO Technical Memorandum ORO-T-8 [EUSAK]; [Chevy Chase, MD]: Operations Research Office, The Johns Hopkins University, 1951), 33. The authors of "Effect of the Armistice on Enemy Logistics in North Korea, Part I: Enemy Transport Facilities" indicated (p. 9) that before the war 815 locomotives and 6,930 cars were operating in North Korea.

19. *North Korean Logistics and Methods of Accomplishment*, 33.

20. "Effect of the Armistice on Enemy Logistics in North Korea, Part I: Enemy Transport Facilities," 9; "Railroads and Highway Transport in North Korea and Their Impact on Enemy Logistics," 28. The Eighth Army G-2 section (*Intelligence Estimate, 27 July 1953*, p. 15) put the number available on 27 July 1953 at 228 locomotives and 5,500 cars.

21. "Railroads and Highway Transport in North Korea and Their Impact on Enemy Logistics," 28–29.

22. "Effect of the Armistice on Enemy Logistics in North Korea, Part I: Enemy Transport Facilities," 16.

23. "Railroads and Highway Transport in North Korea and Their Impact on Enemy Logistics," 29; "Effect of the Armistice on Enemy Logistics in North Korea, Part I: Enemy Transport Facilities," 10.

24. "Effect of the Armistice on Enemy Logistics in North Korea, Part I: Enemy Transport Facilities," 9.

25. Headquarters, Department of the Army, Office of the Assistant Chief of Staff for Intelligence, *Logistical Data for the Chinese Communist Army* (Washington: Headquarters, Department of the Army, Office of the Assistant Chief of Staff for Intelligence, 1959), 6. Data are for models in use in 1959; Korean War era cars may have been somewhat smaller.

26. "North Korean Railroad Security Division," *USAFFE Intelligence Digest*, I, no. 2 (17 January 1953), 25–26.

27. "Railroads and Highway Transport in North Korea and Their Impact on Enemy Logistics," 27–28.

28. "Railroads and Highway Transport in North Korea and Their Impact on Enemy Logistics," 28.

29. "North Korean Railroad Security Division," 27–29 and Chart No. 1; Inclosure 8 ("The North Korean Railroad Recovery Bureau—575th Army Unit") to Headquarters, Eighth United States Army, Office of the Assistant Chief of Staff, G-2, *Periodic Intelligence Report No. 884*, 12 December 1952, 1.

30. "Railroads and Highway Transport in North Korea and Their Impact on Enemy Logistics," 27.

31. Inclosure 8 ("The North Korean Railroad Recovery Bureau—575th Army Unit") to Headquarters, Eighth United States Army, Office of the Assistant Chief of Staff, G-2, *Periodic Intelligence Report No. 884*, 12 December 1952, 1. Robert F. Futrell (*The United States Air Force in Korea, 1950–1953* [rev. ed., Washington: Office of Air Force History, 1983], 338) indicated that there were three brigades of about 7,700 men each, and U.S. intelligence agencies did report three brigades active in early 1955 (see Inclosure 2 to Annex A of Headquarters, United States Army Forces, Far East, and Eighth United States Army, Office of the Assistant Chief of Staff, G-2, *Intelligence Estimate Korea—March 1955* [APO 343: Headquarters, United States Army Forces Far East and Eighth United States Army, Office of the Assistant Chief of Staff, G-2, 3 March 1955]). The total strength of the Railroad Recovery Bureau was about 26,000 men in January 1953 (see "North Korean Railroad Security Division," 26), which would support the existence of three brigades at that time. The third brigade, if it did exist, may have been deployed along the trans-Korea rail line from Kowon to Pyongyang.

32. Gregory A. Carter, *Some Historical Notes on Air Interdiction in Korea* (Santa Monica, CA: The RAND Corporation, September 1966), 14.

33. Samuel B. Griffith II, *The Chinese People's Liberation Army* (New York: McGraw-Hill Book Company for the Council on Foreign Relations, 1967), 222; "Railroads and Highway Transport in North Korea and Their Impact on Enemy Logistics," 28.

34. "North Korean Railroad Security Division," 25–29; Eighth United States Army, G-2, *Periodic Intelligence Report No. 884*, 12 December 1952, 1.

35. "North Korean Railroad Security Division," 27–29. The 5th Regiment was responsible for the rail net from Kowon through Pyongyang to Namchonjom (North and South Hwanghae and South Pyongan Provinces); the 6th Regiment from Pyongyang to Manpojin (North Pyongan and Chakang Provinces); the 7th Regiment from Sinuiju to

Sunchon (Kangwong and South Hamgyong Provinces); and the 8th Regiment from Kowon to Hoeryang (North Hamgyong Province) (see Eighth United States Army, G-2, *Periodic Intelligence Report No. 884*, 12 December 1952, 1). The independent guard battalion controlled by Railroad Security Division headquarters was responsible for railroad security in the immediate vicinity of Pyongyang.

36. "Selected Intelligence Items during Period 16 June-30 June 1952," *FEC Intelligence Digest*, 26 (2 July 1952), 53–54.

37. "Railroads and Highway Transport in North Korea and Their Impact on Enemy Logistics," 36.

38. *Supply and Transportation System of the Chinese Communist and North Korean Forces in Korea*, 69–70. The descriptions of bridges which follow are from this source.

39. See Sketch 8.1 for an expanded view of the Sinuiju bridge complex.

40. "Enemy Motor Transport in North Korea," *USAFFE Intelligence Digest*, I, no. 9 (2 May 1953), 34.

41. "Enemy Motor Transport in North Korea," 35.

42. "Railroads and Highway Transport in North Korea and Their Impact on Enemy Logistics," 38. The peacetime capacity is shown in Table 2.4 in Chapter 2. Note that the peacetime capacity is based on twelve hours of operation per day while wartime capacity is based on ten hours of operation per day. Wartime highway movements were subject to delays caused by enemy action, tactical movement requirements, and increased crew rest and maintenance time.

43. "Railroads and Highway Transport in North Korea and Their Impact on Enemy Logistics," 39.

44. "Effect of the Armistice on Enemy Logistics in North Korea, Part I: Enemy Transport Facilities," 11; "Railroads and Highway Transport in North Korea and Their Impact on Enemy Logistics," 36 and 38. Capacity shown is for a ten-hour-per-day (wartime) operation. Routes 1 through 5 were entry routes; Chongjin connected with points of entry at Musan, Hoeryang, and Unggi.

45. "Railroads and Highway Transport in North Korea and Their Impact on Enemy Logistics," 37.

46. The organization and operational employment of the Military Highway Administration Bureau (also called the Military Roads Administration Bureau) are described in *Supply and Transportation System of the Chinese Communist and North Korean Forces in Korea*, 49–51.

47. *Supply and Transportation System of the Chinese Communist and North Korean Forces in Korea*, 50. The exact number of MHAB regiments is uncertain. The Eighth U.S. Army G-2 section indicated (Inclosure 2 to Annex A, *Intelligence Estimate Korea—March 1955*) that there were only three MHAB regiments in early 1955, each consisting of a headquarters, three road maintenance battalions, and a traffic control battalion.

48. *Supply and Transportation System of the Chinese Communist and North Korean Forces in Korea*, 49–51.

49. Based on 100 percent availability. See "Railroads and Highway Transport in North Korea and Their Impact on Enemy Logistics," 39; "Effect of the Armistice on Enemy Logistics in North Korea, Part I: Enemy Transport Facilities," 13.

50. Headquarters, Far East Command, Military Intelligence Section, Office of the Assistant Chief of Staff, J-2, *Logistical Capability of Communist Forces in Korea to Support a Major Offensive* (APO 500: Headquarters, Far East Command, Military Intelligence Section, Office of the Assistant Chief of Staff, J-2, 28 February 1953), 10–11. The

16,000 trucks represent an estimate of the total number of trucks actually present in North Korea without regard to either the total number authorized or the usual 85 percent availability factor.

51. "Enemy Motor Transport in North Korea," Chart 4 (on p. 34). Table 6.7 shows 100 percent of the authorized vehicles but does not include the quasi-military North Korean trucks known to be present. The 1950 NKPA infantry division was reported to have had a total of 194 trucks, including forty in the organic truck company found in the division Rear Service Section and twenty-three in the supply platoon of each of the three infantry regiments (see "Interrogation Reports—North Korean Forces: Typical North Korean Infantry Division," *ATIS Research Supplement*, Issue No. 1 [19 October 1950], 10 and 30). The 1953 NKPA infantry division was reported to have been authorized only about 100 trucks (see "Enemy Motor Transport in North Korea," 32), but the Far East Command J-2 (*Logistical Capability of Communist Forces in Korea to Support a Major Offensive*, 26) reported 150 trucks per division as well as 150 in the GHQ truck battalions and 200 in the truck regiment supporting each NKPA corps as of January 1953.

52. "Enemy Motor Transport in North Korea," Chart 2 (on p. 31). See Diagrams 6.3 and 6.4. Table 6.8 shows 100 percent of the authorized CCF vehicles, but the vehicles thought to be organic to the CCF Armies, Branch Units, Depots, and Sub-Depots are not included inasmuch as they may have been attached from higher echelons. By mid-1953, each CCF infantry division was authorized an organic truck company of forty-five trucks (see "Effect of the Armistice on Enemy Logistics in North Korea, Part I: Enemy Transport Facilities," 13).

53. "Enemy Motor Transport in North Korea," 32.

54. "Enemy Motor Transport in North Korea," 32.

55. "Railroads and Highway Transport in North Korea and Their Impact on Enemy Logistics," 41.

56. "Railroads and Highway Transport in North Korea and Their Impact on Enemy Logistics," 41 and 43.

57. *Supply and Transportation System of the Chinese Communist and North Korean Forces in Korea*, 93.

58. *North Korean Logistics and Methods of Accomplishment*, 8.

59. "Enemy Motor Transport in North Korea," 36.

60. "Enemy Motor Transport in North Korea," 36; *Supply and Transportation System of the Chinese Communist and North Korean Forces in Korea*, 93; Futrell, 473.

61. *Enemy Tactics, Techniques and Doctrine*, 40.

62. "Enemy Motor Transport in North Korea," 32.

63. The authors of *Supply and Transportation System of the Chinese Communist and North Korean Forces in Korea* (pp. 48–49) reported the existence in 1951 of two regimental-size units each with a strength of approximately 600 men in four companies of five officers and 126 men each and a total vehicular strength of 400 trucks. They also estimated that one such unit was needed to support three NKPA corps. However, the best information seems to be that there were nine independent battalions. See also "Petroleum, Oils and Lubricants Requirements for Communist Ground Forces, Far East," *USAFFE Intelligence Digest*, V, no. 4 (April 1955), 71.

64. "Railroads and Highway Transport in North Korea and Their Impact on Enemy Logistics," 41.

65. "The Enemy Supply System in North Korea," 20. Each NKPA corps truck battalion was authorized 120 trucks (see "Enemy Motor Transport in North Korea," 32).

66. "Interrogation Reports - North Korean Forces: North Korean Logistics," *ATIS Research Supplement*, 18; *Supply and Transportation System of the Chinese Communist and North Korean Forces in Korea*, 58-59.

67. "The Enemy Supply System in North Korea," *USAFFE Intelligence Digest*, II, no. 4 (2 September 1953), 20.

68. "Interrogation Reports—North Korean Forces: North Korean Logistics," 23. NKPA divisional truck companies had about forty trucks, and divisional forward supply dumps were usually located near the regimental rear boundary about 5 to 10 miles behind the front.

69. "Interrogation Reports—North Korean Forces: North Korean Logistics," 18.

70. "Individual Histories, Chinese Communist Support and Service Units," *FEC Intelligence Digest*, 26 (2 July 1952), 51; Russell Spurr, *Enter the Dragon: China's Undeclared War Against the United States in Korea, 1950–51* (New York: Newmarket Press, 1988), 170 and 250. There may have actually been as many as five CCF truck regiments in Korea in October 1950 (see *Supply and Transportation System of the Chinese Communist and North Korean Forces in Korea*, 4–5).

71. *Supply and Transportation System of the Chinese Communist and North Korean Forces in Korea*, 8.

72. "Railroads and Highway Transport in North Korea and Their Impact on Enemy Logistics," 41; "The Enemy Supply System in North Korea," 17.

73. Headquarters, United States Army Forces, Far East (Advance), Office of the Assistant Chief of Staff, G-2, *Chinese Communist Ground Forces in Korea: Tables of Organization and Equipment* (APO 500: Headquarters, United States Army Forces, Far East [Advance], Office of the Assistant Chief of Staff, G-2, Intelligence, 1953), Chart 44.

74. Headquarters, Department of the Army, *Handbook on the Chinese Communist Army* (DA Pamphlet No. 30-51; Washington: USGPO, 1952), 32 and 66.

75. *Chinese Communist Ground Forces in Korea: Tables of Organization and Equipment*, 1 and Charts 44 and 45.

76. *Chinese Communist Ground Forces in Korea: Tables of Organization and Equipment*, Chart 45.

77. *Supply and Transportation System of the Chinese Communist and North Korean Forces in Korea*, 6–7, identifies the 42nd Truck Regiment as the first CCF truck regiment to be reorganized in the Type I format, but also (erroneously) identifies the 42nd Truck Regiment as entering Korea in January 1951. Elsewhere (pp. 10–11) the same source, again erroneously, reports the Type II CCF truck regiment as being organized with six companies and a total complement of 288 trucks. In general, this source is somewhat unreliable, perhaps because of the inadequate intelligence available to UNC in the early part of the war. The authors of *Handbook on the Chinese Communist Army* indicate (p. 66) that the Type I truck regiment had 1,632 officers and men and about 432 trucks while the more common Type II regiment had about 315 trucks.

78. "Chinese Communist Army and North Korean Logistics and Class Supply," 54.

79. "Enemy Motor Transport in North Korea," 29 and 32. In May 1953, seven GHQ CCF truck regiments were reported as being attached to Branch Units. In addition to the independent CCF truck regiments attached to each Branch Unit, the main depots of each Branch Unit were each apparently supported by two truck companies and each subdepot by one truck company, each of which had sixty-five trucks (see Futrell, 337).

80. "Enemy Motor Transport in North Korea," 29; *Supply and Transportation System of the Chinese Communist and North Korean Forces in Korea*, 4.

81. *Supply and Transportation System of the Chinese Communist and North Korean Forces in Korea*, 26; "The Enemy Supply System in North Korea," 17–18.

82. *Supply and Transportation System of the Chinese Communist and North Korean Forces in Korea*, 10 and 15. Originally the truck regiments supporting the Branch Units moved supplies down to the Army depots, but later, when subordinate elements were better equipped with motor transport, they did so only in the case of build-ups for offensives.

83. "Enemy Motor Transport in North Korea," 35. Each CCF Army Group had an organic truck regiment with about 409 trucks.

84. *Handbook on the Chinese Communist Army*, 32 and 66–67. The two truck companies supporting each CCF Army may have been part of the supporting Army Group truck regiment. Those Army units without organic motor transport were supported by trucks from the Army Group truck regiment (see "Enemy Motor Transport in North Korea," 29).

85. *Supply and Transportation System of the Chinese Communist and North Korean Forces in Korea*, 23.

86. *Supply and Transportation System of the Chinese Communist and North Korean Forces in Korea*, 24.

87. *Supply and Transportation System of the Chinese Communist and North Korean Forces in Korea*, 36.

88. *Supply and Transportation System of the Chinese Communist and North Korean Forces in Korea*, 35. The 47th Infantry Division of the 16th CCF Army (itself described as "mobile" or "mechanized") was unusual in that its truck company apparently had sixty-four trucks and supplies were delivered in divisional trucks even down to the line companies, a departure from normal practice (see Headquarters, Eighth United States Army in Korea, Office of the Assistant Chief of Staff, G-2, Order of Battle Branch, *CCF Army Histories* {[Korea]: Headquarters, Eighth US Army in Korea, Office of the Assistant Chief of Staff, G-2, Order of Battle Branch, 1 December 1954}, 12).

89. "Effect of the Armistice on Enemy Logistics in North Korea, Part I: Enemy Transport Facilities," 13.

90. "Effect of the Armistice on Enemy Logistics in North Korea, Part I: Enemy Transport Facilities," 13.

91. "Enemy Motor Transport in North Korea," 48–49.

92. *Supply and Transportation System of the Chinese Communist and North Korean Forces in Korea*, 11.

93. "Enemy Motor Transport in North Korea," 47.

94. *Supply and Transportation System of the Chinese Communist and North Korean Forces in Korea*, 95.

95. *Supply and Transportation System of the Chinese Communist and North Korean Forces in Korea*, 96.

96. "Enemy Motor Transport in North Korea," 47. NKPA-CCF methods for the passive and active defense of MSRs, vehicles, and key facilities against UNC air attack are discussed at greater length in Chapter 8.

97. *Supply and Transportation System of the Chinese Communist and North Korean Forces in Korea*, 96–97.

98. "Enemy Motor Transport in North Korea," 47.

99. "Railroads and Highway Transport in North Korea and Their Impact on Enemy Logistics," 42.

100. *Supply and Transportation System of the Chinese Communist and North Korean Forces in Korea*, 103.

101. Headquarters, United States I Corps, G-2 Section, *CCF Logistical Capabilities: A Study of the Enemy Vehicular Effort on I Corps Front* ([Korea]: Headquarters, United States I Corps, G-2 Section, 28 June 1952), 1.

102. "Chinese Communist Army and North Korean Army Logistics and Class Supply," 54; "The Enemy Supply System in North Korea," 21.

103. "Chinese Communist Army and North Korean Army Logistics and Class Supply," 54.

104. "Enemy Motor Transport in North Korea," 35. The 1950 NKPA infantry regiment, for example, had twenty-three organic trucks.

105. *Supply and Transportation System of the Chinese Communist and North Korean Forces in Korea*, 61.

106. *Chinese Communist Ground Forces in Korea: Tables of Organization and Equipment*, Chart 3.

107. *Chinese Communist Ground Forces in Korea: Tables of Organization and Equipment*, Charts 4, 5, and 15; *Handbook on the Chinese Communist Army*, 67.

108. *Chinese Communist Ground Forces in Korea: Tables of Organization and Equipment*, Chart 17.

109. *Supply and Transportation System of the Chinese Communist and North Korean Forces in Korea*, 91; *North Korean Logistics and Methods of Accomplishment*, 7 and 12. A two-horse wagon could haul a load of about 2,700 lb (see Carter, 5).

110. *Supply and Transportation System of the Chinese Communist and North Korean Forces in Korea*, 91.

111. ROKA and other UNC units also used porters in large numbers. Beginning in August 1950, most U.S. divisions were supported by about 500 paid civilian porters and laborers (see Roy E. Appleman, *South to the Naktong, North to the Yalu* [Washington: Office of the Chief of Military History, Department of the Army, 1961], 388).

112. *Supply and Transportation System of the Chinese Communist and North Korean Forces in Korea*, 91.

113. *North Korean Logistics and Methods of Accomplishment*, Table VI (on p. 27). The normal load/distance was 60 lb for 15 miles in one night (see *North Korean Logistics and Methods of Accomplishment*, 7 and 12). Based on the fact that a U.S. 2 1/2-ton truck could move 4,000 lb 30 miles in one day and return, the equivalent works out to be one U.S. truck = 19.8 porters = 2.2 animal carts (see *North Korean Logistics and Methods of Accomplishment*, 12).

114. *Supply and Transportation System of the Chinese Communist and North Korean Forces in Korea*, 91.

115. Carter, 5.

116. *Supply and Transportation System of the Chinese Communist and North Korean Forces in Korea*, 91.

117. Spurr, 249.

118. "A Statistical Comparison of the Mobility of the US and Communist-Bloc Infantry Divisions in the Far East," *USAFFE Intelligence Digest*, VI, no. 4 (April 1956), 5. The statistical data in this article were based on the slightly larger and more mechanized 1956 structures for all three divisions but utilized Korean War planning data and thus are useful for indicating the order of magnitude.

119. *CCF Logistical Capabilities: A Study of the Enemy Vehicular Effort on I Corps Front*, 15.

120. "A Statistical Comparison of the Mobility of the US and Communist-Bloc Infantry Divisions in the Far East," 3.

121. A distinction should be made between logistical (supply) movements and unit (tactical or administrative) movements.

122. "A Statistical Comparison of the Mobility of the US and Communist-Bloc Infantry Divisions in the Far East," 5.

123. "A Statistical Comparison of the Mobility of the US and Communist-Bloc Infantry Divisions in the Far East," Chart 5.

124. "A Statistical Comparison of the Mobility of the US and Communist-Bloc Infantry Divisions in the Far East," Chart 5.

125. "A Statistical Comparison of the Mobility of the US and Communist-Bloc Infantry Divisions in the Far East," Chart 6. The amounts equate to the U.S. rifleman carrying about 50 percent of his body weight and the NKPA-CCF rifleman carrying about 33 percent of his body weight.

126. "Current Intelligence: Indications and Capabilities, 25 September to 25 December 1955," *USAFFE Intelligence Digest*, VI, no. 1 (January 1956), vi.

127. In 1956, the U.S. division had about four times the lift requirement of the Chinese division and about seven times that of the NKPA division. See "A Statistical Comparison of the Mobility of the US and Communist-Bloc Infantry Divisions in the Far East," Chart 10.

128. "A Statistical Comparison of the Mobility of the US and Communist-Bloc Infantry Divisions in the Far East," Chart 9. Note that "basic load" is not the same as daily resupply requirement.

129. "A Statistical Comparison of the Mobility of the US and Communist-Bloc Infantry Divisions in the Far East," Chart 4c. All figures are based on 1953 data.

130. "A Statistical Comparison of the Mobility of the US and Communist-Bloc Infantry Divisions in the Far East," Chart 8.

131. "A Statistical Comparison of the Mobility of the US and Communist-Bloc Infantry Divisions in the Far East," 1–3. Data on the 1956 CCF and NKPA divisions are from the same source.

132. "A Statistical Comparison of the Mobility of the US and Communist-Bloc Infantry Divisions in the Far East," Charts 15a–15d. U.S. 1/4-ton trucks (jeeps) are not included. The load of the Soviet GAZ-63 truck averaged 3 tons; the Soviet ZIS-150 truck 3.2 tons; and the Soviet ZIS-151 truck 3.8 tons.

133. "A Statistical Comparison of the Mobility of the US and Communist-Bloc Infantry Divisions in the Far East," Chart 4a. Truck requirements are calculated in 2 1/2-ton truck equivalents with thirty men or four animals per truck. Carts were drawn by the trucks required to motorize personnel and animals. The authors of "Chinese Communist Road and Rail Reinforcement Capabilities in Korea," *USAFFE Intelligence Digest*, VI, no. 2 (February 1956), indicated (p. 17) that in addition to organic transport, 4,180 trucks would have been required to move four 1956 CCF Armies by road. In 1956, there were nine CCF truck regiments (417 trucks each) available in Korea and two more regiments available in Northeast China. Those eleven truck regiments with a total of 4,587 trucks were considered adequate to move the four armies.

134. "Chinese Communist Road and Rail Reinforcement Capabilities in Korea," 13.

135. "Chinese Communist Road and Rail Reinforcement Capabilities in Korea," 13.

136. "A Statistical Comparison of the Mobility of the US and Communist-Bloc Infantry Divisions in the Far East," Chart 11. Calculated on the basis of forty U.S. soldiers per boxcar and forty-eight NKPA-CCF soldiers per boxcar.

137. "Chinese Communist Road and Rail Reinforcement Capabilities in Korea," 15. The Type A CCF Army (e. g. - 38th and 63rd CCF Armies) thus required seventy-two forty-car trains, ninety-five thirty-car trains, or 114 25-car trains. The Type B CCF Army with an organic tank regiment (e.g., 46th, 64th, and 65th CCF Armies) required 1,237 boxcars, 1,433 flatcars, and 290 gondolas for a total of 2,960 cars or seventy-four forty-car trains, ninety-nine thirty-car trains, or 119 25-car trains. The Type C CCF Army with both an organic tank regiment and an artillery regiment (e.g., 39th) required 1,274 boxcars, 1,590 flatcars, and 290 gondolas for a total of 3,154 cars or seventy-nine forty-car trains, 106 thirty-car trains, or 127 25-car trains.

138. Avrosimov Chilimuniya and Shih-ku-li-tieh-tzu, *Chinese Communist General Principles of Army Group Tactics* (Manila: General Headquarters, Far East Command, Military Intelligence Section, General Staff, 1951), II, 111.

139. *Chinese Communist General Principles of Army Group Tactics*, II, 111–112.

140. *Chinese Communist General Principles of Army Group Tactics*, II, 112.

141. *Handbook on the Chinese Communist Army, 59-60; Enemy Tactics, Techniques and Doctrine*, 4.

142. *Enemy Tactics, Techniques and Doctrine*, 4.

143. *Handbook on the Chinese Communist Army*, 60.

144. *Handbook on the Chinese Communist Army*, 60.

145. "Enemy Motor Transport in North Korea," 48–49; *Handbook on the Chinese Communist Army*, 64–65.

146. "Railroads and Highway Transport in North Korea and Their Impact on Enemy Logistics," 44–45. For example, NKPA-CCF logistical requirements in April 1953 were estimated to be 4,018 ST/day and logistics imports were estimated to be 4,445 ST/day (2,520 ST/day by rail and 1,925 ST/day by highway). Thus there was a daily surplus at that time of some 427 ST, which could be stockpiled to meet the demands of future defensive and offensive operations.

Railroad marshaling yard on main line south of Wonsan under attack by U.S. B-26 light bombers.

Communist train knocked out by USAF lies accordion-fashion near the Han River, 7 March 1951.

Wreckage of the rail center at Kusong after a USAF bombing raid, 14 October 1950.

Marshaling yard at Masan-ni under attack by a B-26. Rockets and napalm have set fire to the rolling stock and supplies.

Demolished North Korean T-34 tank and two destroyed North Korean trucks. The truck in the foreground is a ZIS-5. The truck in the background appears to be a ZIS-151. Note the gasoline drums. The site may have been a fueling point.

Soldiers of the U.S. 25th Infantry Division using A-frames.

naged NKPA artillery caisson adapted for use with oxen, along the road in Mogong-ni area, 17
tember 1950.

Han River bridge on Route 13 five miles east of Seoul used by the CCF, 26 February 1951.

Vehicular bridge at Kongju showing innovative sandbag repair of a type used by the NKPA-CCF.

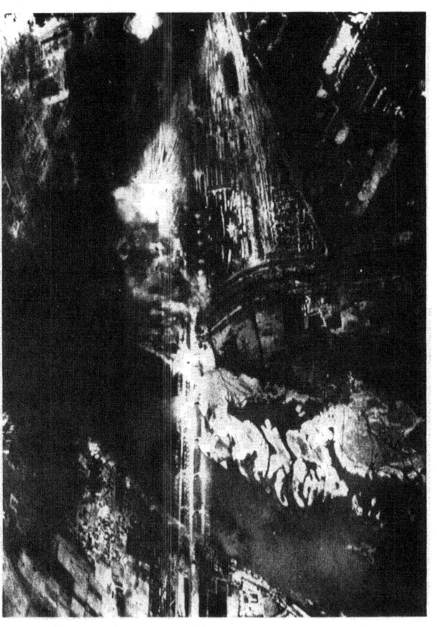

Pyongyang railroad bridges under attack by aircraft from the British-American carrier task force, 3–4 July 1950.

Part II

UNC Interdiction
and
NKPA-CCF Logistics

7

Advances and Retreats,
June 1950–June 1951

The chief problem faced by the North Korean and Chinese Communist forces throughout the Korean War was the development and maintenance of logistical systems adequate to support large numbers of troops over extended lines of communications in the face of intensive interdiction efforts by United Nations forces. Thus distribution, rather than production, storage, or issue, was the most vulnerable link in the Communist logistical system. This fact was soon recognized by the United Nations Command, which applied its considerable air assets in a series of aggressive campaigns designed to deny the enemy the free movement of men and supplies from the Manchurian border down to the fighting front. The UNC tried a variety of methods for achieving its goal of cutting the NKPA-CCF supply lines to the front, but in the end it was unable to degrade Communist logistical support below the level required to support strong defensive action and simultaneously build up supplies for periodic offensive actions, which seriously threatened the UNC defensive line. Indeed, by mid-1953 the Communist logistical system was more effective and more efficient than at any time during the war and was growing stronger.

The history of the NKPA-CCF logistical effort during the Korean War can be divided into three main periods, which differ somewhat from the traditional divisions.[1] The first period began with the sudden attack of North Korean forces on 25 July 1950 and ended with the opening of truce talks in July 1951. That period was characterized by the destruction of the relatively modern logistical organization of the NKPA built up before June 1950 and the subsequent ad hoc organization of NKPA and CCF logistical support following the collapse of the NKPA and the intervention of the CCF in October–November 1950. From October–November 1950 until July 1951, the NKPA and CCF struggled to overcome the defects of their logistical structures and to develop procedures adequate to support large armies operating over a wide area through difficult terrain in the face of UNC air superiority. The second period began in late 1951 and extended to early 1953. During that period, the NKPA-CCF developed their logistical force structure and substantially improved both the means and the methods of supporting their forces in the field. The second period saw the initiation of a program for the standardization and reequipment of Communist forces and the development of effective methods for coming to grips with the intensive UNC air interdiction program. The final phase began in early 1953 and continued until the Armistice on 27 July 1953. This was the period in which Communist logistical structures and methods reached maturity and the NKPA-CCF proved that they were able to keep their extended lines of communications open and operating at a level sufficient to meet both daily consumption and the need to stockpile supplies for high intensity offensive operations.

THE ADVANCE OF THE NKPA, JUNE–SEPTEMBER 1950

The North Korean army, which attacked the Republic of Korea at 0400 hours, 25 June 1950, was a modern, well-led, well-equipped, and well-trained force of some 135,000 men organized into two corps comprising ten infantry divisions, a tank brigade, five brigades of border constabulary, and several independent combat formations. Its modern equipment, mostly of Soviet manufacture, included some 150 aircraft, about 200 T-34 medium tanks, 76-mm self-propelled howitzers, and a variety of other artillery pieces, antitank guns, and mortars as well as about 194 trucks per division. The organization and doctrine of the NKPA, logistical as well as tactical, followed Soviet models, and the North Korean armed forces included many officers who had served either in the Soviet or Communist Chinese armies or who had received formal military training in the Soviet Union. A substantial portion of the noncommissioned officers and soldiers had also served in the Soviet and Chinese Communist armies. Seriously underestimated by the United States, the North Korean forces were well prepared logistically for the quick campaign of conquest which was envisioned.[2]

The speed and precision of the North Korean attack suggests that staff planning and the logistical build-up for the attack had begun at least one year earlier.[3] In fact, the formidable NKPA, which both outnumbered and outgunned its ROK and UNC opponents in the early days of the war, had been created less than three years earlier. The formal establishment of the NKPA with an estimated strength of 30,000 men was celebrated in Pyongyang on 8 February 1948.[4] By the end of that year it had doubled in size, with many of its new divisions formed around nuclei of officers and men transferred from Chinese Communist divisions which had fought for several years in North China and Manchuria against both the Japanese and the Chinese Nationalists.[5] Its size doubled again in 1949 with the addition of some 40,000 conscripts, 20,000 to 22,000

Koreans formerly in the Chinese Communist army, and several thousand men returning from three years of training in the Soviet Union to serve as cadre in air and tank corps.[6] The training of the NKPA shifted into high gear at the beginning of 1950, and the new combat and service units were fleshed out with additional manpower between March and June through an all-out conscription.[7]

In June 1950, the NKPA was equipped principally with Soviet arms and other equipment, and some 3,000 Soviet advisors had helped form and train the NKPA.[8] Soviet occupation forces departing Korea left behind their equipment for the new NKPA. Beginning in April and May 1950, large shipments of arms (including tanks, heavy artillery, trucks, aircraft, and automatic weapons) began to arrive from the Soviet Union in preparation for the planned conquest of the Republic of Korea. These supplies were transported from Manchuria and the Soviet Union by water to Chinnampo and Sinanju on the west coast and Hungnam and Wonsan on the east coast and by rail to Pyongyang and Haeju. Distribution was completed by rail and truck to locations near the 38th Parallel.[9] At the same time, the North Koreans themselves accelerated the production of war matériel, principally small arms, ammunition, and food, by cutting back on planned civilian construction and production.[10] The North Koreans utilized Manchurian and Soviet depots for the storage of war supplies accumulated since 1948 and stockpiled weapons and ammunition in large underground bunkers along the 38th Parallel in preparation for their invasion of the south.[11] By continuously building up their logistical complexes, the North Koreans created a seemingly unlimited capacity to support their combat forces in an invasion of South Korea.

Once underway, the multiple-pronged North Korean attack proved nearly unstoppable. The small, poorly equipped ROK forces virtually disintegrated after the first assaults, and the South Korean capital and key communications center of Seoul fell to the NKPA on 29 June. After a brief pause to reorganize their forces, the North Koreans crossed the Han River and continued to the south at a rapid pace. Remnants of the ROK Army (ROKA) and the feeble U.S. ground forces flown in from Japan were unable to delay the NKPA advance to any significant degree, although the UNC quickly gained air superiority over South Korea and established sea control in Korean waters, which proved effective in delaying the North Korean advance and destroying North Korea's logistical assets. The opposing ROK and UNC ground forces, although initially weak and disorganized, grew stronger by the day, and they too took their toll of NKPA men, vehicles, and other equipment as they were forced south and east into the Pusan Perimeter. With each mile the NKPA advanced into South Korea, its supply lines became longer and thus both less efficient and more vulnerable to UNC air attack. Thus the rapid advance to the south was not without its costs and disadvantages, and indications of logistical problems soon began to appear. As early as 5 July, it was evident that the North Korean tank and infantry columns could advance only about 4 to 8 miles per day before pausing to resupply fuel and ammunition.[12] The growing logistical problems of the NKPA became more apparent after they took Chonan on 8 July, by which date UNC aircraft had forced the NKPA to abandon daylight movements.[13] The combat effectiveness of the crack NKPA 3rd Division, which spearheaded the attack, had been seriously degraded by UNC air attacks, and the division was forced to stop and resupply, thus allowing the battered U.S. 24th Infantry Division a short breathing space and the chance to prepare for the battle of Taejon a week later.[14]

Despite its excellent logistical preparations for the 25 June attack and a maximum use of local resources in the areas through which it moved, after two weeks the NKPA proved incapable of maintaining constant pressure on the crumbling ROK and U.S. forces. Nevertheless, in a series of massive lunges, the NKPA occupied about 85 percent of South Korea in less than thirty days and drove the remaining ROK and U.S. troops behind the Naktong River and into what came to be known as the Pusan Perimeter. Until the stabilization of the Pusan Perimeter on 14 August, the NKPA logistical system remained fairly effective despite the tremendous losses in the attack and from UNC air interdiction. NKPA personnel casualties amounted to some 50,000 men, or about 40 percent, but the losses of equipment, particularly tanks and trucks, were even more serious.[15] By mid-August, NKPA artillery units were at 75 percent of their original strength, the NKPA armored force had been all but annihilated, and the losses of guns, tanks, trucks, fuel, ammunition, and food were greater in transit to the front than in combat action.[16] The NKPA retained the initiative but was already beginning to run out of men, equipment, and supplies. Moreover, UNC air attacks had forced the NKPA to move only at night and to institute strict passive air defense measures during the day as well as to rely more heavily on animal transport and porters for the movement of supplies.[17]

The NKPA logistical situation grew increasingly desperate as the battle for the Pusan Perimeter dragged on, and the NKPA grew increasingly weak while UNC forces garnered strength on a daily basis. Until the middle of July, the NKPA had experienced delays in receipt but no real shortage of supplies, but by mid-August the UNC air interdiction program and the loss of large numbers of transport vehicles began to produce serious shortages.[18] The NKPA units at the far southern end of the supply line were the first to suffer; one NKPA division, for example, reported receipt of eighteen tons of food, ten tons of quartermaster supplies, twelve tons of POL, and 166 tons of ammunition between 25 June and 15 July, but only nine tons of food, five tons of quartermaster supplies, seven tons of POL, and thirty tons of ammunition between 16 July and 15 August.[19] By 26 August, all units had been ordered to conserve ammunition in order to retain sufficient reserves for planned offensives against the Perimeter.[20]

Increasing shortages of all classes of supply required the institution of strict rationing and conservation methods. To protect their irreplaceable heavy weapons, North Korean commanders increasingly adopted conservative combat tactics and were forced to terminate attacks before they could effect a breakthrough.[21] The NKPA also resorted to extreme methods for protecting their supply lines and supply installations in order to permit a minimal flow of critical supplies to reach the front and allow the NKPA to continue to attack the hard-pressed Pusan Perimeter. Trains and trucks moved only at night and were hidden in tunnels during the day. Where bridges had been destroyed, tracks were laid directly over the obstacle or shuttle services were established, and supplies were often ferried across rivers and reloaded on railroad cars or trucks on the other side. Such measures continued to insure the delivery of critical supplies to within easy trucking distance of the front.[22] Large numbers of South Korean civilians were conscripted as porters and were used primarily to move supplies from divisional dumps to forward units along mountain roads and footpaths.[23] Some porters were also used to supplement motor transport operating between the railheads and corps or division depots. Heavy equipment, such as mortars and machineguns, were broken down into individual loads and concealed by camouflage or in the type of pack normally carried by Korean civilians.[24] Truck convoys and supply dumps were carefully camouflaged and were frequently located in tunnels or under bridges and overpasses to protect them from UNC air observation. Smaller battalion and company supply dumps were often hidden in drainage pipes or roadside ditches.[25]

Despite such stringent methods, the NKPA supply situation continued to deteriorate with each passing day. Throughout August 1950, artillery and small arms ammunition and fuel continued to get through to North Korean forces on the Pusan Perimeter, although in reduced quantities. However, motor transport, clothing, and food became increasingly scarce. Trucks were almost impossible to replace, and control over the remaining truck assets was centralized at GHQ NKPA which practically ceased to replace trucks in the later stages of the battle for the Perimeter.[26] The NKPA at the front did, however, receive twenty-one new T-34 tanks and 200 crewmen for the 105th Tank Division in mid-August, and artillery pieces and mortars remained in adequate supply until after the landings of UNC forces at Inchon on 15 September.[27] However, the North Korean self-propelled 76-mm guns were not replaced and subsequently never reappeared.[28] A severe, but unexplained, shortage of small arms occurred in all NKPA combat formations from about the second week of August, and until the first part of September only about 29 percent of divisional requisitions for small arms were filled; after the middle of September, replacement of small arms ceased.[29] NKPA replacements frequently arrived at the front without individual weapons and were instructed to pick up the weapons of the killed and wounded. In some cases, officers gave up their sidearms to arm replacements.[30]

Ammunition of all types remained in sufficient supply during the advance south, but shortages began to develop on the Pusan Perimeter due to both the length of NKPA supply lines and their interdiction by UNC airpower. Small arms ammunition supply remained adequate, but the resupply of artillery ammunition, particularly that for the heavier guns, became increasingly difficult.[31] Ammunition shortages began to affect NKPA combat operations seriously after mid-August. In any event, most of the Soviet-supplied ammunition was four to five years old and in poor condition, and many misfires and duds resulted.[32] On

17 August, during the battle for Obong-ni Ridge in the Naktong Bulge, the U.S. 25th Infantry Division intercepted a North Korean radio message reporting a shortage of ammunition and requesting permission to withdraw across the Naktong.[33]

Petroleum products also remained plentiful until the assault on the Pusan Perimeter was well underway, and large stocks had been captured from ROK and U.S. sources during the move south.[34] Severe shortages began to be reported by frontline units around 10 September due primarily to destruction of the large refinery at Wonsan and the depletion of captured stocks rather than solely due to transport difficulties.[35]

Although shortages in major items of equipment, ammunition, and fuel were troublesome, more serious shortages were experienced by the NKPA in such troops support items as clothing and food. By mid-August, most NKPA troops were in rags or captured U.S. fatigues, and new NKPA draftees were being issued ROK, U.S., and nonmilitary items of clothing.[36] The most critical supply problem, however, was food. As the NKPA advanced south, it requisitioned foodstuffs from the local areas but quickly exhausted the available supplies, and little or no food was received from the rear.[37] By the end of August, NKPA soldiers were receiving only one or two meals per day at best and were beginning to show evidence of malnutrition, resulting in a loss of stamina and impaired combat effectiveness due to inadequate rations.[38] For example, by the last week of August half the personnel of the NKPA 13th Infantry Division were no longer able to fight in mountainous terrain.[39]

As their supply difficulties increased, the combat effectiveness of NKPA units fell proportionately. Having crossed the Naktong River and penetrated the Pusan Perimeter, Major General Lee Kwon Mu's NKPA 4th "Seoul" Division faced a desperate situation due to logistical deficiencies. Food was in short supply, ammunition was very difficult to move across the Naktong, half the replacements had no weapons, and medical treatment was practically nonexistent.[40] The NKPA 18th Regiment holding the critical Obong-ni Ridge against determined counterattacks by the U.S. Marines and U.S. 24th Infantry Division received no ammunition resupply after 14 August, and on 18 August the U.S. Marines and Army forces decisively defeated the enemy penetration and forced the NKPA 4th Division back across the Naktong with heavy personnel and equipment losses.[41]

The logistical situation of the NKPA 12th Division, driving south to capture Pohang on the isolated east coast, was even more perilous. Exhausted by its movement through the difficult mountainous terrain south of Andong, the 12th Division had at the end of July replaced its Japanese rifles with captured U.S. M-1 rifles and carbines, for which there was adequate ammunition although it was not always to be found at the front.[42] However, in early August the 2nd Battalion of the division's artillery regiment had to send all of its artillery pieces back to Tanyang on the upper Han River because it could no longer supply them with ammunition.[43] For five days after 12 August, the division received no resupply of rations and was forced to forage.[44] Lacking sufficient logistical support, the remnants of the NKPA 12th Division were ultimately forced to retreat northward under heavy ROKA pressure.[45]

The NKPA 6th Division on the far southern end of the Pusan Perimeter fared little better. Moving south rapidly from the Han River, the division concentrated at Suchon, 90 air miles west of Pusan, on 25 July and prepared for a final drive eastward toward that critical port.[46] But the 6th Division was at the extreme far end of the NKPA supply line and was poorly prepared logistically for its offensive, particularly with respect to rations.[47] Opposed by the U.S. 25th Infantry Division in the mountains west of Masan, the 6th Division still had about twelve T-34 tanks but lacked fuel, the men were hungry, and all supplies had to be carried forward by A-frame porters.[48] A captured officer of the 6th Division reported at the end of August that ammunition was supplied to the division by truck and immediately distributed to subordinate units because there was no central division supply dump.[49] The prisoner also reported that only about 100 rounds had been delivered each night for the entire regiment, which tried to maintain a reserve of twenty to thirty rounds per piece for emergencies.

The last ten days of August saw a lull in NKPA operations against the Pusan Perimeter as the Communists attempted to build up units for a final offensive scheduled to begin on 1 September.[50] But the North Korean drive to conquer the Republic of Korea, originally planned to last ten days, had already lasted two months. The North Korean forces were exhausted, had lost large numbers of trained personnel and most of their tanks and heavy artillery, and faced severe shortages of ammunition, fuel, and rations. The loss of motorized transport was particularly acute and severely restricted both tactical mobility and the amount of supplies that could be moved forward from advanced railheads. As might be expected, the 1 September assault soon petered out.

INITIAL UNC INTERDICTION EFFORTS

By 15 September 1950, the NKPA logistical situation was already far more critical than UNC intelligence agencies could conceive.[51] The NKPA attack had passed its apogee and was vulnerable to the heavy blow which was soon to fall at Inchon. The North Korean logistical system, complete and modern on 25 June, had deteriorated under the pressure of increasingly effective UNC air and sea interdiction, which ensured that the NKPA could no longer replace its serious losses in men and matériel inflicted by UNC ground forces. The long, and indeed overextended, NKPA supply lines were particularly vulnerable to UNC air attack, and that, perhaps more than any other single factor, contributed to the ultimate collapse of the North Korean attack.

Sea Interdiction and Blockade

Prior to the start of hostilities, the North Koreans were able to import significant quantities of matériel from Manchuria and the Soviet Union by water to the ports of Chongjin, Hungnam, Wonsan, and Chinnampo. Once the war began, however, UN domination of the seas around the Korean peninsula all but eliminated seaborne supply of Communist forces in Korea. The small ROK naval forces were quickly augmented by UNC naval forces at the beginning of the war, and UNC patrols on both coasts of Korea soon denied the use of the seas for logistical purposes to the North Korean invaders. The blockade of North Korea was recommended by the U.S. Chief of Naval Operations on 30 June and was ordered into effect by President Truman the following day.[52] Separate East and West Coast Support Groups were established for the coastline north of the 37th Parallel, and the minuscule ROK Navy was assigned responsibility for the area south of that line. The northern limits of the blockade were set at 41° N on the east coast and 39° 30' N on the west coast to keep well clear of Manchurian and Soviet waters.[53] By the end of July, UNC naval units were attacking North Korean water transport wherever it was found and had already destroyed approximately one third of the vessels originally available to the North Koreans.[54]

The effectiveness of UNC air interdiction of rail and highway routes caused the North Koreans to seek to increase the amount of supplies moved by sea, and between 13 and 20 August the ROK Navy fought five coastal engagements between Kunsan and the southwestern tip of Korea. On 15 August a ROK patrol vessel, the *YMS 503*, met forty-five small craft between the tip of the peninsula and the off-shore islands, sinking fifteen and capturing the remaining thirty.[55] By the end of August, the naval blockading forces had effectively stopped all coastal water movement of enemy troops and supplies and had seriously damaged North Korean supply lines by naval gunfire, air attack, and raids.[56] The NKPA 12th Division driving toward Pohang on the east coast was particularly hard hit by UNC naval forces. The NKPA soon abandoned its efforts to move supplies down from the north by sea, and efforts to move men and supplies by small boat in the south and southwest were stymied by UNC naval action.[57] Indeed, the UNC naval blockade soon eliminated any significant seaborne logistical movement by the Communist forces for the rest of the war.

Air Interdiction

In the first months of the war, the majority of sorties flown by UNC air forces were to provide close-air support for the harried, outmanned, and outgunned UNC ground forces, but the attention of UNC airmen soon turned to interdiction, which in U.S. Air Force doctrine came to be given second place on the priority list right after the "be-all" of airpower doctrine, air superiority.[58] During the crucial period of the defense of the Pusan Perimeter, between 3 August and 23 September, 24 percent of all sorties flown by the U.S. Fifth Air Force were

for interdiction.[59] Eventually 47.7 percent of all sorties flown by the U.S. Far
East Air Forces (FEAF) during the Korean War were for interdiction.[60] From
their experience in World War II, U.S. airpower advocates had drawn the lesson
that strategic bombardment offered the most effective method for defeating an
enemy, but in Korea the sources of NKPA (and later CCF) industrial production
were for the most part safely north of the Yalu River and off limits to UNC
bombers. Thus, in Korea the UNC air forces turned to interdiction as the principal method of reducing the enemy's ability and will to continue the fight. As
defined in 1950 Air Force doctrine, air interdiction envisioned the employment
of airpower to prevent, delay, or destroy enemy soldiers, supplies, and equipment from reaching the battlefield.[61] World War II had taught that to achieve
maximum effectiveness, any air interdiction campaign had to be carefully and
thoroughly planned and patiently sustained and would also involve the cutting of
enemy supply routes far from the frontlines.[62] There were, in effect, two types
of interdiction campaigns in the Korean War: *General*, which included the
normal, day-to-day, daylight armed reconnaissance and night intrusion missions;
and *Special Purpose*, which involved specific operations of relatively short duration against more or less specific objectives.[63]

Initially, UNC air forces were hampered in their attempts to interdict NKPA
supply lines by poor maps, poor intelligence procedures, and a policy which
stressed disruption of enemy communications immediately behind the frontline.[64] The first UNC (U.S.) air missions in support of the ROKA were flown
on 27 June. The North Koreans were unprepared to deal with unopposed UNC
airpower, but they subsequently developed effective methods and training to
counter air attacks.[65] Although poorly planned and coordinated, the ad hoc UNC
air interdiction efforts in July 1950 produced significant results in the destruction of NKPA transport and other equipment and did much to delay the forward
movement of the NKPA against the weak and disorganized UNC ground forces.
Between 7 and 9 July, U.S. Fifth Air Force crews claimed 197 trucks and forty-
four tanks destroyed on the roads between Pyongtaek and Seoul. On 10 July, all
available aircraft were concentrated on a large enemy convoy stalled north of a
bombed-out bridge near Pyongtaek and destroyed 117 trucks, thirty-eight tanks,
seven half-tracks, and a large number of personnel.[66] UNC aircraft were also
credited with delaying the NKPA assault on Taejon, allowing the U.S. 24th Infantry Division to establish a hasty defense of that key town.

The sporadic air interdiction efforts throughout July delayed, but did not stop,
the forward movement of the invading NKPA, and the movement of supplies
north of Seoul remained practically unimpeded.[67] A formal, comprehensive air
interdiction program was required but did not begin until 2 August 1950, more
than a month after the war started. "Interdiction Campaign No. 1" assigned responsibility for air interdiction north of the 38th Parallel (but including the key
transportation center of Seoul) to the FEAF Bomber Command. In early
August, the medium bombers (B-29s) concentrated on the destruction of North
Korean transportation centers and equipment, including marshaling yards at

Seoul, Pyongyang, Wonsan, Hamhung, Chongung-ni, Chinnampo, Kilchu, Oro-ri, Chongjin, Sigjin-ni, Sinanju, and Sariwon, and by mid-August the North Korean transportation centers were a shambles.[68] Attention then shifted on 12 August to key bridges, and by the end of August suitable bridge targets for the medium bombers were also becoming scarce.[69] The final results of "Interdiction Campaign No. 1" were calculated on 4 September, and FEAF Bomber Command reported that it had destroyed all but seven of the forty-four bridges on the original target list.[70] In early September, the medium bombers initiated a special rail interdiction operation in which each day one medium bomber group made maximum-effort strikes against marshaling yards while the other two groups concentrated on effecting multiple cuts of rail lines in areas where repairs would be difficult.[71] Targets in the latter case included tracks, trestles, bridges, and tunnels in a triangular area from Seoul to Wonsan to Pyongyang. In an all-out effort on 13 September, FEAF bombers attacked marshaling yards and tracks on all lines south of Anju and Hungnam, cutting the lines in forty-six places.[72]

The FEAF B-29s also carried out a limited program of strategic bombing against North Korean industrial facilities. The U.S. Strategic Air Command prepared a plan for the destruction of major industrial targets in North Korea which envisioned both incendiary attacks and the use of high-explosive bombs in precision attacks.[73] The list of key industrial targets included the two munitions plants and railway facilities in Pyongyang, three chemical plants at Hungnam (Konan), the oil refinery and railway facilities at Wonsan, and the naval oil-storage tank farm at Najin (Rashin).[74] On 15 August, the Joint Chiefs of Staff added the railway and port facilities at Chongjin; the railway yards, the "Tong Iron Foundry," and the "Sam Yong Industrial Factory" at Chinnampo; the rail, dock, and storage facilities at Songjin; and railway facilities at Hamhung and Haeju.[75]

The major North Korean explosives and chemicals complex at Konan (near Hungnam) was obliterated in three B-29 strikes at the end of July and beginning of August, and by the end of August the medium bombers had severely damaged chemical plants, iron works, electric power plants, tank assembly plants, port facilities, and other industrial targets as well as transportation complexes in Pyongyang, Hamhung, Hungnam, Wonsan, Songjin, Chinnampo, Chongjin, and Rashin (Najin).[76] By 15 September, the Pyongyang arsenal was reported as 70 percent destroyed, the largest chemical complex in the Far East at Hungnam (Konan) had been reduced by 80 percent, the oil refinery at Wonsan was 95 percent destroyed, damage to the iron and steel plants at Chongjin, Songjin, and Kyomipo was reported at 30 to 90 percent; and aluminum and magnesium production at Chinnampo had suffered destruction in the range of 50 to 80 percent.[77] FEAF Bomber Command all but ran out of strategic industrial and transportation targets, and the strategic bombing campaign ended on 26 September with strikes against the Fusen hydroelectric generating plant.[78]

Meanwhile, the U.S. Fifth Air Force was responsible for air interdiction operations south of Seoul.[79] Until 15 September, the Fifth Air Force commander,

Major General Earle E. Partridge, was required to give first priority for the use of his light bombers and fighter-bombers to close-air support for the hard-pressed UNC ground forces but tried to commit about one third of his aircraft to the interdiction mission.[80] The Fifth Air Force interdiction effort focused on the destruction of major road and railroad bridges on routes to the front used by the North Koreans, particularly the railways south of Seoul. By the end of August the Fifth Air Force, aided by naval carrier aircraft, had made forty-seven rail cuts, destroyed some ninety-three highway bridges, and put another 140 bridges out of service.[81] Systematic armed reconnaissance coverage of North Korean highway routes to the front also began in early August and significantly reduced both the combat power and logistical mobility of the North Korean forces.[82] Night intruder missions flown by specially equipped B-26 light bombers further complicated the North Korean efforts to maintain their overextended supply lines and slowed, but could not stop, the movement of reinforcements and supplies to the front along the Pusan Perimeter.[83]

Once placed on a comprehensive coordinated basis in early August, UNC air and naval interdiction, coupled with heavy fighting along the Pusan Perimeter, quickly disrupted the NKPA logistical system, forced less efficient and more difficult nighttime travel, and destroyed irreplaceable combat vehicles, locomotives, railroad cars, trucks, and other transport equipment as well as bridges, track, repair facilities, and other facilities needed to maintain the lines of communications in full operation. Between June and September 1950, the North Korean rail system handled about 200,000 tons per month, principally between Pyongyang and Seoul, but after July 1950 UNC air interdiction began to take its toll and the system became unreliable.[84] The resulting shortage of critical supply items also began to affect North Korean tactical operations, causing attacks to be of limited duration and conducted at night without sufficient artillery and armored support. North Korean morale also declined with the loss of men, equipment, and tactical flexibility.[85] Thus the beleaguered UNC ground forces were able to hold onto their tenuous bridgehead along the Naktong and to prepare an offensive blow which would entirely reverse the strategic and tactical situation.

RETREAT OF THE NKPA, SEPTEMBER–NOVEMBER 1950

Already critically weakened, the NKPA logistical system collapsed and with it the entire North Korean armed forces, following the amphibious invasion at Inchon by the U.S. X Corps and the coordinated breakout of the UNC forces from the Pusan Perimeter, which began on 15 September 1950. The key transportation hub and South Korean capital of Seoul was retaken by UNC forces on 29 September, severing the North Korean lines of communications at their midpoint. The battered North Korean forces retreated northward helter-skelter or reformed as guerrilla units in territory controlled by the UNC. No longer compelled to concentrate their efforts on close-air support for hard-pressed UNC ground forces, the UNC air forces shifted their attention to increasing interdiction and completing the destruction of the retreating NKPA from the air. Anticipating their future use by advancing UNC forces, in early October the UNC Commander-in-Chief, General Douglas MacArthur, prohibited the destruction of railways south of the 38th Parallel (unless being actively used by the enemy) and of enemy airfields south of the 40th Parallel.[86] UNC air forces subsequently concentrated on the bombing of bridges, marshaling yards, highways, and rail lines north of Seoul, and the resulting disruption of the NKPA supply lines north of Seoul served to retard further the North Korean withdrawal and prevent the removal of their heavy equipment.[87] General MacArthur was thus able to report that "the seizure of the heart of the enemy's distributing system in the Seoul area has completely dislocated his logistical supply to his forces in South Korea and has quickly resulted in their disintegration."[88]

On 9 October, UNC forces moved north of the 38th Parallel in pursuit of the routed North Korean forces, facing only scattered resistance and capturing large numbers of prisoners and great quantities of equipment and supplies. UNC air forces continued to pound North Korean logistical routes and command, communication, and supply installations in the steadily decreasing area of North Korea remaining under NKPA control, and UNC naval forces continued to prevent enemy reinforcement or resupply by sea.[89] On 20 October, elements of the U.S. X Corps began landing in the Wonsan area on Korea's east coast, and on 29 October the U.S. 7th Infantry Division and ROK Army units landed at Iwon, 178 miles north of Wonsan.[90] Naval aircraft from the UNC carriers offshore provided cover for the landings and concentrated their attacks on moving transport and the roads and rail lines on the east coast north of Wonsan.[91] Meanwhile, on the western side of the peninsula the U.S. Eighth Army prepared to continue the attack to the Yalu River to eliminate the remnants of the NKPA and gain control over all of North Korea. The back of the NKPA appeared to have been broken, and on 21 October 1950 General MacArthur reported that the tide of battle had completely changed.[92]

However, toward the end of October North Korean resistance stiffened in what appeared to be a final desperate attempt to halt the UNC forces. At the same time, it became obvious that the UNC efforts to prevent reinforcement and resupply of the remaining North Korean forces from Manchuria were hampered by restrictions on air operations close to the North Korean–Manchurian border or against Communist base areas and supply centers in Manchuria.[93] The immunity of Communist installations in Manchuria ultimately proved to be only a minor constraint on the efforts of the already fully committed UNC air forces to interdict Communist lines of communications and prevent the movement of men and supplies to the battle area in Korea and thus did not materially affect the outcome of the war.

On 27 December 1950, General MacArthur reported that by late November 1950 the personnel of the NKPA had been eliminated, their equipment captured or destroyed, and all but the far northern borders of Korea held by UNC forces. "For all practical purposes," he stated, "the conflict with the armed forces of the former North Korean regime had been terminated."[94] However, on 1 November 1950, elements of the Chinese Communist 124th Division were identified on the front and UNC aircraft were attacked for the first time by Soviet-made MIG-15 jet aircraft in the Sinuiju area.[95] Moreover, although apparently disintegrating and in head-long retreat, the NKPA was still able to undertake an amazing reorganization during October and November 1950, which eventually resulted in the formation of twenty-nine divisions under eight corps headquarters.[96] Nine of those divisions were in Manchuria and had never been committed, approximately ten were scattered in rear areas nominally under UNC control, and the remaining ten were holding in northern Korea. The units in Korea itself were reduced to about 60,000 effectives, but the units in Manchuria were up to strength and probably numbered another 60,000.[97] The Korean War was not over; it was only just beginning, and a new opponent, far more formidable than the NKPA had ever been, was about to appear.

THE INTERVENTION OF COMMUNIST CHINA

Neither the Soviet Union nor the People's Republic of China were willing to permit the total destruction of their North Korean ally or the occupation of the Manchurian border by UNC forces. Although willing to supply arms and equipment and to provide other support, the Soviet Union was not prepared for a direct confrontation with the United States. The People's Republic of China, however, entered the war under the thinly veiled subterfuge of a "volunteer" army which was to aid the North Koreans in defeating and eliminating the UNC forces from Korea.

Preparations of the CCF

The Chinese Communist decision to intervene militarily in the Korean conflict was apparently taken at a conference in Peking on 6 August 1950 attended by representatives of the Soviet Union, North Korea, and the PRC.[98] The Chinese representatives are believed to have indicated their willingness to intervene to save the North Koreans if the Russians would undertake to supply modern weapons, vehicles, and aircraft. In any event, Chinese intentions were clearly signaled in September 1950 with the creation of a "Chinese Peoples' Volunteer Army" and the massive movement of Chinese ground forces into Manchuria from central, east, and south China.[99] Preparations for intervention had not been made earlier because the Chinese believed the North Koreans could win their war alone. More importantly, considerations of logistics may have caused the Chinese to wait until the fighting reached the Korean-Manchurian frontier in order to shorten their lines of communications and allow additional time for preparation.[100] In any event, the rapid advance of UNC forces and the deteriorating condition of the NKPA after 15 September precipitated the Chinese intervention even before the Soviets could supply significant quantities of arms and other supplies; such matériel would make itself felt only later in the war.[101]

The logistical difficulties of intervening in Korea were well recognized by Chinese military leaders, who anticipated that both the rugged Korean terrain and UNC airpower would pose significant problems. At the August meeting, General Ye Jian-ying is reported to have estimated that four months would be required to move a significant Chinese Communist force into Korea.[102] The man destined to command the CCF in Korea, General Peng Teh-huai, also noted the fact that the farther the Chinese advanced against UNC forces in Korea, the farther they would be from their sources of supply.[103]

On 10 September, General Peng conducted a one-day staff conference to discuss plans for the forthcoming intervention. He is reported to have remarked that the war in Korea would not be won by manpower alone but that it would be "a battle of supply."[104] Staff officers also noted the difficulties of moving forward large numbers of artillery weapons over the limited roads, the need for better communications equipment, and a requirement for three additional engineer regiments just to repair roads and railway lines. The chief supply officer spoke of the need for more than three regiments of porters to carry food and ammunition and for four times as many trucks as were then assigned to each Chinese division.[105] The Chinese officers no doubt also discussed the vulnerability of their prospective supply lines, which were already identified by the UNC and which would funnel Chinese men and supplies over six bridges crossing the Yalu, the most important of which was the twin 3,098-foot-long highway and railroad spans linking Antung and Sinuiju.[106] In view of the limited experience of his staff officers in handling large-scale long-distance movements, the known deficiencies of his forces, and the lack of adequate transport facilities General Peng proposed that, if the UNC forces moved into North Korea, the CCF should conduct a limited attack to halt the UNC forces north of Pyongyang at the narrow neck of the Korean peninsula.[107]

Before the start of the Korean War, Chinese Communist military forces, including the major portion of General Lin Piao's Fourth Field Army, had been concentrated in south and central China in anticipation of an invasion of Taiwan. However, in the spring of 1950 the Chinese began to redeploy major forces from south and central China to Shantung and Manchuria.[108] The crack 38th, 40th, and 42nd Armies of the Fourth Field Army returned to Manchuria between mid-June and July, and the Third and First Field Armies relocated to training areas south and east of Shenyang in early July.[109] The 50th and 66th Armies, along the Yangtze River in central China, were moved by rail to camps near Shenyang.[110] The seasoned 27th and 39th Armies returned to their home province of Shandong in eastern China, where they waited to entrain for Manchuria on 48 hours' notice, and the 20th and 26th Armies, preparing for the invasion of Taiwan, were also alerted for movement.[111]   The simultaneous movement of so many large units brought the Manchurian rail system close to collapse.[112]

Movement of CCF into Korea

The movement of Chinese "volunteers" into Korea began on 14 October 1950, and by late November some 300,000 Chinese soldiers had infiltrated into North Korea undetected by UNC intelligence agencies or air observers.[113]   The lead elements of the 38th CCF Army began crossing the Yalu River at Antung (Sinuiju) on 14 October, and 160 kilometers farther east the 42nd CCF Army crossed at Manpojin and advanced beyond Kanggye to Mupyong-ni to serve as a flank guard against a potential UNC advance up the east coast.[114]   Between 14 and 20 October, the 39th and 40th CCF Armies crossed at Antung and established blocking positions north of the Chungchon River, some 100 kilometers south of the Yalu, where they were joined by the 50th and 66th CCF Armies which crossed at Sakchu, 20 kilometers upstream from Sinuiju, later in October.[115]   Farther east the 20th, 26th, and 27th CCF Armies, each augmented by a division from the 30th CCF Army, entered Korea via Manpojin and Singalpajin during the first week in November.[116]

The traffic from Antung through Sinuiju into North Korea was so heavy in early November that UNC pilots reported "tremendous" and even "gigantic" convoys moving south.[117]   Accordingly, UNC air forces undertook the delicate task of dropping the Yalu bridges on the Korean side and had knocked out about half of them and damaged the remainder before the third week in November, when the Yalu froze sufficiently to support vehicular traffic.[118]   The effort against the Yalu bridges achieved less than the expected results, but heavy incendiary attacks against North Korean supply centers by the B-29 medium bombers produced better results, and by the end of November most of the key North Korean communications and supply centers were in ruins.[119]

The CCF units moving down into North Korea from Manchuria remained relatively safe from UNC air attacks during the actual period of their crossing and movement to the assembly areas in Korea and as long as they remained relatively close to the frontier. In most cases, this movement could be effected in one long night march.[120]   The logistical problems of the CCF increased, however, as they moved southward. As General MacArthur himself stated the problem,

> By breaking contact with the enemy and rapidly withdrawing to the south when our advance of 24 November exposed the secret build up of Communist Chinese forces in the forward battle area south of the Yalu River, the enemy, following in pursuit, was forced to extend his lines of supply over 300 miles. Each mile of this forward extension rendered him increasingly vulnerable to air attack, expanded correspondingly our power by maneuver to overcome the handicap of numerically superior ground forces and terrain

favorable to the enemy tactic of infiltration, and reduced proportionately our own logistical difficulties.[121]

By mid-November, the CCF IXth Army Group, 120,000 strong and commanded by Lieutenant General Song Shi-lun, consisted of three CCF armies (the 20th, 26th, and 27th), each augmented by one division from the 30th CCF Army, and was assigned the mission of destroying the UNC forces (principally the U.S. X Corps) in northeastern Korea.[122] On the western plain facing the U.S. Eighth Army (including ROKA and other UNC forces as well as U.S. troops) was the XIIIth Army Group under the command of General Li Tian-yu. Composed of some 180,000 men in six CCF Armies (the 38th, 39th, 40th, 42nd, 50th, and 66th) reinforced by the elements of three artillery divisions, a motor transport regiment, and a cavalry regiment, the XIIIth Army Group was prepared to attack the advancing UNC forces and pursue them down the peninsula in the direction of Seoul.[123]

The massive deployments of CCF troops into Korea testified to both the competence of Chinese staff planners and the discipline and endurance of the individual Chinese soldier.[124] The CCF soldiers, accompanied by porters carrying the heavier equipment, held to the strenuous march schedules despite growing shortages of food, moving at night with excellent march discipline and resting by day in well-camouflaged assembly areas.[125] The CCF divisions in the initial deployment had little or no logistical "tail" and had to make do with what could be carried along by the troops and attached porters, obtained locally, or captured from UNC forces. Most of the Chinese "volunteers" crossed the Yalu carrying eighty rounds of rifle ammunition, four or five grenades, and perhaps a few extra clips for the automatic rifles and submachineguns, some belted ammunition for the machineguns, one or two mortar rounds, or some TNT for satchel charges.[126] Each soldier also carried an emergency food supply consisting of rice, tea, and salt sufficient for five days.[127] The operative logistical concept, a legacy of centuries of Chinese warfare, was that when the food carried by the soldiers gave out, it would be replaced by the time-honored practice of foraging on the countryside, and when a unit used up its ammunition, it could either gather up and use that of the enemy or it could retire from the frontline to resupply and be replaced in the line by a fresh unit.[128]

While the individual Chinese "volunteer" was hardy and capable of surprising endurance on long and difficult marches, the Chinese armies deployed in Korea in 1950 had several important defects. They lacked aircraft, modern communications equipment, and motor transport; they were armed with a hodgepodge of old American, Japanese, and Soviet weapons; and they lacked artillery support, essential in facing the modern UNC forces.[129] Perhaps their most critical defect was that their logistical systems were inadequate to support large numbers of troops engaged in heavy, continuous combat deep in Korea against a technologically superior UNC force, which enjoyed almost total command of the air.[130]

In the first few months, the Chinese sought to solve their logistical problems with a few trucks, an army of Manchurian and impressed Korean porters, and foraging and self-transport by the Chinese combat units.[131] Indeed, the lack of motorized transport was something of an advantage in that it permitted off-road movement over difficult terrain and thus increased the ability of the CCF to avoid detection and attack by UNC air forces.[132] In the long term, however, the CCF and their North Korean allies would be forced to reorganize and modernize their logistical support systems.[133]

CCF OFFENSIVES, OCTOBER 1950–JUNE 1951

On 26 November 1950, the CCF launched their first major offensive against UNC forces with fourteen divisions on a wide front.[134] Achieving tactical surprise and greatly outnumbering their UNC opponents, the Communist forces employed highly effective infiltration and flanking tactics and precipitated a rapid, deep withdrawal south to the 38th Parallel of the U.S. Eighth Army, ROKA, and other UNC forces in western Korea and the retreat of the U.S. X Corps from the Changjin (Chosin) Reservoir and other advanced points in northeastern Korea to the port of Hungnam, from which all UNC forces in northeastern Korea were evacuated by sea on 24 December. Despite their initial success, the CCF were badly shaken themselves and forced to regroup and re-supply before continuing the attack.[135]

The initial onslaught of the CCF failed to destroy the forward UNC forces, which were badly mauled but managed to withdraw in good order. It also exposed the deficiencies in the CCF logistical system and the serious threat to CCF logistics posed by UNC dominance of the air. The farther south the Chinese advanced, the more desperate their supply situation became and the more they were exposed to UNC air interdiction efforts. In their eagerness to catch and destroy the retreating UNC forces, the advancing CCF troops abandoned their usual methods of moving only at night under strict march and camouflage discipline. They failed to appreciate fully the threat from the air, and UNC air forces inflicted terrible damage on them until mid-December, when they again began to move only at night and under the strictest march and camouflage discipline.[136] Nevertheless, the CCF were able, thanks to heroic maintenance and repair efforts, to keep a minimum number of trucks and trains moving forward with critical supplies, but for the most part the Chinese divisions moved forward on foot, depending on large numbers of porters.[137] Only a trickle of critical supplies got through however, and the CCF troops staved off absolute starvation with meager rations foraged from the desolate North Korean countryside or captured from retreating UNC troops. The hodgepodge of Communist weaponry was also kept in minimal operation by using captured U.S. ammunition. Many UNC soldiers noted that in every attack the Chinese soldiers were quick to stop and loot whatever food, ammunition, or other items had been abandoned.[138]

By December 1950, the Chinese "volunteers" were suffering terribly from hunger and from the lack of adequate winter clothing. The troops of the CCF IXth Army Group in the isolated mountains on the eastern side of the peninsula found themselves in particularly bad condition logistically. The Chinese divisions attacking the U.S. 1st Marine Division and U.S. 7th Infantry Division near the Changjin (Chosin) Reservoir in late November and early December 1950 lacked transport, food, ammunition, medical support, and adequate winter clothing. A document captured from the 26th CCF Army noted that,

> A shortage of transportation and escort personnel makes it impossible to accomplish the mission of supplying the troops. As a result, our soldiers frequently starve. From now on, the organization of our rear service units should be improved. . . . The troops were hungry. They ate cold food, and some had only a few potatoes in two days. They were unable to maintain the physical strength for combat; the wounded personnel could not be evacuated. . . . The fire power of our entire army was basically inadequate. When we used our guns there were no shells and sometimes the shells were duds.[139]

The haste with which the CCF IXth Army Group had moved into position, its dispersion, and active UNC air support of the Marines and Army troops withdrawing from the Changjin Reservoir contributed to the adverse CCF supply situation. Artillery was scarce and there were few shells available, and in any event many of those were duds.[140] In the absence of a functioning resupply system, the CCF divisions, having expended the supplies of small arms ammunition which they carried forward with them, were withdrawn as a body and replaced by new formations.[141] However, the most serious problem was the lack of adequate food and winter clothing. One Chinese medic captured during the campaign reported that 70 percent of all the Chinese combat troops suffered from frostbite and 5 percent of the cases required amputation.[142] Over 90 percent of the personnel of the 26th CCF Army were reported to have been frostbite casualties, and the 27th CCF Army had 10,000 noncombat casualties in its four divisions.[143] It was not unusual for the Marines to find Chinese soldiers frozen to death in their foxholes.[144]

Although sufficiently prepared for a "hit-and-run" attack, the massive CCF forces proved to be inadequately supplied for conducting a sustained offensive against well-supplied UNC troops in the below-zero temperatures of the Korean winter and were thus unable to trap and annihilate the UNC forces in November and December 1950.[145] By the time the CCF troops reached Pyongyang, they were half-starved and incapable of further operations without major resupply.[146] The new U.S. Eighth Army commander, General Matthew B. Ridgway, estimated that the CCF was too lightly equipped, too poorly supplied, and too far from its sources of supply to aim for anything but a quick victory.[147]

Contemporary Chinese military doctrine based on the thoughts of Mao Tse-tung envisioned highly mobile operations by large guerrilla armies spread widely among a friendly and supportive civilian population.[148] Such conditions did not pertain in the narrow Korean peninsula, where the native population, especially near and below the 38th Parallel, was indifferent or actively hostile. Nor did Mao's military precepts fully account for the firepower and airpower of modern Western armies. Nevertheless, General Zhou Chun-quan, the director of the CCF Rear Services Department, promised the mobilization of 180,000 men, women, and children for moving supplies by the end of the year as well as railway troops from China to keep the rail lines from Manchuria in operation.[149] Such actions, he said, should provide the CCF XIII Army Group with at least a thousand tons of supplies per day, well beyond the 50 tons per day estimated to be required by each CCF army.[150]

Despite the logistical problems associated with further movement to the south, the plans for a continuance of the Communist offensive were issued on 19 December, and on 1 January 1951 the CCF renewed its attacks on UNC forces with the main effort by elements of the CCF XIII Army Group toward Seoul supported by secondary efforts in the center of the peninsula toward Chunchon and by the reconstituted NKPA II Corps on the east coast.[151] By 4 January 1951, Seoul was retaken and UNC forces had been driven south of the Han River. However, the massive Communist offensive ground to a halt by the middle of January due to logistical problems made worse by intensive UNC air attacks on NKPA-CCF supply lines.[152] General MacArthur estimated that at that time the Chinese could supply as many as one and one-half million men at the Yalu from bases in Manchuria but that the CCF would loose 50 percent of their frontline strength by the time they crossed the 38th Parallel and another 10 percent as they moved 50 miles farther south.[153]

For most of December 1950, the UNC air forces had been the only significant force capable of delaying the Communists and destroying their men, equipment, and supplies and they had performed their task with great effect, flying some 7,654 armed reconnaissance and interdiction sorties in addition to providing close-air support for the retreating UNC ground forces.[154] On 15 December 1950 FEAF initiated "Interdiction Campaign No. 4," which divided Korea north of the 37th Parallel into eleven zones and designated 172 principal targets, including forty-five railway bridges, twelve highway bridges, thirteen tunnels, thirty-nine railroad marshaling yards, and sixty-three supply centers, for air attack.[155] The medium bombers were also scheduled to participate in "Interdiction Campaign No. 4," but on 23 December General MacArthur directed that two thirds of the B-29s be used in direct attacks against towns and villages sheltering NKPA-CCF troops.[156]

"Interdiction Campaign No. 4" hardly got off the ground before a renewal of the CCF offensive on 1 January 1951 spurred the UNC air forces to even greater efforts. The evacuation of the U.S. X Corps from Hungnam at the end of December 1950 provided an unexpected bonus by releasing dedicated ground support aircraft for use in the interdiction effort, and between 19 and 31 January 1951 UNC air forces conducted the most massive and sustained air operations of the war against NKPA-CCF lines of communications with attacks against more than eighty key rail and highway bridges and other transportation facilities.[157]

The inability of the CCF to sustain their offensive to the south logistically in the face of such massive air attacks enabled the battered UNC forces, commanded and revitalized since 27 December by the new Eighth Army commander, Lieutenant General Matthew B. Ridgway, to stabilize their lines in mid-January and to initiate aggressive patrolling and offensive actions, which brought them back to the south bank of the Han River by the middle of February and which eliminated the CCF bridgehead south of the Han by the end of February. On 16 February General Peng Teh-huai issued orders for his troops to defend their line along the 38th Parallel pending receipt of additional Soviet support and expected resumption of offensive action in May.[158] Seoul was retaken by UNC forces on 14 March, and, having suffered very heavy casualties in the March fighting, all CCF and NKPA forces east of the Imjin River were driven out of South Korea by 8 April, at which point the Communists regrouped and forcefully opposed further UNC advances.

With typical dissimulation, on 20 February 1951 General MacArthur took credit for the collapse of the Communist January offensive, stating that

> our field strategy, initiated upon Communist China's entry into the war, involving a rapid withdrawal to lengthen the enemy's supply lines with resultant pyramiding of his logistical difficulties and an almost astronomical increase in destructiveness of our air power, has worked well. The enemy is finding it an entirely different problem fighting 350 miles from his base than when he had this "sanctuary" in his immediate rear and our air and naval forces practically zeroed out.[159]

During late March and early April, while stiffening their resistance to further UNC advances, the CCF and NKPA prepared for yet another offensive by moving large numbers of reinforcements to the front and stockpiling supplies in forward areas. UNC aircraft reported increasing numbers of vehicle sightings, and it was not uncommon to observe 2,000 enemy vehicles during a 24-hour period. Following an intensive artillery preparation, the Communists launched yet another general offensive on the night of 22–23 April with heavy attacks across the entire western half of the line from Munsan to the Hwachon Reservoir involving the largest force ever to participate in a single Communist offensive during the entire war, some 337,000 troops.[160] By 29 April, skillful handling of the UNC defense and the usual logistical difficulties caused by deep UNC withdrawals caused the Communist drive to pause once again for reorganization and resupply.

The April NKPA-CCF offensive was aided significantly by improvements in the Communist logistical system. Between February and April, the CCF managed to reorganize their logistical support and assemble some 500,000 civilian and military personnel to support the seventy divisions in Korea.[161] The resulting system was effective, but not efficient, and continued to limit both the number of frontline divisions which could be actively employed and the duration of Communist offensives.[162] By minimizing supply expenditures during defensive periods, the CCF was able to stockpile sufficient supplies to permit offensives to take place. These stockpiles were, of course, vulnerable to UNC air attack and the Communists struggled strenuously to protect them. In forward areas, supplies were dispersed in small quantities in every conceivable hiding place. Caves, tunnels, ditches, ravines, houses, and simple holes in the ground were utilized and proved very difficult for UNC air forces to identify and destroy from the air. Rear area supply installations were naturally larger and more difficult to protect from air attack, and in mid-March 1951 FEAF medium bombers obtained good results in attacks on NKPA-CCF depots and storage areas at Hamhung, Yonghung, Chunchon, Pyongyang, Kumwha, Chorwon, and Wonsan.[163] Such attacks forced the CCF and NKPA to resort to further dispersal with attendant decreases in supply responsiveness. They also prompted further improvements in Communist air defense systems and an increase in the number of anti-aircraft guns deployed around logistical installations. At the same time, however, the number of Communist motor vehicles was also increasing and the UNC air forces continued to sight and destroy or damage large numbers of them.[164]

The NKPA-CCF offensive was resumed with twenty-one divisions on 16 May and focused on the eastern front. The Communist attack gained 10 to 15 miles along the front but had ground to a halt by 21 May. The UNC forces immediately seized the initiative, and on 23 May the U.S. I, IX, and X Corps began a coordinated counteroffensive designed to cut the enemy's main supply routes and destroy him.[165] The Communist withdrawal assumed the proportions of a rout before UNC pursuit ended on 2 June, having forced the NKPA-CCF to give up the southern reaches of the Pyonggang-Chorwon-Kumwha triangle and pushing them back 30 to 50 miles while inflicting some 105,000 Communist casualties.[166] The 60th CCF Army, for example, lost an estimated 75 percent of its personnel, and most NKPA divisions were reduced to an average strength of only 6,000 men.[167]

Although subject to the vagaries of the weather, enemy deception, and observer error, UNC aerial observation reports provided some indication of the magnitude of the NKPA-CCF logistical effort during the Communist offensives in the first half of 1951. Between 1 March and 31 August 1951, UNC aerial observers reported a total of 249,827 motor vehicle sightings on the roads in North Korea.[168] The distribution of total enemy vehicular traffic during the months of March through August 1951 is shown on Table 7.1.

Table 7.1
UNC Vehicle Sightings, March–August 1951[169]

Month	Vehicles Headed North	Vehicles Headed South	Vehicles Headed East	Vehicles Headed West	Direction Unknown	Total
March	1,998	10,430			6,229	18,657
April	9,261	22,927			8,225	30,413
May	10,093	33,119			10,083	53,295
June	11,946	32,209	3,489	1,540	3,788	52,972
July	9,907	24,504	4,337	3,424	2,079	44,251
August	9,642	34,499	4,121	1,791	1,186	50,239
Total	52,847	157,688	12,947	6,755	32,590	249,827

Aerial sightings of NKPA-CCF trucks proved useful for predicting forthcoming enemy offensives due to the enemy practice of stockpiling supplies in advance of any offensive action. Analysis of Communist highway movements by UNC intelligence agencies in early 1951 also revealed that the enemy consistently telegraphed its readiness to resume the offensive by sharply decreasing the number of vehicles used to transport supplies to forward areas during the last two to four days before the attack was to begin.[170] For example, a decided drop in truck sightings was noticed on 20 April and continued until 22 April, when the NKPA-CCF offensive was launched.[171] POW interrogations, agent reports, and captured enemy documents relating to the issue of rations and ammunition by NKPA-CCF were also used as indicators of forthcoming attacks and their expected duration.[172] The issue of combat rations and additional ammunition usually signaled a forthcoming offensive action, and the amounts issued could be used to calculate the approximate expected duration of the offensive, especially when POWs reported being issued rations and ordered not to consume them until a certain date (i.e., the beginning date of the offensive). For example, prior to the 22 April 1951 CCF offensive, POWs stated that they had been issued rations for six days; the offensive lasted six days.[173]

THE UNC AIR INTERDICTION PROGRAM, JANUARY–JULY 1951

Much of the credit for halting the southward movement of the NKPA-CCF in the first half of 1951 must go to the UNC air interdiction campaign, which demonstrably slowed the pace of the Communist advance and prevented the exploitation of breakthroughs by limiting the supplies reaching the forward CCF and NKPA units. In the first months of 1951, "Interdiction Campaign No. 4," begun on 15 December 1950, continued to devastate North Korean railway and highway facilities, NKPA-CCF supply installations, and thousands of locomotives, railway cars, trucks, and carts as well as "horses, camels, mules, donkeys, burros, and Mongol ponies."[174]

UNC air forces routinely emphasized daylight armed reconnaissance during periods of slack ground attacks when the Communist forces were reorganizing and resupplying.[175] Following the end of the NKPA-CCF offensive in January 1951, the fighter-bombers shifted from close-air support to armed reconnaissance but found that the enemy was beginning to hide its men and equipment effectively during daylight hours, making the job of finding and hitting them very difficult. Thus in mid-February 1951, the Fifth Air Force established three armed reconnaissance areas in the band of territory 50 miles north of the frontlines.[176] A specific air unit was assigned to each area, allowing pilots to become intimately familiar with the area for which they were responsible. Intelligence methods were also improved, and new "truck-busting" tactics achieved good success.

Having forced the Communist forces to move mainly at night, the UNC air forces increased their attention on night intruder missions, but suitable specially equipped aircraft were scarce, and such missions faced major problems, including the lack of adequate illumination or other target detection devices and the inability to assess target damage accurately.[177] The sophisticated sensors and night-vision devices available today were, of course, not available during the Korean War. Expedients such as flares and even searchlights mounted on the aircraft proved unworkable or merely inadequate. Even so, the UNC night intruder missions produced results; in July 1951 alone, the 3rd and 452nd Bombardment Wings claimed 1,011 vehicles destroyed and another 1,573 damaged.[178]

FEAF's medium bombers also participated in the interdiction campaign and were assigned some sixty bridges, thirty-nine marshaling yards, and thirty-five supply centers as targets.[179] In view of the heavy enemy traffic in north central and northeastern Korea, on 6 February 1951 the FEAF commander, Lieutenant General George E. Stratemeyer, ordered the medium bombers to concentrate on bridges, choke points, and tunnels in those areas while the Fifth Air Force fighter-bombers attacked rolling stock.[180] The B-29 attacks on the key bridges in North Korea demonstrated both the difficulty of hitting such point targets and the enemy's growing ability to bypass and repair damaged bridges.[181] Pending more effective fighter cover to protect the bombers against the increasing number of Communist MIG fighters, the B-29 attacks on bridges and other facilities in the northwestern corner of Korea were suspended on 12 April 1951, having put out of action forty-eight of the sixty bridges and twenty-nine of the thirty-nine marshaling yards assigned to it under "Interdiction Campaign No. 4."[182] The medium bombers continued to participate in the campaign at a high sortie rate until early May, when General Stratemeyer, acting on complaints by the Air Force Chief of Staff General Hoyt Vandenberg about the small return being obtained by expensive and difficult methods (i.e., the use of vulnerable medium bombers) and intelligence reports that the NKPA-CCF had shifted their attention from bringing supplies southward to protecting their stockpiles in forward areas, redirected the medium bombers to destroy marshaling yards and supply and communications centers while the Fifth Air Force continued the interdiction of enemy railroads and highways.[183]

The naval carrier aircraft of Task Force 77 were also actively involved in the UNC air interdiction effort and were assigned responsibility for the three zones of "Interdiction Campaign No. 4" in northeastern Korea. Although concentrating in early 1951 on close-air support and the control of the sea approaches to Korea, the Task Force 77 carrier planes were shifted to the interdiction effort on 16 February and Admiral Turner Joy subsequently reported that his efforts "got the interdiction line effective on about 8 March 1951."[184] Navy planners reduced the 395 major bridges in eastern North Korea to a list of forty-eight "key" targets, and in March and April Navy carrier planes, facing ever-increasing Communist flak, attacked the North Korean choke points with a high degree of success.[185] The railway system along the east coast of Korea, which had carried two thirds of North Korean rail traffic in February, moved less than half the total in March and less than a third in April, while road traffic in eastern North Korea was also significantly reduced.[186] By 8 April, after thirty-eight days of intensive interdiction efforts by Task Force 77 aircraft, fifty-four rail and thirty-seven highway bridges had been put out of operation, forty-four others damaged, and the railroads cut in more than 200 places.[187] The air interdiction operations of Task Force 77 were supplemented by naval gunfire bombardment and even by special operations, such as the daring but unproductive raid by Navy frogmen and British Royal Marine commandos against North Korean rail facilities near Sorye-dong on 7 April 1951.[188]

Operation STRANGLE I (May–September 1951)

By May 1951, it was becoming increasingly difficult to locate and strike enemy interdiction targets in daylight. The CCF and NKPA were beginning to implement even more effective camouflage discipline and habitually moved their men and vehicles into cover and concealment during the daytime and moved only at night. On 31 May 1951, concurrent with the UNC counteroffensive, the UNC air forces initiated Operation STRANGLE, perhaps the best known of the special-purpose air interdiction campaigns.[189] The objective of Operation STRANGLE was to stop all NKPA-CCF highway traffic from railheads near the 39th Parallel to the frontlines. A one-degree-of-latitude strip (38° 15' N to 39° 15' N) was selected, and various component elements of the UNC air forces (i.e., Fifth Air Force and Task Force 77) were assigned to destroy all trucks and bridges found on the seven major highway routes which crossed the strip. The three routes south and southeast of Pyongyang were taken by the Fifth Air Force, the two central routes south from Yangdok and Majon-ni by Navy flyers from Task Force 77, and the two east coast routes south from Wonsan and Kojo by the 1st Marine Air Wing.[190] Even while Operation STRANGLE was in progress, FEAF bombers and fighters and Task Force 77 carrier aircraft continued to attack key rail bridges and other transportation targets in North Korea. STRANGLE slowed and diverted, but did not stop, Communist highway movements, and STRANGLE began to decrease in effectiveness in mid-June (after only thirteen days) when UNC ground pressure on the NKPA-CCF eased.[191] Although Operation STRANGLE was generally assessed a failure, principally due to the halt in the Eighth Army's advance and the enemy's ability to repair road cuts quickly, it continued into September 1951.[192]

Even though Operation STRANGLE did not produce the desired results, overall FEAF statistics for the first year of the war were impressive. Between 25 June 1950 and 10 July 1951, FEAF pilots alone flew some 72,740 interdiction sorties and claimed some 130,495 enemy troops killed, 966 rail cuts completed, and 1,463 tanks, 993 locomotives, 15,607 railroad cars, 25,952 vehicles, and 1,129 railroad bridges destroyed or damaged.[193] FEAF bombers also neutralized the eighteen major strategic targets in North Korea, the enemy was compelled to move only at night, and the flow of enemy men and supplies to the frontlines was significantly restricted.

CONCLUSION

The failure of the NKPA-CCF May 1951 offensive and the stabilization of the front near the 38th Parallel in early June 1951 ended Communist hopes of unifying Korea on their terms. With their combat power seriously reduced and with little prospect of being able to mount a decisive offensive in the near future, the Communist leaders found it expedient to open negotiations which might produce at the conference table what had eluded them on the battlefield. The truce talks began formally at Panmunjom on 18 July 1951, thus bringing to a close the first period of the war from a NKPA-CCF logistical point of view.

Between June 1950 and July 1951, some serious defects in the Communist logistical systems in Korea and their vulnerability to UNC air interdiction were revealed. Overextension in the face of UNC air superiority coupled with hard fighting on the Pusan Perimeter and the severance of NKPA supply lines by the Inchon landings in September 1950 led to the near total destruction of the NKPA and its withdrawal to the far north of Korea. The CCF, which came to the aid of their North Korean allies in October 1950, initially enjoyed a high level of success, but it quickly became apparent that, despite limited requirements, the CCF logistical systems could not efficiently support a very large number of troops at a distance from their protected bases in Manchuria and North China. The hodgepodge of weapons and equipment, the lack of modern communications equipment and artillery, and the restriction on ammunition supplies caused by the primitive logistical system limited the tactical flexibility and ability of the NKPA-CCF to sustain their attacks against the UNC ground forces. The rugged Korean terrain and reliance on large numbers of porters due to the significant lack of motor transport, although initially considered advantages, proved greater handicaps as the distance from Manchuria lengthened. Moreover, the farther south the CCF advanced, the more they exposed their supply lines to UNC air interdiction and the less they were able to support their forward forces adequately. Nevertheless, from January 1951 until they were stopped by strong, revitalized UNC ground forces in early June 1951, the CCF and the reorganized NKPA were able, through tremendously costly efforts, to supply their forces with sufficient basic matériel to carry them forward, albeit slowly and in short increments limited by the amount of supplies amassed.

From their entry into the war until the truce talks began in July 1951, the CCF and their North Korean allies generally remained "underequipped and poorly serviced, relying on superior numbers and tactics to compensate for [their] shortcomings in logistics and ordnance."[194] The Chinese and North Korean soldiers were frequently hungry, often ill clad, and always tired, and their morale and combat efficiency suffered accordingly.[195] Although able to introduce into Korea some seventy divisions, the CCF was incapable of moving them all to the front and supporting them all in offensive operations at the same time.[196] Supply restrictions and limited tactical mobility also served to make it difficult, if not impossible, for the CCF to sustain attacks beyond a limited period or to exploit local breakthroughs. General MacArthur predicted that the "Chinese superiority in numbers will be nullified by Chinese problems of supply," and General James A. Van Fleet expressed the same idea on 10 June 1951 when he observed that "the enemy is not capable of bringing in enough Chinese to drive us out of Korea."[197] Whether or not such prognostications were overly optimistic would only be discovered in the two years of war which followed.

NOTES

1. Historians have traditionally divided the Korean War into three main phases based on the changes in the strategic and tactical situation which took place: from the beginning of the war to the defeat of the NKPA (25 June 1950–November 1950); from the intervention of the Chinese Communists to the opening of the truce talks (November 1950–July 1951); and the period of static warfare ending with the Armistice (July 1951–27 July 1953). See "Review and Analysis of Enemy Operations, 1 January–27 July 1953," Inclosure 5 to Headquarters, Eighth United States Army in Korea, Office of the Assistant Chief of Staff G-2, *Periodic Intelligence Report No. 1111*, 27 July 1953, 1.

2. Roy E. Appleman (*South to the Naktong, North to the Yalu* [Washington: Office of the Chief of Military History, Department of the Army, 1961], 119) has quoted Major General William Dean, commander of the 24th Infantry Division, as saying on 8 July 1950, "I am convinced that the North Korean Army, the North Korean soldiers, and his status of training and quality of equipment have been under-estimated."

3. Russell Spurr, *Enter the Dragon: China's Undeclared War Against the United States in Korea, 1950–51* (New York: Newmarket Press, 1988), 50. By early 1949, it was obvious to North Korean Communist leaders that efforts to subvert the Republic of Korea by propaganda and coercion were not going to succeed and the two parts of Korea could be united under Communist North Korean control only by force of arms.

4. "Brief History of the Korean War," Inclosure 7 to Headquarters, Eighth United States Army in Korea, Office of the Assistant Chief of Staff G-2, *Periodic Intelligence Report No. 1000*, 7 April 1953, 1.

5. "Brief History of the Korean War," 1; Samuel B. Griffith II, *The Chinese People's Liberation Army* (New York: McGraw-Hill Book Company for the Council on Foreign Relations, 1967), 113–114. The NKPA 3rd Division was formed from Korean elements of the Chinese Communist 164th and 166th Divisions in October 1948, and the NKPA 4th Division was formed with officers and men from the Chinese Communist 15th and 156th Divisions. Similarly, the NKPA 5th, 6th, and 7th (later redesignated the 12th) Divisions were almost entirely composed of veterans of the Chinese Communist armies.

6. "Brief History of the Korean War," 1.

7. General Headquarters, Far East Command, Military Intelligence Section, General Staff, *History of the North Korean Army* ([Tokyo]: General Headquarters, Far East Command, Military Intelligence Section, General Staff, 31 July 1952), 4.

8. Joseph C. Goulden, *Korea: The Untold Story of the War* (New York: Times Books, 1982), 35.

9. E. L. Atkins, H. P. Griggs, and Roy T. Sessums, *North Korean Logistics and Methods of Accomplishment* (ORO Technical Memorandum ORO-T-8 [EUSAK]; [Chevy Chase, MD]: Operations Research Office, The Johns Hopkins University, 1951), 4.

10. "Brief History of the Korean War," 1.

11. *History of the North Korean Army*, 4.

12. Goulden, 113-114.

13. Eduard Mark, *Aerial Interdiction in Three Wars: Air Power and the Land Battle in Three American Wars* (Washington: Center for Air Force History, 1994), 273.

14. Robert Frank Futrell, *The United States Air Force in Korea, 1950–1953* (rev. ed., Washington: Office of Air Force History, 1983), 90; James A. Field, Jr., *History of United States Naval Operations: Korea* (Washington: USGPO, 1962), 96.

15. Spurr, 61; T. R. Fehrenbach, *This Kind of War: A Study in Unpreparedness* (rev. ed., New York: Bantam Books, 1991), 160.

16. "Brief History of the Korean War," 2; Fehrenbach, 160; Spurr, 61. On 4 August, the NKPA had no more than forty tanks left from an initial complement of about 200.

17. *North Korean Logistics and Methods of Accomplishment*, 2.

18. General Headquarters, Far East Command, Military Intelligence Section, Allied Translator and Interpreter Service, "Interrogation Reports—North Korean Forces: North Korean Logistics," *ATIS Research Supplement*, Issue No. 1 (19 October 1950), 24.

19. Mark, 281 (Table 14).

20. "Interrogation Reports—North Korean Forces: North Korean Logistics," 24.

21. Futrell, 171.

22. "Interrogation Reports—North Korean Forces: North Korean Logistics," 24.

23. A captured North Korean lieutenant from the NKPA 2nd Division's 247th Artillery Regiment reported that artillery ammunition was transported by truck from the corps ASP but that around 600 "volunteers" were used to transport other supplies for the divi-

sion, including twelve bags of rice per day per regiment (about 1,800 lb for 1,000 men). He also reported that his artillery regiment used about 50 tons of POL in moving from Hamhung to the Changnyong area near Taegu, and that the regiment expended as much as 1,000 rounds of ammunition per day but averaged about 500 rounds per day when firing (see *North Korean Logistics and Methods of Accomplishment*, 37).

24. "Interrogation Reports—North Korean Forces: North Korean Logistics," 25.

25. "Interrogation Reports—North Korean Forces: North Korean Logistics," 24.

26. "Interrogation Reports—North Korean Forces: North Korean Logistics," 27.

27. Appleman, 264 and 354; "Interrogation Reports—North Korean Forces: North Korean Logistics," 26. The number of serviceable pieces was, however, greatly reduced. On 5 August, the NKPA 4th Division apparently had only twelve guns left out of an initial complement of twenty-four 76-mm guns and twelve 122-mm howitzers. The 105th Tank Brigade was redesignated the 105th Tank Division in late July.

28. "Interrogation Reports—North Korean Forces: North Korean Logistics," 26. The 15th NKPA Division, for example, was without its 76-mm SP guns from the end of August.

29. "Interrogation Reports—North Korean Forces: North Korean Logistics," 26. The problem was perhaps systemic rather than a direct result of UNC interdiction efforts since individual weapons could have been carried forward by the arriving replacements.

30. "Interrogation Reports—North Korean Forces: North Korean Logistics," 26.

31. *North Korean Logistics and Methods of Accomplishment*, 9; "Interrogation Reports—North Korean Forces: North Korean Logistics," 25; Appleman, 394.

32. Appleman, 264 note 60. Until about October 1950 the NKPA used only two types of artillery ammunition, high explosive and armor piercing. The shells had a point detonating fuze to which a nose cap could be attached to give a slightly delayed burst.

33. Appleman, 315.

34. *North Korean Logistics and Methods of Accomplishment*, 8.

35. "Interrogation Reports—North Korean Forces: North Korean Logistics," 25; *North Korean Logistics and Methods of Accomplishment*, 8. The captured motor officer of the NKPA 8th Infantry Division reported that by 20 September, only seven liters of gasoline remained for each of the division's thirty trucks (see Mark, 282).

36. Fehrenbach, 196; "Interrogation Reports—North Korean Forces: North Korean Logistics," 27.

37. *North Korean Logistics and Methods of Accomplishment*, 78–79.

38. Appleman, 394; "Interrogation Reports—North Korean Forces: North Korean Logistics," 25-26; *North Korean Logistics and Methods of Accomplishment*, 78–79 and 83. The usual issue was one to three balls of rice and perhaps a bit of soy sauce per day. Food was even in short supply in rear areas such as Seoul, and in the absence of a rationing system a blackmarket in food thrived (see *North Korean Logistics and Methods of Accomplishment*, 83).

39. Reported by the captured chief of staff of the NKPA 13th Infantry Division (see Mark, 281).

40. Appleman 310; Fehrenbach, 180–181.

41. Appleman, 310; Fehrenbach, 180–181; United States Senate, Committee on Armed Services, *Military Situation in the Far East: Hearings before the Committee on Armed Services and the Committee on Foreign Relations, United States Senate, Eighty-second Congress, First Session, to Conduct an Inquiry into the Military Situation in the Far East and the Facts Surrounding the Relief of General of the Army MacArthur from*

His Assignments in That Area (Washington: USGPO, 1951), V, 3399 (CINCUNC Fourth Report, 17 September 1950, for period 16–31 August 1950).

42. Appleman, 333.

43. Appleman, 321.

44. Fehrenbach, 192.

45. Fehrenbach, 192.

46. Appleman, 211.

47. Appleman, 211. Rations had been cut in half, and on some days no rations were issued.

48. Appleman, 287–288.

49. *North Korean Logistics and Methods of Accomplishment*, 82–83. The POW reported that a corps truck unit delivered ammunition from the corps ASP at Yongdok directly to the regimental areas, taking three nights to make the 54-mile trip. The normal procedure was for corps transport to deliver ammunition to division dumps, and the divisional artillery ammunition platoon would pick it up there. Impressed civilians and troops not engaged in combat were used to carry ammunition to the frontlines.

50. Field, 155.

51. Fehrenbach, 240. For example, the NKPA 13th Division on the Perimeter had less than half its original guns and equipment, and one battalion of the NKPA 7th Division reported only six officers, thirty-four NCOs, and 111 privates remaining with only three pistols, nine carbines, fifty-seven rifles, thirteen automatic rifles, ninety-two grenades, and six light machineguns with less than 300 rounds per gun.

52. Field, 58.

53. Field, 59.

54. *Military Situation in the Far East*, V, 3386 (CINCUNC First Report, 25 July 1950, for the period 25 June–19 July 1950).

55. Field, 153.

56. *Military Situation in the Far East*, V, 3391 (CINCUNC Second Report, 16 August 1950, for the period 20–31 August 1950), and V, 3400 (CINCUNC Fourth Report, 17 September 1950, for the period 16–31 August 1950).

57. Field, 157.

58. Gregory A. Carter, *Some Historical Notes on Air Interdiction in Korea* (Santa Monica, CA: The RAND Corporation, September 1966), 1. Even with the emphasis on close-air support, FEAF flew 7,863 interdiction sorties between 25 June and 30 September 1950 (see Mark, 274).

59. Mark, 279.

60. Carter, 6.

61. Futrell, 700.

62. Futrell, 700. The theory was that it was easier to attack the enemy as it concentrated enroute to the front and that such action would best limit the strength of the enemy's frontline effort.

63. Carter, 7. Air interdiction missions in Korea were carried out by fighter-bombers (P-51, F-80, F-82) and light bombers (B-26) assigned to FEAF's tactical unit, the U.S. Fifth Air Force; medium bombers (B-29) assigned to FEAF's strategic Bomber Command; ROKAF and tactical air elements from other UN participants; USMC ground-based aircraft; and U.S. and British naval carrier aircraft. Most of the U.S. aircraft used for air interdiction missions were no longer in production, and the number of tactical

aircraft available in Korea were never sufficient to meet the simultaneous requirements of air superiority, interdiction, and close-air support (see Mark, 262).

64. Futrell, 52. Major General Otto P. Weyland, commander of FEAF tactical air forces, characterized the original policy as being like "trying to dam a stream at the bottom of a waterfall."

65. Futrell, 85.

66. Futrell, 86 and 91.

67. Futrell, 125.

68. Futrell, 129–130; *Military Situation in the Far East*, V, 3396–3397 (CINCUNC Third Report, 5 September 1950, for the period 1–15 August 1950). The plan called for the medium bombers to establish primary cut points at Pyongyang, Hamhung, Wonsan, and Seoul to prevent rail movement from North Korea to the front and also to destroy key highway bridges between the principal transportation centers of Pyongyang, Seoul, and Hamhung (see Futrell, 125–126); Mark, 276.

69. Futrell, 130. FEAF Bomber Command estimated that 13.3 runs (four bombs each run) were required to destroy the average bridge.

70. Futrell, 130. The seven bridges still standing were damaged and impassable.

71. Futrell, 157.

72. Futrell, 157–158.

73. Futrell, 184 and 186.

74. Futrell, 186–187.

75. Futrell, 187.

76. Futrell, 188–189; *Military Situation in the Far East*, V, 3401 (CINCUNC Fourth Report, 17 September 1950, for the period 16–31 August 1950).

77. *Military Situation in the Far East*, V, 3409 (CINCUNC Fifth Report, 5 October 1950, for the period 1–14 September 1950).

78. Futrell, 194. The B-29s caused an average of 55 percent destruction of all the strategic targets except one, the port of Najin (Rashin), only 17 miles from the Soviet border, which was placed off limits to the medium bombers on 1 September for fear of accidentally bombing Soviet territory (see Futrell, 193). Although the effect of the strategic bombing campaign was constrained by the restrictions on bombing Manchuria, the damage in North Korea itself was significant. For example, NKPA POWs attributed the increasingly serious shortage of POL to the destruction of the large refinery at Wonsan (see Futrell, 195–196).

79. Futrell, 126. The plan called for the Fifth Air Force to destroy all enemy transportation facilities in a zone between the 38th and 37th Parallels.

80. Futrell, 131.

81. Futrell, 131–132; Mark, 279–280. FEAF also claimed 280 locomotives, 1,314 railroad cars, and 875 motor vehicles of various types destroyed as of 12 September.

82. Futrell, 132–135.

83. Futrell, 134–136. Despite the destructive power of UNC air operations, cuts in roads or railway lines seldom delayed the movement of supplies more than one or two days, although the cumulative effect of such delays seriously hampered the North Korean support of units at the front (see Futrell, 174).

84. *North Korean Logistics and Methods of Accomplishment*, 34. By the end of July, the North Koreans had lost about 350 locomotives, approximately the same number they had operational at the start of the war (in the meantime, they had restored others to service and had captured a number of ROK locomotives and rail cars). They had also lost

about 20 percent of their freight cars to UNC air attacks. North Korean POWs reported that more than half of the supplies destined for the front were destroyed enroute (see Futrell, 174). The diminished capacity of the railroads required the NKPA to rely more heavily on less efficient and even more vulnerable motor transport (see Mark, 283).

85. By mid-November, North Korean prisoners of war had reported some 452 NKPA tanks, 637 trucks, and 301 artillery pieces destroyed and about 49,527 enemy personnel casualties due to UNC air attacks and another 143 tanks, 146 trucks, 112 artillery pieces, and 56,270 enemy personnel due to UNC ground action (see Futrell, 175). The same survey of 825 North Korean POWs showed that 21.4 percent attributed their low morale to a shortage of food, 9.8 percent to a lack of arms and equipment, 1.2 percent to inadequate clothing, and 17.9 percent directly to the effects of UNC aircraft (see Futrell, 173).

86. Futrell, 168.

87. *Military Situation in the Far East*, V, 3415 (CINCUNC Sixth Report, 21 October 1950, for the period 15–30 September 1950).

88. *Military Situation in the Far East*, V, 3411 (CINCUNC Sixth Report, 21 October 1950, for the period 15–30 September 1950).

89. *Military Situation in the Far East*, V, 3421–3422 (CINCUNC Seventh Report, 3 November 1950, for the period 1–15 October 1950), and V, 3434 (CINCUNC Ninth Report, 27 December 1950, for the period 1–15 November 1950).

90. *History of the North Korean Army*, 33.

91. *Military Situation in the Far East*, V, 3427 (CINCUNC Eighth Report, 6 November 1950, for the period 16–31 October 1950).

92. *Military Situation in the Far East*, V, 3418 (CINCUNC Sixth Report, 21 October 1950, for the period 15–30 September 1950).

93. *Military Situation in the Far East*, V, 3441 (CINCUNC Tenth Report, 27 December 1950, for the period 16–30 November 1950).

94. *Military Situation in the Far East*, V, 3436–3437 (CINCUNC Tenth Report, 27 December 1950, for the period 16–30 November 1950).

95. "Brief History of the Korean War," 2.

96. "Brief History of the Korean War," 3.

97. "Brief History of the Korean War," 3.

98. Edgar O'Ballance, *The Red Army of China: A Short History* (New York: Frederick A. Praeger, 1963), 194; Spurr, 59–60.

99. O'Ballance, 194.

100. Griffith, 351 note 17, quoting a 6 November 1950 cable to the State Department from the U.S. Ambassador to Nationalist China, Karl Lott Rankin. Shorter lines of communication were important in view of UNC air and sea superiority. Additional time was also needed to replace equipment and supplies provided to the North Koreans from stocks in Manchuria.

101. Allen S. Whiting, *China Crosses the Yalu: The Decision to Enter the Korean War* (RAND Study; New York: Macmillan, 1960), 126. Not only did the promised weapons have to be delivered, the Chinese had to be trained to use them.

102. Spurr, 59–60. Mao Tse-tung is reported to have said the task could be accomplished in three weeks at most.

103. Spurr, 68. General Peng was generally regarded as the CCF's most logistically minded commander (see Robert B. Rigg, *Red China's Fighting Hordes* [rev. ed., Harrisburg, PA: The Military Service Publishing Company, 1952], 41).

104. Spurr, 80.

105. Spurr, 83. On 10 September 1950, the Chinese Fourth Field Army had only eight fuel tankers in various states of repair.

106. Whiting, 122–123. Moreover, the Yalu would not freeze over sufficiently to support heavy traffic until November.

107. Spurr, 76 and 82. General Peng is reported to have said (see Spurr, 169) "We must content ourselves for the moment with establishing a line just beyond the 39th Parallel. We do not have the logistic backup to advance much more."

108. Griffith, 106.

109. Spurr, 79; Griffith, 106.

110. Spurr, 83.

111. Spurr, 79.

112. Spurr, 83.

113. The failure of UNC intelligence agencies to detect the massive movement of Chinese Communist forces into Korea, or to believe the fact even after it was proven by the taking of Chinese POWs, stands as one of the great intelligence failures of all time. The refusal of MacArthur's intelligence staff to recognize and report what was actually happening owed much to their proven capacity for procrastination and self-delusion when the situation involved telling their chief things he did not want to hear. An overestimation of the capabilities of air reconnaissance and a decided lack of reliable human intelligence also contributed to the problem.

114. Spurr, 117. The 42nd CCF Army was subsequently replaced by the CCF IXth Army Group in the vicinity of the Changjin (Chosin) Reservoir.

115. Spurr, 117.

116. Spurr, 118.

117. Griffith, 134.

118. Futrell, 226.

119. Futrell, 226. By 28 November, Manpojin was reported 95 percent, Hoeryang 90 percent, Kanggye 75 percent, and Sinuiju 60 percent destroyed.

120. *Military Situation in the Far East*, V, 3432 (CINCUNC Ninth Report, 27 December 1950, for the period 1–15 November 1950), and V, 3449 (CINCUNC Twelfth Report, 23 February 1951, for the period 16–31 December 1950).

121. *Military Situation in the Far East*, V, 3456 (CINCUNC Fifteenth Report, 26 March 1951, for the period 1–15 February 1951).

122. Spurr, 167 and 249–250.

123. Spurr, 167–168 and 250; Griffith, 129.

124. Griffith, 129. The staff of Lin Piao's Fourth Field Army, which supplied many of the key CCF armies to the effort in Korea, was judged more "logistics-minded" than that of any other Chinese Communist field army, having had considerable experience in large-scale railway operations during the Chinese Civil War (see Rigg, 93–94).

125. Griffith, 129; Spurr, 154.

126. Griffith, 138.

127. Griffith, 138.

128. Futrell, 261–262. Ninety years before, both sides in the American Civil War had also replaced entire units in the line as they ran low on ammunition.

129. Fehrenbach, 305. The lack of modern communications equipment, motor transport, and artillery was largely overcome by the end of 1951 by deliveries from the Soviet Union.

130. Spurr, 118–119. In any event, the CCF logistical system proved sufficiently effective to allow the CCF to keep the field until improved support organizations and methods were devised.

131. Spurr, 118.

132. Spurr, 119. The CCF habitually marched 18 or more miles per night with excellent march discipline and camouflage (see Fehrenbach, 275), and in early 1951 one CCF army of three divisions footmarched 286 miles from their base in Manchuria to North Korea in just nineteen days (see James A. Huston, *Guns and Butter, Powder and Rice: U. S. Army Logistics in the Korean War* [Selinsgrove, PA: Susquehanna University Press, 1989], 352).

133. The Chinese Communists were only gradually weaned from their basic military philosophy of "men over weapons," and then only because they were forced to recognize that they could not succeed in fighting a modern, technologically sophisticated Western army with copious manpower alone. By the time an armistice was signed on 18 July 1953, the CCF had itself developed a dependence on technology and had developed effective, "modern" logistical organizations, facilities, and methods. On the "men over weapons" philosophy, see Alexander L. George, *The Chinese Communist Army in Action: The Korean War and Its Aftermath* (New York: Columbia University Press, 1967), vii–ix.

134. O'Ballance, 194. The following account of the strategic and tactical situation in Korea from 26 November 1950 through mid-July 1951 follows closely the account given in "Brief History of the Korean War," 2–5.

135. O'Ballance, 194–195.

136. Futrell, 262–263. UNC airmen estimated that by late December they had killed or wounded nearly 40,000 Chinese Communist soldiers, the equivalent of almost five full CCF divisions.

137. Spurr, 284.

138. Spurr, 289.

139. Quoted by John Gittings, *The Role of the Chinese Army* (New York: Oxford University Press, 1967),133–134; Whiting, 61; Griffith, 257.

140. The historian S. L. A. Marshall reported (*CCF in the Attack, Part II: A Study Based on the Operations of 1st Marine Division in the Koto-ri, Hagaru-ri, Yudam-ni Area, 20 November–10 December 1950* [ORO Staff Memorandum ORO-S-34 [EUSAK]; APO 500: Operations Research Office, The Johns Hopkins University, 1951], 1) that on only six occasions during the 1st Marine Division's withdrawal from the Chosin Reservoir did the CCF support their attacks with artillery, and then no more than two or three guns were firing at any one time and the shelling was limited in the number of rounds fired.

141. Marshall, 1.

142. Griffith, 146. The incidence of tetanus and night blindness induced by vitamin deficiencies was also high among the Chinese soldiers.

143. Gittings, 134.

144. Marshall, 9.

145. Whiting, 161.

146. Spurr, 252–253. The 50th CCF Army, for example, reached Pyongyang on 5 December but had been unfed for the last two days of its march, had only a meager three-days' supply on hand, and required at least ten days to replenish its supplies before resuming the advance (see Spurr, 234).

147. Spurr, 277.

148. Whiting, 122.

149. Spurr, 253.

150. Spurr, 253. The North Koreans, who had demonstrated a notable lack of success in supplying a smaller army from nearer bases during the previous summer, concurred.

151. Spurr, 251–252.

152. Futrell, 282.

153. Cited by Rigg, 301.

154. Futrell, 261.

155. Futrell, 261 and 313; Mark, 294–295. Carrier-based naval air forces were responsible for the three zones along the east coast of Korea from Wonsan north to the Soviet border.

156. Futrell, 263.

157. Field, 309; Futrell, 314.

158. Futrell, 360.

159. Quoted by Futrell, 315. The UNC "withdrawal strategy" was perhaps more a policy born of necessity than a premeditated strategy.

160. George, 8.

161. Futrell, 339.

162. Futrell, 339.

163. Futrell, 339. Meanwhile, UNC naval forces continued to deny to the enemy the use of Korean waters through aggressive patrol and reconnaissance coupled with interdiction of east coast rail lines and highways by naval gunfire from surface vessels offshore (see *Military Situation in the Far East*, V, 3461 [26 March 1951, for the period 16–28 February 1951]).

164. During the April offensive, the CCF had again exposed their supply lines to daylight air attack and UNC air forces claimed some 2,336 Communist vehicles destroyed and 1,496 damaged in April 1951 alone (see Futrell, 335). Fifth Air Force claimed 2,761 vehicles destroyed in March 1951 and 827 vehicles destroyed in June 1951 (see Mark, 301).

165. George, 9; Futrell, 368.

166. George, 9.

167. George, 9.

168. *Supply and Transportation System of the Chinese Communist and North Korean Forces in Korea*, 103. The highest vehicle count on any one night in late 1952 was just over 9,000 vehicles, and toward the end of active fighting in Korea as many as 11,000 vehicles might be on the road each night (see "Effect of the Armistice on Enemy Logistics in North Korea, Part I: Enemy Transport Facilities," *USAFFE Intelligence Digest*, IV, no. 6 [August 1954], 13).

169. *Supply and Transportation System of the Chinese Communist and North Korean Forces in Korea*, 103.

170. Headquarters, United States IXth Corps, G-2 Section, *Enemy Tactics, Techniques and Doctrine* ([Korea]: Headquarters, United States IXth Corps, September 1951), 50–51.

171. *Enemy Tactics, Techniques and Doctrine*, 51.

172. *Enemy Tactics, Techniques and Doctrine*, 49.

173. Similarly, POWs captured before the 16 May 1951 CCF offensive stated that they had been issued rations for fifteen days on or about 10 May before leaving their

assembly areas to march to the front. On 16 May, each soldier would have had nine days of rations remaining; the CCF May offensive was broken up by a UNC counterattack after seven days (see *Enemy Tactics, Techniques and Doctrine,* 49).

174. Griffith, 156.

175. Futrell, 331.

176. Futrell, 332.

177. Futrell, 326–329 *passim*; Mark, 300. According to Mark (p. 278), the greatest operational limitation of the USAF in Korea was its limited capability for conducting tactical ground attack operations at night. The night intruder mission was assigned to the 3rd and 452nd Bombardment Wings, which never had their full authorization of B-26 aircraft (which were considered "marginal" for the mission in any event). Marine pilots from VMF(N)-513 also flew night intruder missions in Korea in night-fighter versions of the old Navy F4U Corsair, which was called "most unsatisfactory for night operations" (see Futrell, 325).

178. Futrell, 331.

179. Futrell, 318.

180. Futrell, 314.

181. Futrell, 320–321 and 323. Futrell cites the 3,500-foot railroad bridge across the Chongchon River at Sinanju as a case in point. The bridge was destroyed by UNC ground forces as they retreated from the area in November–December 1950. By 4 February 1951, the Communists had a bypass bridge in operation. It was destroyed by FEAF bombers on 1 March, but on 7 March the Communists began to construct a bypass to the bypass and the original bypass bridge was itself back in operation by 26 March. On 1 April, the original bypass was again knocked out by the B-29s but was back in operation by 15 April, only to be knocked out yet again on 24 April, at which time the second bypass was almost completed. Both bypasses were hit again on 2 May, but the Communists immediately began to repair them, and by the end of 1951 there would be a total of four rail bridges across the Chongchon at Sinanju.

182. Futrell, 322.

183. Futrell, 323. The B-29s were also very vulnerable to attack by Communist MIG fighters, which constituted "a major obstacle to Fifth Air Force attempts to interdict Chinese supply lines" (Mark, 293).

184. Quoted by Futrell, 318.

185. Field, 332–338 *passim*.

186. Field, 338.

187. Field, 336.

188. Field, 338–339.

189. Carter, 9; Futrell, 324 and 437.

190. Field, 357–358.

191. Carter, 9; Futrell, 437. The key to effective air interdiction was found to be a concurrent heavy pressure by ground combat forces, which caused the enemy to expend supplies at a higher rate than they could be brought forward (see Griffith, 157–159). For various reasons, such continuous pressure on the enemy was not forthcoming and its lack contributed in a substantial way to the ultimate failure of UNC air interdiction to cut off the logistical support of the NKPA-CCF.

192. Carter, 9; Futrell, 437.

193. Billy C. Mossman, "The Effectiveness of Air Interdiction during the Korean War" (CMH Draft Study No. 2-3.7 AD.H; Washington: Office of the Chief of Military

History, Department of the Army, March 1966), Tables "USAF Close Support and Interdiction Sorties by Phase During the Korean War" and "U.S. AIR FORCE Pilot Claims by
Phase During the Korean War." Futrell (p. 371) reported that between 27 June 1950 and
30 June 1951, FEAF aircraft inflicted some 120,000 NKPA and CCF personnel casualties
and destroyed or damaged 391 aircraft, 893 locomotives, 14,200 railroad cars, 439 tunnels, 1,080 rail and highway bridges, 24,500 vehicles, 1,695 tanks, 2,700 artillery pieces,
and 125,000 buildings.

194. Gittings, 134.

195. Futrell, 340. One captured Chinese sergeant from the 26th Army noted during
interrogation that the chief problems in Korea were the shortage of provisions, frostbite
or illness due to the lack of adequate footwear, the nonsupply of weapons and ammunition, and being forced to move and fight mainly at night, all of which he attributed to
UNC air superiority (see George, 165). The CCF commander, Peng Dehuai, and other
senior Chinese officers cited the shortage of food as a major factor in the failure of the
CCF offensives in the spring of 1951 (see Mark, 303 note 28).

196. Futrell, 340.

197. Both quoted by Rigg, 298–299. Rigg (p. 300) enumerated the principal logistical weaknesses of the Chinese Communist army in general as being (1) an insufficient
number of trained logistical staff officers; (2) incomplete organization and training of its
logistical establishment; (3) the lack of effective air and water transport; (4) the necessity
of importing all its oil; (5) the limited extent and efficiency of its rail and highway networks; (6) an inadequate medical service; and (7) the fact that the PLA was too large for
its existing logistical support system.

8

Stalemate, July 1951–July 1953

The second phase of the war in Korea began with the opening of the truce talks at Kaesong on 10 July 1951. From July 1951 until the beginning of 1953, both sides jockeyed for position while improving their strength and the organization of their combat and logistical forces. The NKPA-CCF accelerated their efforts to reorganize their combat units and reequip them with Soviet-supplied matériel, which was appearing in increasing quantity. They also exerted strong efforts to reorganize and improve the efficiency of their logistical support activities and to accumulate stockpiles of supplies in forward areas which could be used for future offensives. At the same time, considerable attention was devoted to protecting and maintaining their rail and highway supply lines against continued heavy UNC interdiction efforts, which included several special interdiction campaigns.

From mid-January 1951, the principal concern of the CCF and NKPA leaders was the problem of how to provide adequate logistical support to their forces in the face of UNC air superiority. Some Chinese leaders, notably General Lin Piao and the Chinese air commander, General Liu Ya-lou, maintained that in order to protect their supply lines the CCF would have to gain air superiority, but General Peng Teh-huai was apparently determined to establish a logistical system in North Korea capable of supporting his forces even with UNC air superiority. The creation of such an effective supply system required three things: the reorganization and augmentation of the NKPA-CCF logistical support structure; the build-up of Communist air defenses; and an energetic and efficient rail and highway repair system accompanied by effective passive defense measures.[1] During the second phase of the war, General Peng implemented his three-point program for the improvement of NKPA-CCF logistics with notable success and proved that his estimation of the ability of the Communist forces to prevail against UNC airpower was correct.

REORGANIZATION OF THE NKPA-CCF LOGISTICAL SYSTEM

The Chinese armies which crossed the Yalu in October and November 1950 were not much more sophisticated than their guerrilla predecessors, and although the North Koreans and Chinese were skillful improvisers, they lacked a concept of modern military logistics. However, Soviet advisors and the pressures of the Korean War soon changed that.[2] As the war progressed, perhaps the most notable feature of the NKPA-CCF supply system was its ability to reorganize and shift supply and transport units according to immediate needs and the dictates of the military situation.[3] The logistical system of the CCF in particular made great progress after July 1951. Initially hampered by a shortage of trained logistical personnel and the lack of uniform logistical procedures, the Chinese quickly established supply training centers and gained experience on the battlefield, which substantially improved all aspects of their logistical support.[4] Although they never reached the level considered acceptable by Western standards, their commander, Peng Teh-huai, is reported to have said that they "not only rapidly improved and raised the level of their equipment, added new formations and various new types of arms, but also acquired rich experience in modern warfare, thus daily increasing their fighting power."[5]

The Chinese leaders were determined to modernize their armies, especially those forces committed in Korea, and the piecemeal attempts at reorganization and modernization undertaken in the first year of the war evolved into a systematic program once the Communists had established themselves behind a nearly impregnable defensive barrier by mid-1951.[6] Major improvements in CCF and NKPA logistical capabilities resulted from deliveries of Soviet matériel and the arrival of Soviet and East European advisors. Although Soviet support began to trickle in soon after the Communist offensive in December 1950, it did not reach significant proportions until the autumn of 1951.[7] By June 1952, the CCF and NKPA had largely been reequipped with weapons, vehicles, and other matériel produced in the Soviet Union, and there appeared to be no shortage of infantry weapons in frontline units, although ammunition continued to be rationed to some extent and the CCF continued to make maximum use of captured UNC weapons and ammunition.[8] The improvement in CCF and NKPA artillery capabilities was particularly noticeable, and for the first time in the war the CCF was able to support its attacks with accurate and often heavy artillery fire.[9]

Improvements in NKPA-CCF Logistical Capabilities

The presence of Soviet and East European advisors was almost as important as the delivery of Soviet equipment in that their expertise aided both the Chinese and North Koreans in reforming and streamlining their logistical support systems along modern lines. Although the CCF and NKPA rear areas remained chaotic for some time, General Peng's logistical reorganization and improvement efforts soon began to meet with success, and by the fall of 1951 the flow of supplies to the front exceeded the daily consumption requirements and thus allowed for serious stockpiling and the establishment of numerous dumps in forward areas.[10] The U.S. Eighth Army assessment was that "the enemy has been successfully supplying his troops despite the UN air interdiction program. The means of transportation and the available supplies have adequately served his logistical requirements."[11] Indeed, the NKPA-CCF transport situation in particular had been substantially improved. By the winter of 1951–1952, the 800,000 Communist troops in Korea were supported by some 6,000 to 7,000 motor vehicles, 275 locomotives, and 7,700 railroad cars.[12] The substantial improvement in the NKPA-CCF transport situation permitted a slow but steady accumulation of supplies in forward areas during the winter of 1951–1952 as the Communists demonstrated their ability to support an army of over 800,000 men with roughly half the logistical establishment of the smaller UNC force.[13]

The truce talks at Panmunjom continued to produce little or no progress in 1952, but the NKPA-CCF logistical situation continued to improve throughout the year. The Communists were not only able to keep their frontline troops in operation but also stockpiled sufficient supplies to create numerous forward area supply dumps. In April 1952, they had major depots at Sopo, Pyongyang, and Yangdok and forward depots at Mulgae-ri, Koksan, Singosan, Sepo-ri, and Hoeryang.[14] The extremely high number of vehicles sighted by UNC aerial observers in May (approximately 4,000 per night) as well as POW interrogations and agent reports indicated a high level of enemy logistical activity, possibly in preparation for a renewed general offensive.[15] Although enemy troop and supply accumulations reached extraordinary levels in June 1952, the threat of an all-out Communist offensive failed to materialize. By November 1952, UNC intelligence agencies were noting not only high levels of vehicle sightings but the fact that the enemy had apparently shifted its transportation effort north of the 39th Parallel in order to replenish its rear area depots and that it was using trucks to transport troops into the forward areas, an indicator that its supply status in the frontlines was of little immediate concern.[16]

There were several indicators of the improvements in the NKPA-CCF logistical systems after July 1951. The improved physical condition of captured Chinese and North Koreans in 1952 and 1953 testified to improved NKPA-CCF ration stocks, and record-breaking vehicle sightings (4,623 during the night of 5–6 September 1952 alone) demonstrated the new-found ability of the CCF and NKPA to replace destroyed or damaged vehicles as well as the adequacy of their POL supply.[17] When hostilities in Korea ended on 27 July 1953, UNC intelligence agencies estimated that Communist ground forces in Korea numbered some 1,057,100 officers and men, of which 263,800 belonged to the NKPA, 783,300 belonged to the CCF, and 10,000 were Soviet and satellite support troops and advisors.[18] The principal crew-served weapons systems available to the NKPA and CCF at the time of the Armistice are tabulated in Table 8.1.

Table 8.1
NKPA and CCF Crew-Served Weapons Systems in Korea, 27 July 1953[19]

Weapons System	CCF Combat Forces	CCF Support Units	NKPA Combat Forces	NKPA Support Units
7.62-mm Heavy Machinegun	3,231		2,759	
12.7-mm AA Machinegun	2,181	598	730	
37-mm AA Gun	588	276	192	396
76-mm AA Gun				12
85-mm AA Gun		528		128
14.5-mm Antitank Rifle			1,215	
3.5-in Rocket Launcher	3,363			
45-mm Antitank Gun			620	
57-mm Recoil-less Rifle	1,062			
57-mm Antitank Gun		72		
60-mm Mortar	3,498			
82-mm Mortar	2,655		2,266	
120-mm Mortar	708		544	120
70-mm Pack Howitzer	708			
75-mm Pack Howitzer	708			
75/76.2-mm Gun/Howitzer	816	240	572	12
76-mm SP Gun (SU-76)			96	62
105-mm Howitzer	228	216	12	
107-mm Gun			42	
122-mm Howitzer		264	240	48
122-mm. SP Gun (JSU)		16		
132-mm. Rocket Launcher		72		
150/155-mm. Howitzer		72	8	
T-34/T-85 Tank		144	32	298
JS-11 Tank		16		

Increased NKPA-CCF Artillery Usage

The constant improvement in Communist logistical capabilities after the truce talks began in July 1951 is perhaps best reflected in the increase in NKPA-CCF artillery employment after the middle of 1951 as new weapons, including 152-mm guns, were received from the Soviet Union and improvements were made in the supply of artillery ammunition. The growth of NKPA-CCF artillery deployments compared to those of UNC forces is shown in Table 8.2. Both the number of guns and the number of artillery battalions deployed peaked in January 1953, and on 1 July 1953 UNC intelligence agencies estimated that the Communists had deployed some 270 artillery battalions with about 2,753 artillery pieces.

Table 8.2
UNC vs. NKPA-CCF Field Artillery Weapons in Korea, July 1951–July 1953[20]

Date	UNC Total		NKPA-CCF On MLR		In Rear Areas		Total	
	Pieces	Bns	Pieces	Bns	Pieces	Bns	Pieces	Bns
1 Jul 51	912	52	366	est. 31	?	140	?	est. 171
1 Oct 51	1,050	58	530	est. 50	?	144	?	est. 194
1 Jan 52	1,182	66	852	71	1,279	145	2,131	216
1 Apr 52	1,294	73	934	95	1,197	121	2,131	216
1 Jul 52	1,433	80	1,246	125	1,103	112	2,349	237
1 Oct 52	1,470	82	1,307	131	1,215	126	2,522	257
1 Jan 53	1,642	95	1,448	142	1,337	131	2,785	273
1 Apr 53	1,754	99	1,469	144	1,254	123	2,723	267
1 Jul 53	1,862	106	1,570	154	1,183	116	2,753	270
Increase	104%	104%	329%	397%	-	-17%	-	58%

Inasmuch as the quantities of artillery and mortar ammunition fired were directly proportional to the amounts which could be produced and brought forward to the guns, the substantial increases in Communist expenditures of artillery and mortar ammunition after July 1951 are an excellent indicator of the steady improvement of the NKPA-CCF logistical system. In July 1951, the NKPA and CCF fired only about 8,000 artillery and mortar rounds, but as shown in Table 8.3 they fired 43,000 rounds in November 1951, 104,700 rounds in September 1952, and about 375,400 rounds in the last month of the war.[21] The increase in NKPA-CCF artillery ammunition expenditures was particularly striking in 1952, as shown in Chart 8.1.[22]

Chart 8.1
Communist Artillery and Mortar Shells Expended in 1952[23]

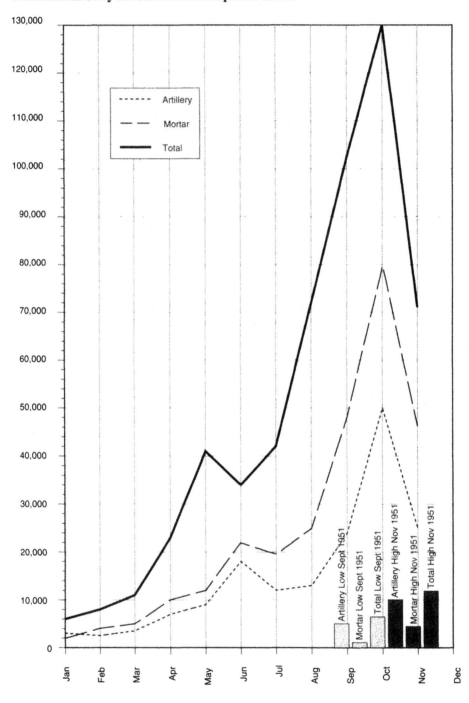

Table 8.3
NKPA-CCF Monthly Artillery Expenditures, August 1951–July 1953[24]

Month	Rounds Expended
August 1951	16,300
September 1951	18,400
October 1951	37,400
November 1951	43,200
December 1951	19,700
January 1952	17,500
February 1952	11,900
March 1952	18,500
April 1952	29,200
May 1952	43,500
June 1952	77,300
July 1952	57,000
August 1952	70,400
September 1952	104,700
October 1952	220,600
November 1952	106,700
December 1952	51,000
January 1953	36,700
February 1953	37,800
March 1953	69,400
April 1953	51,700
May 1953	99,300
June 1953	329,100
July 1953	375,400
Increase (From Oct 1951)	**904%**

Improved NKPA-CCF Anti-Aircraft Defenses

An important part of General Peng's plan to strengthen his logistical support was the improvement of Communist air defenses. In November 1950, the NKPA-CCF had few anti-aircraft artillery weapons, particularly in forward areas, but during the course of the war deliveries of Soviet-made weapons rectified that defect, and UNC flyers faced increasingly heavy flak, especially along transportation routes and around key bridges, tunnels, and supply installations. Although weak by World War II standards, the NKPA-CCF flak, coupled with the MIG-15s, progressively degraded the effectiveness of both routine and special UNC air interdiction operations.[25]

From early January 1951, special "hunter groups" of Chinese infantrymen specialized in trying to destroy UNC aircraft, decoys (or "flak traps") were employed, and aircraft warning guards were posted at intervals of 300 to 600 meters along main supply routes.[26] From April 1951 onward, these ad hoc measures were supplemented by the increasing deployments of regular anti-aircraft artillery units armed with newly issued Soviet 12.7-mm anti-aircraft machineguns and even heavier weapons.[27] By 1 July 1951, the CCF and NKPA had some 329 anti-aircraft guns and 945 anti-aircraft automatic weapons in Korea, many of which were deployed to protect vital supply lines and supply installations.[28] Stabilization of the front lines after June 1951 led to additional increases in the number of anti-aircraft weapons and the preparation of coordinated air defenses.[29] Table 8.4 portrays the increase and distribution of NKPA-CCF anti-aircraft artillery weapons from July 1951 to July 1953.

Table 8.4
NKPA-CCF Anti-Aircraft Guns and Automatic Weapons, July 1951–July 1953[30]

	Line of Comm		Front		Miscellaneous		Total	
Date	Heavy	AW	Heavy	AW	Heavy	AW	Heavy	AW
1 Jul 1951	-	-	-	-	-	-	329	945
1 Oct 1951	-	-	-	-	-	-	329	1,360
1 Jan 1952	-	-	-	-	-	-	351	1,455
1 Apr 1952	96	487	20	246	250	330	366	1,063
1 Jul 1952	100	751	12	288	197	270	309	1,309
1 Oct 1952	128	616	0	220	257	298	385	1,134
1 Jan 1953	204	628	11	263	453	423	668	1,134
1 Apr 1953	223	475	10	153	486	354	619	982
1 Jul 1953	146	345	57	244	517	320	720	909
						Increase	119%	-4%

From the beginning of the war, the Communists employed a considerable portion of their anti-aircraft artillery to protect their main supply routes. The MSR from Sinuiju to Pyongyang, for example, was extremely well protected from the beginning, and protection of other routes was developed after the first few months of 1951.[31] Most of the Communist anti-aircraft artillery was of the automatic weapons type in fixed positions rather than railway or vehicle mounted. In May 1951, FEAF intelligence officers plotted the location of 252 anti-aircraft guns and 673 automatic anti-aircraft weapons; most of these were in fixed locations, but a few mobile 37-mm automatic weapons were found along the main supply routes.[32]

From July 1951 to the end of 1952, the CCF and NKPA made great strides in improving both their active and passive air defense with the assistance of new Soviet weapons and better techniques. With the initiation of the intensive UNC air interdiction campaigns against North Korean rail lines in August 1951, the Communists began to concentrate their anti-aircraft automatic weapons along the rail lines, and in September 1951 UNC sources estimated some ninety-one heavy AA guns and ninety-eight AA automatic weapons in the Sinuiju and adjacent Antung (Manchuria) area, with another twenty heavy guns and seventy-nine automatic weapons around Sinanju and some sixty-eight heavy guns and 165 automatic weapons in the Pyongyang area. By June 1952, the Communists were using over half their anti-aircraft artillery to protect key bridges and rail lines.[33] By 1 May 1953, UNC intelligence officers estimated that the Communists had deployed sixty-six anti-aircraft gun battalions and 116 anti-aircraft automatic weapons battalions in Korea.[34]

UNC AIR INTERDICTION, JULY 1951–JULY 1953

Even as the NKPA-CCF were improving their logistical organization and the air defenses of their lines of communications, the UNC air forces were seeking better techniques for the exploitation of UNC air superiority. From the beginning of the truce talks at Kaesong in July 1951 to the Armistice in July 1953, UNC air planners constantly shifted the focus of the UNC air interdiction effort, trying to find the ideal method which would decisively cripple NKPA-CCF logistical support of their frontline troops. In the end, UNC air interdiction was unable to stop Communist rail and highway movements, but some success was achieved in slowing the flow of supplies to the NKPA-CCF, thus limiting the Communist freedom of action.

Operation STRANGLE II (August–December 1951)

Concurrent with the opening of truce talks at Kaesong in mid-July 1951, UNC air forces launched a limited program to destroy key logistical targets in the vicinity of Pyongyang and the east coast port city of Najin (Rashin), which had been put off limits in September 1950 in view of its proximity to the Soviet border. These attacks produced results, but political considerations connected with the truce talks limited the full exploitation of UNC air power.[35] Intelligence reports of Communist supply build-ups for a renewed offensive in the event the peace talks failed focused the attention of UNC planners on a renewed and intensified air interdiction campaign, but it was recognized that the effectiveness of such a campaign, given the reduced ground action resulting from the ongoing attempts to obtain a truce, would be limited.[36]

One approach was to employ UNC air assets in another special interdiction operation directed against a limited, specific target. As Operation STRANGLE began to produce fewer results in late June 1951, FEAF planners had concluded that the rail system was the key to the Communist supply system, and so on 18 August 1951 UNC air forces began another ninety-day campaign, also called

STRANGLE, to "destroy the enemy rail system."[37] The idea behind the operation was that if UNC air forces could reduce NKPA-CCF rail movements significantly, the Communists would be forced to use more vulnerable motor transport and would be unable to sustain a steady loss of trucks (potentially as many as 250 per day, according to UNC estimates).[38]

Once again, the Navy and FEAF Bomber Command joined Fifth Air Force fighter-bombers in the interdiction operation, with the Navy assuming responsibility for the lateral rail line across Korea from Samdong-ni to Kowon and the east coast line from Kilchu south through Hungnam and Wonsan to Pyonggang, while the FEAF medium bombers were assigned to interdict the key rail bridges at Pyongyang, Sonchon, Sunchon, and Sinanju.[39] The Fifth Air Force B-26s and fighter-bombers concentrated on enemy rail facilities in northwestern Korea, particularly the double-tracked rail line between Sonchon and Sariwon.[40]

The UNC rail interdiction program produced good results in August and September 1951, and the enemy was forced to move greater quantities of cargo by truck, resort to circuitous routings, cannibalize other sections to keep critical rail segments in operation, and take other drastic corrective measures.[41] In October and November 1951, the UNC planes destroyed the North Korean railways faster than the Communists could repair them, but the improving NKPA-CCF air defenses and other countermeasures were beginning to take effect.[42] In November, the Communists managed to repair most rail cuts within twenty-four hours; in December, they had reduced the average time required to eight hours.[43] By December the UNC airmen began to tone down their claims for the effectiveness of STRANGLE II, calling it a program designed to "interfere with and disrupt" rather than "destroy" or "cripple" the enemy's rail lines of communications.[44] In early December, Communist progress in repairing the nearly destroyed rail line between Pyongyang and Sariwon was so rapid that on 23 December 1951, Fifth Air Force intelligence had to admit that the enemy had "broken our railroad blockade of Pyongyang and...won...the use of all key rail arteries."[45] Even at the height of STRANGLE II, the CCF were still able to move an estimated 1,000 to 2,000 tons a day from Manchuria by rail, thus supplying about half their total requirements.[46] Not for the last time NKPA-CCF countermeasures proved effective and their ability to repair cuts quickly was fully demonstrated.

STRANGLE II ended on 23 December 1951, another failure, although the FEAF commander, General Otto P. Weyland, announced on 26 December that STRANGLE II had all but destroyed the North Korean railway network and destroyed or damaged some 40,000 trucks.[47] Considering the shift to a defensive policy by UNC ground forces in mid-November, which took the pressure off the NKPA-CCF logistical system, the Communists apparently remained fully capable of moving supplies forward in sufficient quantities to support an active defense, and, given sufficient time, they could stockpile enough war matériel to support limited major offensive actions. Nevertheless, UNC commanders recommended the continuance of the rail interdiction program and sought improved methods for making it more effective.[48]

In January 1952, the Fifth Air Force shifted its fighter-bomber interdiction attacks north of the Chongchon River to avoid the growing concentration of CCF flak south of the river, but the attacks on rail lines between the Yalu and the Chongchon achieved only limited success in January and February, in part due to the frozen ground.[49] At the same time, another attempt was made to use the medium bombers of FEAF Bomber Command in an interdiction role. In late January 1952, FEAF intelligence officers identified a bottleneck in the enemy rail system running across central North Korea near the village of Wadong. Between 26 January and 11 March 1952, seventy-seven B-29 and 125 B-26 sorties dropped some 3,938 500-lb bombs on the so-called "Wadong Choke Point."[50] The results were disappointing, with only eighteen rail and fifteen highway cuts recorded; the rail line was blocked for only seven days and the road net for only four days out of the 44-day operation.[51] The conclusion was that the proper targets for interdiction were rail lines and highways, bridges, and rolling stock and that the medium bombers ought to be concentrated on such point targets.[52]

Operation SATURATE (March 1952)

UNC air planners continued to search for more effective methods of air interdiction, and on 25 February 1952 the Fifth Air Force Director of Intelligence recommended implementation of Operation SATURATE, a program which involved the concentration of available air interdiction assets against short segments of railway track to destroy them by round-the-clock attacks.[53] Four main railway lines were targeted for this program: those running from Kunu-ri to Huichon, Sunchon to Samdong-ni, Sinanju to Namsi-dong, and Pyongyang to Namchonjom.[54] Operation SATURATE began on 3 March 1952, and during April UNC air forces succeeded in keeping the rail line between Sinuiju and Sinanju out of operation continuously; however, the number of available fighter-bombers was too small to permit simultaneous interdiction of all four lines.[55] In the end, the effort failed because the UNC air forces simply did not have enough planes to maintain around the clock the number of rail cuts required to shut down the NKPA-CCF rail network.[56] Effective Communist countermeasures also lessened the impact of even concentrated attacks on limited stretches of track, and ultimately SATURATE, too, was rated a failure, and other methods for interdicting the enemy line of supply had to be sought.

The "Air Pressure" Concept

Concurrent with the beginning of Operation SATURATE, the FEAF commander, General Frank P. Everest, set two of his staff officers, Colonel Richard L. Randolph and Lieutenant Colonel Ben I. Mayo, to make a study of FEAF operations. The results of their study were submitted on 12 April 1952 and concluded that after December 1951 the UNC rail interdiction program had reached a point at which destruction by FEAF's limited air assets was matched by the enemy's ability to repair its damaged rail lines.[57] They also pointed out that the intensive railway interdiction effort was probably not worth its cost and that in the future small but periodic air attacks could keep the North Korean rail system operating at only a marginal capacity.[58] Subsequently, the UNC air forces began to shift away from interdiction beginning in May 1952 and instead adopted the concept of "air pressure," which was aimed at maintaining a constant pressure on all facets of the enemy logistical and combat systems through destruction of the enemy's men, equipment, vehicles, and supplies in forward areas as well as in the rear.[59] The new policy was incorporated in the FEAF operational policy directive of 10 July 1952, and the "air pressure through selective attacks" tactic proved somewhat more effective overall and was continued until the armistice terms were agreed on in July 1953.[60]

Even before the "air pressure" strategy was adopted, the UNC air forces had struck hard against NKPA-CCF accumulations of men and supplies. On 11 March 1952, the CCF depot behind the frontlines at Mulgae-ri was hit by 254 fighter-bomber sorties; and on 8 May 1952, the Communist supply depot at Suan was hit by 485 fighter-bomber sorties in the most massive single attack since the beginning of the war.[61] Beginning in late October, carrier aircraft from Task Force 77 conducted massed fighter-bomber attacks against troop and supply concentrations near the frontlines under the rubric of "Cherokee strikes."[62] Meanwhile, the Fifth Air Force sought to find one "special" target per day, against which it placed 100 fighter-bomber sorties; the remaining aircraft were directed against enemy personnel and supply concentrations in the area south of the Pyongyang-Wonsan line.[63] The medium bombers also participated again, and in late October and early November FEAF Bomber Command aircraft made numerous strikes against the Sopo supply complex a few miles north of Pyongyang as well as their usual industrial and communications targets.[64]

The advent of the "air pressure" strategy did not mean that the NKPA-CCF rail and highway interdiction targets were neglected. In November 1952, the Fifth Air Force obtained good results from a main supply route interdiction plan called "Choke," which involved the coordinated use of fighter-bombers and night-intruder B-26s.[65] The fighter-bombers and night-intruders again cooperated successfully in December, with "Truck Killer" operations against Communist roads and vehicles and "Spotlight" against Communist rail traffic.[66] Some idea of the level of success obtained by UNC air interdiction efforts is provided in Table 8.5 which presents the claims of vehicles destroyed made by Fifth Air Force pilots from September 1951 through December 1952.

Table 8.5
Fifth Air Force Claims of Vehicles Destroyed, September 1951–December 1952[67]

Month	Vehicles Destroyed
September 1951	5,318
October 1951	6,761
November 1951	4,571
December 1951	4,290
January 1952	2,489
February 1952	2,397
March 1952	1,750
April 1952	1,723
May 1952	2,532
June 1952	1,804
July 1952	594
August 1952	169
September 1952	2,167
October 1952	2,502
November 1952	3,139
December 1952	2,321

While some success was achieved against Communist highway targets, maintaining railroad cuts proved as difficult as ever. In mid-October 1952, the Communists already had three railroad bridges in operation across the Taeryong River at Yongmi-dong, about 10 miles northwest of Sinanju, and were building a fourth.[68] Yongmi-dong was an obvious bottleneck on a key railway line, and some 114 UNC fighter-bombers attacked the bridges on 1 November 1952. Another 100 planes returned on 6 November to find that the Communists had already repaired the three operational bridges and had begun to construct a fifth bypass bridge as well as having moved in additional anti-aircraft artillery.

The Final Accounting

Although restricted in its application and ultimately failing to achieve all of its objectives, the UNC air interdiction effort in Korea was massive and did have measurable effects on NKPA-CCF combat power. As shown in Table 8.6, about one quarter of all UNC air combat sorties in the Korean War were devoted to interdiction, the greatest portion flown by U.S. Air Force pilots.

Table 8.6
UNC Air Forces Interdiction Sorties, 25 June 1950–27 July 1953[69]

Organization	Total Sorties	Interdiction Sorties
U.S. Air Force (FEAF)	720,980	192,581
U.S. Navy	167,552	
U.S. Marines	107,303	47,873
Friendly Foreign	44,873	15,359
Total	**1,040,708**	**254,813**

At best, the UNC air interdiction campaign achieved only limited success against an enemy with low supply requirements, a relatively primitive logistical system, and considerable flexibility, but the damage to enemy personnel, supplies, and equipment was extensive even when due allowance is made for the expected exaggeration of claims made by UNC pilots, as shown in Table 8.7.

Table 8.7
UNC Pilot Claims, 25 June 1950–27 July 1953[70]

Claim Category	USAF and Friendly Foreign	USN and USMC	Totals
Enemy Troops Killed	145,416	86,265	231,681
Tanks Destroyed	988	249	1,237
Tanks Damaged	979		
Locomotives Destroyed	869	391	1,260
Locomotives Damaged	1,085		
Railroad Cars Destroyed	14,906	5,896	20,802
Railroad Cars Damaged	21,090		
Vehicles Destroyed	74,589	7,437	82,026
Vehicles Damaged	29,597		
Buildings Destroyed	116,839	44,828	161,667
Buildings Damaged	77,406		
Bridges Destroyed	827	2,005	2,832
Supply Installations Destroyed		1,900	
Power Plants Destroyed		33	
Enemy Vessels Destroyed		2,464	
Railcuts Completed	22,828	13,000	35,828

Although the NKPA-CCF continued to be able to supply their forces with at least a minimum amount of supplies and equipment throughout the conflict, the UNC air interdiction took a terrible toll and had a profound effect on the ability of the Communists to support dynamic combat operations. Air interdiction degraded the Communist logistical systems and forced reliance on more difficult and less reliable methods of local supply and primitive transportation at night over difficult terrain. The NKPA-CCF were forced to decentralize and disperse their supply operations and to adopt the somewhat inflexible practice of distributing large amounts of all types of supplies equally in the terrain compartments leading to the front.[71]

NKPA AND CCF COUNTERMEASURES

Although the UN air interdiction campaign destroyed great quantities of NKPA-CCF supplies and transport equipment, forced movement at night and off-road movement of supplies by animal and man transport, and generally hampered NKPA-CCF offensive operations, one authority assessed the enemy's success at overcoming the massive UNC interdiction effort as "little short of fantastic."[72] This was due to four factors: low requirements; use of off-road animal and man transport to supplement rail and motor movements; effective masking of movements; and effective methods for the repair of transportation facilities.[73] Of these four factors, the two most important were the masking of movements and effective methods for maintaining transportation facilities.

Masking of Movements

One major reason for Communist success in minimizing the effects of UN interdiction was the Communists' superior ability to mask their movements. Although initially stunned by UNC airpower, the NKPA and CCF soon devised operational techniques to minimize the probability of UNC air attack and the effects of air strikes when they did occur. The Communists also consistently made maximum use of cover and concealment and demonstrated a very high level of camouflage and march discipline.

Operational techniques which lowered the probability of detection included movement at night and during poor flying weather, dispersal of supply installations and dispersal of supplies within depots and supply dumps, light discipline during night marches, and an extensive air warning system.[74] During daylight hours railroad trains, trucks, and other equipment were hidden in tunnels or other protected areas.[75] Highway traffic was dispersed to the maximum extent possible over a wide area using every road capable of handling vehicles in order to make UNC air detection more difficult and air strikes less effective.[76] Detection was made even more difficult by the employment of very small march units such as convoys of only four or five trucks operated by drivers who remained assigned to the same area, knew it well, and could drive at night without lights. The NKPA-CCF also developed trucking schedules which facilitated their efforts to avoid detection and destruction.[77] Convoys moved from areas in the north heavily protected by anti-aircraft artillery to bunkers in the intermediate zone on one night. The following night, they delivered their cargoes to the frontlines and returned to the bunkers. The next night, they returned to the protected rear area.

The Communists also developed a highly effective air warning system consisting of air guards located at short intervals along railroads and main supply routes. With the approach of UNC aircraft, the guards gave warning by means of rifle shots, whistles, or sirens, and defensive measures were taken.[78] Normally, NKPA-CCF drivers drove with their lights on until an air warning was received, at which time they extinguished their lights and either pulled off the road or continued at a reduced speed. An enemy document captured by the U.S. 25th Infantry Division in March 1951 provided regulations for the night movement of convoys and their conduct when under attack.[79] The document stressed the necessity for strict light and movement discipline on the part of drivers and set the priorities for movements through restricted areas or when under attack. In all situations, motor vehicles were to be given priority over marching troops or animal transport. The document also warned against the possibility of accidents when convoys were operating under blackout conditions.

Other operational techniques, such as shuttling around rail and highway breaks and the construction of bypasses in advance, further reduced the effect of UNC air strikes. The use of trucks and porters to shuttle supplies around destroyed sections of railroad tracks or roadways was common, but it was also time-consuming and manpower intensive. Shuttle operations also had a number of less obvious disadvantages. For example, although large numbers of military and civilian porters could be mobilized for shuttling activities, it was necessary to load cargo in small packages which could be manhandled. This resulted in inefficient loading of boxcars and trucks and thereby reduced the amount of supplies moved forward by vulnerable transport assets.[80] Flatcars loaded with sandbags and placed in front of the locomotive also helped to minimize damage from guerrilla sabotage, and when a bridge had been damaged to the extent that it was too weak to support both the locomotive and cars, the Communists pushed several cars at a time over the bridge and they were picked up by another locomotive on the other side.[81]

Supplies and vehicles were located in protected areas whenever possible. The natural protection provided by ravines, ditches, caves, and even holes in the ground were utilized to the maximum possible extent, as were man-made revetments, culverts, tunnels, mine shafts, buildings, and other structures.[82] In some cases, supplies were placed in shallow water.[83] Systematic use of villages to provide cover and concealment for men, supplies, and equipment was standard procedure.[84] During daylight hours, movement in bivouac areas was restricted to lessen the chances of detection.[85]

By necessity, the Communists practiced a very strict camouflage discipline. Maximum use was made of natural cover and concealment to hide supplies, but North Korean and Chinese soldiers became very adept at camouflaging their vehicles and supply stocks. In towns or villages, small supply dumps were located in huts or covered with rubble to give the appearance of a destroyed building.[86] In the countryside, supply dumps were camouflaged to resemble cultivated fields or rice paddies.[87] Haystacks were a favored place of concealment for supplies.[88] Fresh foliage was maintained at all times on trucks moving in daylight, and the windshield and other reflecting surfaces were removed, covered, or painted.[89] When UNC aircraft appeared, the trucks were pulled off the road and concealed in gullies or woods. Deceptive techniques, such as the construction of dummy bridges and other facilities or the removal of bridge sections during the daytime, were also widely practiced.[90] Railroad tracks and highways were frequently camouflaged to appear to have been impassable. In some respects the Communist devotion to camouflage techniques produced unexpected results. In some cases, the enemy cleared the surrounding area of its trees and bushes to heavily camouflage a vehicle, thus leaving it very obvious. On several other occasions, UNC pilots observed NKPA-CCF troops in column carrying bushes for individual camouflage. When the UNC aircraft approached, the Communist soldiers dutifully hid under their bushes but remained in the middle of the road![91]

Maintenance and Repair of Lines of Communication

The ability to repair the damage to railroads and highways caused by UNC air attacks was perhaps the single greatest factor in the success of the NKPA-CCF in countering the UNC interdiction program. Despite massive air interdiction, the Communists were able, by means of rapid, simple repairs carried out with minimal equipment and large numbers of men, to keep their railroads and highways in operation and to insure the flow of sufficient supplies to the frontlines.

The NKPA-CCF methods for work-arounds and repairs to fixed transport facilities such as roads, railroads, and bridges were ingenious and highly effective. In most cases, adequate repair supplies were available and the lack of mechanized repair equipment was compensated by the use of large numbers of military and civilian laborers.[92] Destroyed bridges and railroad tracks were replaced with multiple bypasses (four, five, or even as many as ten).[93] A striking example was the key Yalu crossing at Sinuiju, which was supplied with at least ten temporary railroad bridge bypasses. The bypasses, shown in Sketch 8.1, were seasonal but required the UNC to keep four bridges down at all times to cut service between Manchuria and North Korea.[94] Underwater bridges and removal spans made detection by UN air observers more difficult.[95] In some cases, temporary river and stream crossings consisted only of improved fords, and the bottom was built up with rocks, logs, and sandbags.[96] The average time required to repair a medium-sized bridge was five or six days, but some key bridges were repaired

Sketch 8.1
Bridge Bypasses in the Sinuiju Area[97]

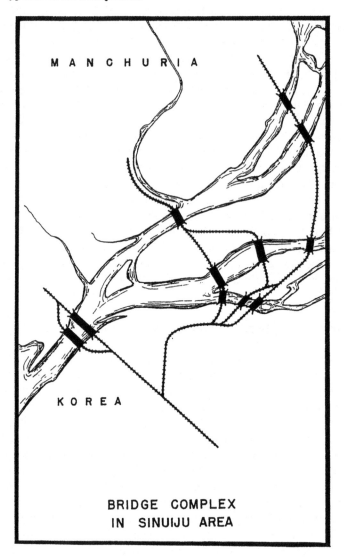

BRIDGE COMPLEX
IN SINUIJU AREA

overnight and others in only one to four days using nearly unlimited manpower and supplies stockpiled nearby.[98] The time needed to repair a bridge was reduced through the use of wooden pilings, wooden cribbing, sandbags, and prefabricated bridge sections.[99]

The principle governing railroad repairs was to achieve early use of the damaged section with a minimum expenditure of time and matériel; thus repairs tended to be temporary rather than permanent.[100] Simple rail cuts were repaired expeditiously, but more time was required when the lines were sufficiently damaged to require the enemy to bring in heavy repair equipment.[101] Such heavy equipment was scarce, but apparently the Soviets supplied sufficient numbers of essential items to enable the NKPA-CCF to make all necessary repairs.[102] Repairs to ordinary cuts were made in two to six hours and "max effort" cuts in four to seven days.[103] In World War II, the average repair time for a rail cut was one day; in Korea it was ten hours.[104] The actual repair times achieved by CCF repair crews on various types of projects included two hours to lay 30 meters of track; twelve hours to repair a major rail cut and cratering; forty-eight hours to repair 200 feet of bridge; and seventy-two hours to repair 330 feet of bridge (using 150 workers and with a five-hour delay before the start of repairs).[105] Delays were further reduced by anticipating the destruction of key rail lines and bridges and the preparation of bypasses or other arrangements in advance.[106] Strenuous efforts were also made to protect maintenance supplies and repair equipment. They were often hidden in railroad tunnels during the day, with the entrances blocked by several railroad cars to minimize damage from skip-bombing attacks.[107]

THE THIRD PERIOD: JANUARY–JULY 1953

From the point of view of NKPA-CCF logistics, the final phase of the war from 1 January to 27 July 1953 was anticlimactic. The battle to organize adequate supply and transportation systems and protect them against UNC airpower, to reequip and modernize combat units, and to overcome other deficiencies in the Communist logistical systems had already been won in the seventeen months from August 1951 through December 1952. By the beginning of January 1953, the logistical systems of the NKPA and CCF were reaching their maturity and would prove their new-found effectiveness and efficiency in the hard fighting which took place between March 1953 and the concluding of an armistice agreement on 27 July 1953.

For the first three months of 1953, the NKPA and CCF continued to improve their lines of communications, to build up their logistical stockpiles, and to expend supplies cautiously. Consequently, combat activity on the front in Korea remained light. Beginning on 23 March, however, the Communists began a series of battalion-sized attacks which sharply increased in size and extent in the last half of May, with regimental-sized attacks with heavy mortar and artillery support against the U.S. I Corps and ROK II Corps and to a lesser extent against the U.S. X Corps.[108] The enemy attacks intensified to divisional size in June and shifted from the eastern sector of the front (1–10 June) to the central sector (10–20 June) and finally to the western sector (after 20 June). Heavy Communist offensive actions continued until 19 July, apparently in an attempt to gain an advantage before the armistice agreement was concluded and a cease-fire went into effect.

The extended Communist offensives in June and July 1953 demonstrated the degree to which the Communist logistical situation had been improved.[109] By early June, the stockpile of rations had reached its highest level since the beginning of the war, and NKPA-CCF soldiers who had existed throughout 1952 on only two meals per day were again permitted three meals per day.[110] Clothing supplies were adequate. The supply of weapons and other equipment continued to increase throughout 1953, and POL stocks were apparently sufficient to maintain necessary motor vehicle and combat operations.[111] The heavy attacks in June and July were supported by very high levels of ammunition expenditure, and their duration bespoke a logistical system which was fully functional and capable of supporting a high level of offensive action over a considerable period.[112] POWs reported that all forward ammunition storage areas were filled to capacity, and in June 1953 the Communists expended 40 percent more ammunition than they had in October 1952.[113]

The series of NKPA-CCF attacks beginning in March did not involve the entire front simultaneously, and thus the rate at which supplies were expended was probably well below the 6,070 short tons per day that UNC intelligence agencies estimated would be required to support a general Communist offensive.[114] Table 8.8 shows UNC estimates of NKPA-CCF supply expenditures at various times in 1953 and reflects the increased expenditure of supplies, particularly ammunition as the tempo of Communist offensive activity increased after 23 March. Data for January 1952 is provided for comparison.

Table 8.8
UNC Estimates of NKPA-CCF Supply Expenditures, January–July 1953
   (Average ST/Day)[115]

Class of Supply	January 1952	January 1953	January–March 1953	April–July 1953	In Event of a General Offensive
I (Rations)	1,508	2,062	2,102	2,143	2,062
II & IV (Equip)	884	1,080	1,177	1,291	2,738
III (POL)	292	408	486	515	497
V (Ammo)	72	276	253	416	773
Total	2,756	3,826	4,018	4,365	6,070

The Communist build-up for the 1953 offensives was made possible by an excess of transport capability beyond the requirements of normal consumption. The extent of this excess is depicted in Table 8.9.

Table 8.9
NKPA-CCF Logistics Requirements vs. Transport Capabilities, January–July 1953 (Average ST/Day)[116]

Month	Estimated Requirement	Estimated Transport Capability	Excess Available for Stockpiling
January 1953	3,826	4,328	502
April 1953	4,018	4,445	427
July 1953	4,365	4,800	435

Through strenuous efforts, the NKPA-CCF continued to improve the capabilities of their distribution system throughout 1953 as both rail and highway movements were facilitated by improvements in NKPA-CCF repair and construction capabilities. Between January and 15 April 1953, the Communists were able to construct an entirely new 70-mile rail line connecting Kusong, Kunu-ri, and Sinpyong-ni to link the Namsan-Chongju line with the Sinanju-Manpojin line.[117] As a result of such improvements, UNC intelligence agencies estimated that by 27 July 1953 an average of 3,500 ST of supplies were entering North Korea by rail each day, 39 percent more than during the first quarter of 1953.[118] The increased capacity of North Korean railroads in 1953 also released trucks from "import runs" for movement of supplies into forward areas, resulting in a steadier flow of supplies to the frontline.[119]

At the end of combat operations in Korea on 27 July 1953, the Communist forces were in better logistical condition than they had been at any time since the war began. The improvements in the NKPA-CCF logistical systems since July 1951 gave the Communist forces the ability to launch sustained heavy offensives in June and July 1953 with troops that were well fed, adequately equipped, and strongly supported by artillery and mortar fire.[120] Just prior to the Armistice on 27 July 1953, the NKPA-CCF is estimated to have had on hand in forward areas sufficient ammunition to support their forces for forty days and thirty-five days stockage of other supplies, amounts considered sufficient for the enemy to support logistically a general ground offensive of seventeen to twenty-four days duration.[121]

CONCLUSION

The focal point of the story of Communist logistics in the Korean War was the battle of distribution, and that struggle revolved around the UNC interdiction effort and the passive and active measures adopted by the Communists to neutralize the effects of UNC air superiority and an intensive air interdiction effort. In the end, the battle was won by the Communists. Despite superior airpower, superior technology, and a first-rate effort, the UNC air forces in Korea were unable to destroy, or even interdict decisively, the NKPA-CCF logistical system, and the NKPA-CCF were able to provide their forward forces with sufficient men and matériel to conduct an active defense and, with time to stockpile supplies, to undertake limited offensive actions.

In the final analysis, the success of the UNC air interdiction effort was limited by a number of factors, including low overall enemy supply requirements, inadequate UNC aircraft resources, the lack of an effective night capability, the insufficient use of delay-fused and antidisturbance weapons, the existence of an off-limits sanctuary in Manchuria and North China, and the failure of UNC ground forces to maintain a constant pressure against the enemy sufficient to force the enemy to consume its supplies at a rate greater than they could be replenished.[122]

Above all, the impact of the UNC air interdiction program was reduced by aggressive NKPA-CCF countermeasures, both passive and active. Dispersion, movement at night, excellent camouflage and march discipline, innovative use of cover and concealment, effective air warning networks, a growing air defense artillery capability, the availability of large numbers of construction and repair personnel, and an aggressive program for the repair and maintenance of transportation lines and facilities combined to permit the Communists to reduce the impact of UNC air interdiction to tolerable levels.

As even General Mark Clark, the UNC commander in the later stages of the war, later had to admit,

> The Air Force and the Navy carriers may have kept us from losing the war, but they were denied the opportunity of influencing the outcome decisively in our favor.... Our air power could not keep a steady stream of enemy supplies and reinforcements from reaching the battle line. Air could not isolate the front.[123]

NOTES

1. Robert Frank Futrell, *The United States Air Force in Korea, 1950–1953* (rev. ed., Washington: Office of Air Force History, 1983), 316.

2. James A. Houston, *Guns and Butter, Powder and Rice: U.S. Army Logistics in the Korean War* (Selinsgrove, PA: Susquehanna University Press, 1989), 351; "Individual Histories, Chinese Communist Support and Service Units," *FEC Intelligence Digest*, 26 (2 July 1952), 44.

3. E. L. Atkins, H. P. Griggs, and Roy T. Sessums, *North Korean Logistics and Methods of Accomplishment* (ORO Technical Memorandum ORO-T-8 [EUSAK];

[Chevy Chase, MD]: Operations Research Office, The Johns Hopkins University, 1951), 5.

4. "Chinese Communist Army Supply System," *USAFFE Intelligence Digest*, IV, no. 4 (June 1954), 38.

5. Samuel B. Griffith II, *The Chinese People's Liberation Army* (New York: McGraw-Hill Book Company for the Council on Foreign Relations, 1967), 182.

6. John Gittings, *The Role of the Chinese Army* (New York: Oxford University Press, 1967), 120–121.

7. Edgar O'Ballance, *The Red Army of China: A Short History* (New York: Frederick A. Praeger, 1963), 195. The flow of Soviet equipment was at first restricted mostly to trucks and small arms, and the Russians apparently were reluctant to supply large quantities of equipment before they were sure the Chinese were able to handle them.

8. Gittings, 135.

9. Gittings, 135. In late November and December 1950 the artillery regiments organic to the NKPA divisions were reconstituted with a battalion of 120-mm mortars, a battalion of 76-mm guns, and a battalion of 122-mm guns, and the NKPA 76-mm self-propelled gun battalions ceased to exist. At the same time, the CCF in Korea, already augmented by three tank regiments in December 1950, added an additional artillery division, bringing total CCF artillery strength to about 115 battalions. Between the end of May and the beginning of the truce talks in mid-July 1951, another independent CCF artillery regiment entered Korea and the NKPA organized one independent howitzer regiment and one independent mortar regiment (see "Brief History of the Korean War," Inclosure 7 to Headquarters, Eighth United States Army in Korea, Office of the Assistant Chief of Staff G-2, *Periodic Intelligence Report No. 1000*, 7 April 1953, 3–5).

10. Headquarters, Eighth United States Army, Assistant Chief of Staff G-2/Headquarters, United States Fifth Air Force, Assistant Chief of Staff A-2, *Supply and Transportation System of the Chinese Communist and North Korean Forces in Korea* ([Tokyo]: Headquarters, Eighth United States Army, Assistant Chief of Staff G-2/Headquarters, United States Fifth Air Force, Assistant Chief of Staff A-2, 23 September 1951), iv.

11. *Supply and Transportation System of the Chinese Communist and North Korean Forces in Korea*, iv.

12. James A. Field, Jr., *History of United States Naval Operations: Korea* (Washington: USGPO, 1962), 427 (Table 22). At the same time, the 600,000 UNC troops had some 22,000 motor vehicles, 486 locomotives, and 8,314 railroad cars.

13. Field, 427.

14. Futrell, 471.

15. Field, 433.

16. Inclosure 6 to Eighth United States Army, *Periodic Intelligence Report No. 833*, 11 December 1952, 2. The same source notes that vehicle sightings in November 1952 were the highest since May of that year.

17. *Supply and Transportation System of the Chinese Communist and North Korean Forces in Korea*, 104.

18. Headquarters, Eighth United States Army, Office of the Assistant Chief of Staff, G-2, *Intelligence Estimate, 27 July 1953* (APO 301: Headquarters, Eighth United States Army, Office of the Assistant Chief of Staff, G-2, 27 July 1953), 5.

19. Headquarters, United States Army Forces, Far East, and Eighth United States Army (Rear), Office of the Assistant Chief of Staff, G-2, *Order of Battle Handbook—*

Chinese Communist Forces, Korea, and the North Korean Army (APO 343: Headquarters, United States Army Forces, Far East, and Eighth United States Army [Rear], Office of the Assistant Chief of Staff, G-2, 1 January 1956), 58–62.

20. Adapted from Headquarters, Eighth United States Army in Korea, Office of the Assistant Chief of Staff, G-2, *Weekly Intelligence Summary No. 6*, 6 September 1953, Table No. 4 to Annex 1 to Inclosure No. 5. NKPA-CCF battalions are estimated at 75 to 85 percent of authorized strength. The percentage of increase shown is for the period from 1 July 1951 to 1 July 1953.

21. Headquarters, Eighth United States Army in Korea, Office of the Assistant Chief of Staff, G-2, *Weekly Intelligence Summary No. 6*, 6 September 1953, Table 5 to Annex 1 to Inclosure 5; Futrell, 471; Field, 419.

22. The enormous increase in NKPA-CCF artillery capability was made clear during an action on 21 June 1952, when an estimated enemy regiment unsuccessfully attempted to recapture outposts taken by the U.S. 45th Infantry Division in the Mabang area of the western front. Although the enemy was routed after a six-hour battle, over 10,000 rounds of enemy artillery and mortar rounds fell on 45th Infantry Division positions, the largest amount on a single day in one division sector during the war. See "Selected Intelligence Items during Period 16 June–30–June 1952," *FEC Intelligence Digest*, 26 (2 July 1952), v.

23. Inclosure 8 to Headquarters, Eighth U.S. Army in Korea, Office of the ACS, G-2, *Periodic Intelligence Report No. 879*, 7 December 1952.

24. Headquarters, Eighth United States Army in Korea, Office of the Assistant Chief of Staff, G-2, *Weekly Intelligence Summary No. 6*, 6 September 1953, Table 5 to Annex 1 to Inclosure 5; Futrell, 471; Field, 419.

25. Futrell, 474.

26. Futrell, 337-338.

27. Futrell, 338 and 335. The principal heavy anti-aircraft gun used by the NKPA and CCF was the Soviet 85-mm model which had a range of up to 25,000 feet. The principal anti-aircraft automatic weapons were the Soviet 12.7-mm anti-aircraft machinegun and the Soviet 37-mm automatic cannon, which could fire up to 160 rounds per minute and had a range of up to 4,500 feet (see Harry G. Summers, Jr., *Korean War Almanac* [New York: Facts on File, 1990], 48).

28. Headquarters, Eighth U.S. Army in Korea, Office of the Assistant Chief of Staff, G-2, *Weekly Intelligence Summary No. 6*, 6 September 1953, Table No. 6 to Annex 1 to Inclosure No. 5. See also Futrell, 338; "Railroads and Highway Transport in North Korea and Their Impact on Enemy Logistics," *USAFFE Intelligence Digest*, I, no. 13 (2 July 1953), 30.

29. *Supply and Transportation System of the Chinese Communist and North Korean Forces in Korea*, 82.

30. Adapted from Headquarters, Eighth U.S. Army in Korea, Office of the Assistant Chief of Staff, G-2, *Weekly Intelligence Summary No. 6*, 6 September 1953, Table No. 6 to Annex 1 to Inclosure No. 5. During the same period, UNC anti-aircraft artillery resources expanded by 78 percent for guns (from 49 to 87) and 63 percent for automatic weapons (from 504 to 823).

31. *Supply and Transportation System of the Chinese Communist and North Korean Forces in Korea*, 82–85.

32. Futrell, 335.

33. Futrell, 473–474.

34. "Railroads and Highway Transport in North Korea and Their Impact on Enemy Logistics," 30.

35. Futrell, 433–435 *passim*. In addition to restrictions on the use of tactical airpower arising from the truce talks, the UNC air forces continued to be prohibited for diplomatic and strategic reasons from attacking the factories, assembly areas, supply depots, and transportation facilities in Manchuria which supported the Communist forces in Korea. General MacArthur and others argued forcefully that such action was necessary to defeat the CCF and NKPA and that otherwise the UNC air interdiction effort could only hamper and delay the movement of Communist men and matériel to the front in Korea (see United States Senate, Committee on Armed Services, *Military Situation in the Far East: Hearings before the Committee on Armed Services and the Committee on Foreign Relations, United States Senate, Eighty-second Congress, First Session, to Conduct an Inquiry into the Military Situation in the Far East and the Facts Surrounding the Relief of General of the Army MacArthur from His Assignments in That Area* [Washington: USGPO, 1951], *passim*). UN political and higher level military leaders were also reticent to approve attacks against North Korea's hydroelectric facilities and irrigation systems, but in late June 1952 permission was finally given to attack the North Korean hydroelectric plants and a joint Air Force–Navy operation produced excellent results, causing an almost total power outage that lasted almost two weeks. The loss of the generators at the Sui-ho plant, the world's fourth largest hydroelectric plant, alone represented a loss of nearly one fourth of the electric power requirements of northeastern Korea (see Field, 437–438; Futrell, 480–482, 488, and 666–667).

36. Futrell, 435–436. The Communists were estimated to be stockpiling over 800 tons of supplies per day in forward areas behind the front.

37. Gregory A. Carter, *Some Historical Notes on Air Interdiction in Korea* (Santa Monica, CA: The RAND Corporation, September 1966), 10. Operation STRANGLE II is also known as the Rail Interdiction Program (see Eduard Mark, *Aerial Interdiction in Three Wars: Air Power and the Land Battle in Three American Wars* [Washington: Center for Air Force History, 1994], 293).

38. Mark, 309.

39. Futrell, 439–440.

40. Futrell, 442.

41. Futrell, 443–445 *passim*.

42. Futrell, 445.

43. Futrell, 447.

44. Futrell, 441–442.

45. Futrell, 447.

46. Griffith, 158.

47. Carter, 11; Futrell, 447; Mark, 316.

48. Futrell, 447–448.

49. Futrell, 448–449. Along the six main rail lines south of the Chongchon, the CCF anti-aircraft automatic weapons positions were distributed about every 4 miles.

50. Futrell, 450. The "Wadong Choke Point" was a narrow gorge near the village of Wadong just west of Yangdok through which passed the rail line and highway connecting Wonsan with Sinanju and Pyongyang.

51. Futrell, 450.

52. Futrell, 450.

53. Futrell, 451; Carter, 11.

54. Futrell, 451.
55. Futrell, 453.
56. Futrell, 473.
57. Futrell, 478–479.
58. Futrell, 479.
59. Futrell, 471–472, 479–480, and 703–704.
60. Futrell, 533. According to Mark (pp. 323–324), the "air pressure campaign" was essentially a "political strategy designed to bring the Communists to a truce by inflicting an intolerable level of damage on the economic infrastructure of North Korea."
61. Futrell, 483.
62. Futrell, 619.
63. Futrell, 619.
64. Futrell, 617–618.
65. Futrell, 620.
66. Futrell, 622.
67. Futrell, 455–456, 459, and 622; Patrick M. Dowling, Thomas H. Tudor, and Theodore G. Schad, *The Vulnerability of Army Supply to Air Interdiction* (ORO Technical Memorandum ORO-T-46 [FEC]; APO 500: Operations Research Office, The Johns Hopkins University, March 1954), 182–183 (Table A1-1). For the months of May–August 1952, only estimated B-26 night intruder claims are listed.
68. For the operations against the Yongmi-dong bridges, see Futrell, 536 and 620.
69. Billy C. Mossman, "The Effectiveness of Air Interdiction during the Korean War" (CMH Draft Study No. 2-3.7 AD.H; Washington: Office of the Chief of Military History, Department of the Army, March 1966); Futrell, 692. U.S. Marine Corps interdiction sorties are included with U.S. Navy interdiction sorties. Friendly foreign sorties are for ground-based aircraft only; friendly foreign carrier-based sorties are included with U.S. Navy sorties. UNC ground-based tactical aircraft included units from the Republic of Korea, Australia, and South Africa.
70. Mossman, "The Effectiveness of Air Interdiction during the Korean War," Table "Total Pilot Claims During the Korean War." See also Carter, 2; Futrell, 692. The claim of 988 tanks destroyed by USAF and friendly foreign pilots probably includes land-based U.S. Marine Corps pilot claims. The "USAF and Friendly Foreign" column probably also includes "Supply Installations Destroyed" and "Power Plants Destroyed" under "Buildings Destroyed." The 13,000 rail cuts claimed by USN and USMC pilots include only those made by fast carrier aircraft.
71. "The Enemy Supply System in North Korea," *USAFFE Intelligence Digest*, II, no. 4 (2 September 1953), 24.
72. Carter, 13.
73. Mark (pp. 263, 317, and 323) also mentions action by the Chinese Air Force, effective NKPA-CCF anti-aircraft defenses, flexible and redundant Communist communications, and the limited number of USAF tactical aircraft, especially night intruders, as factors contributing to the reduced effectiveness of the UNC interdiction effort.
74. For a good general discussion of NKPA-CCF passive defense measures, see Dowling et al., 315–320.
75. "Railroads and Highway Transport in North Korea and Their Impact on Enemy Logistics," 32.
76. *Supply and Transportation System of the Chinese Communist and North Korean Forces in Korea*, 88.

77. Futrell, 334.

78. *Supply and Transportation System of the Chinese Communist and North Korean Forces in Korea*, 85.

79. *Supply and Transportation System of the Chinese Communist and North Korean Forces in Korea*, 97–99. The document was dated 11 January 1951, but the procedures described were applicable at other times.

80. "Railroads and Highway Transport in North Korea and Their Impact on Enemy Logistics," 34.

81. "Railroads and Highway Transport in North Korea and Their Impact on Enemy Logistics," 32 and 34.

82. "Chinese Communist Army and North Korean Army Logistics and Class Supply," *USAFFE Intelligence Digest*, VI, no. 4 (April 1956), 58.

83. *Supply and Transportation System of the Chinese Communist and North Korean Forces in Korea*, 86.

84. S. L. A. Marshall, *CCF in the Attack, Part II: A Study Based on the Operations of 1st Marine Division in the Koto-ri, Hagaru-ri, Yudam-ni Area, 20 November–10 December 1950* (ORO Staff Memorandum ORO-S-34 [EUSAK]; APO 500: Operations Research Office, The Johns Hopkins University, 1951), 9; Headquarters, United States IX Corps, G-2 Section, *Enemy Tactics, Techniques and Doctrine* ([Korea]: Headquarters, United States IX Corps, September 1951), 4. Chinese and North Korean troops usually stayed within 500 yards from the route of roads and trails.

85. *Enemy Tactics, Techniques and Doctrine*, 4. The enemy was taught not to fire on UNC aircraft or patrols during the day unless absolutely necessary.

86. *Enemy Tactics, Techniques and Doctrine*, 41.

87. *Enemy Tactics, Techniques and Doctrine*, 41.

88. *Supply and Transportation System of the Chinese Communist and North Korean Forces in Korea*, 87.

89. *Supply and Transportation System of the Chinese Communist and North Korean Forces in Korea*, 86.

90. "Railroads and Highway Transport in North Korea and Their Impact on Enemy Logistics," 32.

91. *Supply and Transportation System of the Chinese Communist and North Korean Forces in Korea*, 86.

92. *Supply and Transportation System of the Chinese Communist and North Korean Forces in Korea*, iv. The various NKPA and CCF organizations involved in rail and highway maintenance and repair are discussed in Chapter 6.

93. Carter, 13.

94. "Railroads and Highway Transport in North Korea and Their Impact on Enemy Logistics," 32.

95. Futrell, 132; "Train Sightings in North Korea Period 270600 Nov–040600 Dec 1952," Inclosure 7 to EUSAK G-2, *Periodic Intelligence Report No. 884*, 12 December 1952, paragraph 5 (pp. 1–2).

96. *Supply and Transportation System of the Chinese Communist and North Korean Forces in Korea*, 89.

97. "Railroads and Highway Transport in North Korea and Their Impact on Enemy Logistics," 33.

98. Dowling et al., 304; Carter, 14.

99. Dowling et al., 304.

100. "Railroads and Highway Transport in North Korea and Their Impact on Enemy Logistics," 34.

101. Futrell, 451.

102. *Supply and Transportation System of the Chinese Communist and North Korean Forces in Korea*, 89.

103. Carter, 14.

104. Carter, 16.

105. Dowling et al., 304 (Table J-6).

106. *Supply and Transportation System of the Chinese Communist and North Korean Forces in Korea*, 88.

107. "Railroads and Highway Transport in North Korea and Their Impact on Enemy Logistics," 34.

108. The progress of the tactical situation in 1953 is outlined in "Review and Analysis of Enemy Operations, 1 January–27 July 1953," Inclosure 5 to EUSA G-2, *Periodic Intelligence Report No. 1111*, 27 July 1953.

109. "The Enemy Supply System in North Korea," 15.

110. "Review and Analysis of Enemy Operations, 1 January–27 July 1953," 7. UNC estimates were that enemy Class I stockage levels in forward areas were sixty to ninety days of supply for CCF units and 45-60 days of supply for NKPA units after March 1953. One POW reported that stockpiling of rations ceased in April 1953 because the required level of eight months' supply had been achieved and only sufficient supplies to maintain that level would be brought forward thereafter (see "The Enemy Supply System in North Korea," 18).

111. The supply of POL remained difficult for the Communist forces throughout the war, and such measures as strict rationing, movement of trucks by rail, and the conversion of gasoline-powered vehicles to charcoal-burners continued to the end (see "Effect of the Armistice on Enemy Logistics in North Korea, Part II: Enemy Supply System and Logistics Requirements in North Korea," *USAFFE Intelligence Digest*, IV, no. 8 [October 1954], 14).

112. In June 1953, UNC ground forces reported the largest number of incoming rounds of any month during the war and the enemy was estimated to have expended a daily total of 600 ST of Class V supplies (see "Effect of the Armistice on Enemy Logistics in North Korea, Part II: Enemy Supply System and Logistics Requirements in North Korea," 29).

113. "Review and Analysis of Enemy Operations, 1 January–27 July 1953," 8.

114. "Effect of the Armistice on Enemy Logistics in North Korea, Part II: Enemy Supply System and Logistics Requirements in North Korea," 29.

115. "Effect of the Armistice on Enemy Logistics in North Korea, Part II: Enemy Supply System and Logistics Requirements in North Korea," 28–30; General Headquarters, Far East Command, Military Intelligence Section, General Staff, *Logistical Capability of Communist Forces in Korea to Support a Major Offensive* (APO 500: GHQ, FEC, OACS, J-2, 28 February 1953), 4 and *passim*.

116. "Effect of the Armistice on Enemy Logistics in North Korea, Part II: Enemy Supply System and Logistics Requirements in North Korea," 31–32.

117. Futrell, 627.

118. "Effect of the Armistice on Enemy Logistics in North Korea, Part I: Enemy Transport Facilities," *USAFFE Intelligence Digest*, IV, no. 6 (August 1954), 5. The

average was 2,520 ST/day in March 1953. The average train density also increased from eleven trains per day in March to fourteen trains per day in July 1953.

119. "Effect of the Armistice on Enemy Logistics in North Korea, Part I: Enemy Transport Facilities," 11. Imports by truck decreased by 40 percent in the second quarter of 1953.

120. "Military Supply in North Korea," *USAFFE Intelligence Digest,* V, no. 10 (October 1955), 40.

121. "Effect of the Armistice on Enemy Logistics in North Korea, Part II: Enemy Supply System and Logistics Requirements in North Korea," 25–26.

122. Carter, 15–16.

123. Quoted by Griffith, 157.

9

Conclusion

The war in Korea from 25 June 1950 to 27 July 1953 was above all a war of logistics for both sides. The strategy and operational decisions of both the United Nations Command and Communist forces were based largely on logistical considerations. The principal difficulty faced by the North Korean People's Army and the Chinese Communist Forces in Korea was to provide adequate logistical support to their forces in the field, and the focal point of that difficulty was the Communist distribution system. From the UNC perspective, the principal difficulty lay in trying to deny to the Communists the minimal resources needed to pursue active combat operations. This the UNC forces were unable to do, and although the Communists were never strong enough logistically to employ their maximum combat manpower to defeat the UNC forces and eject them from the Korean peninsula, they were able to maintain a flow of supplies to frontline units sufficient to enable them to conduct a static defense strong enough to prevent a UNC victory and, in the last months of the war, to mount strong sustained offensive actions.

From the point of view of NKPA-CCF logistical activities, the Korean War can be divided into three main periods. From June 1950 to July 1951, the Communists struggled to keep their forces supplied in the face of intensive UNC air interdiction efforts and aggressive UNC ground operations. Consequently, the NKPA and CCF were unable to exploit their initial operational successes by sustained offensive action. In the second period from July 1951 through December 1952, the NKPA and CCF reorganized and strengthened their logistical forces and developed effective methods for coping with the UNC air interdiction program. In the final period, from January 1953 through July 1953, NKPA-CCF logistical systems achieved maturity and demonstrated an ability not only to meet the requirements of a strong static defense but to stockpile in forward areas the supplies necessary to sustain prolonged offensive operations as well.

A number of factors influenced the ability of the NKPA and CCF to support their forces in the field adequately. In the first instance, the logistical requirements of both the NKPA and the CCF in Korea were extremely low in comparison to those of UNC forces. The minimal provision of food, clothing, and medical support to frontline Communist troops sometimes caused great hardship and suffering but apparently did not cause a significant deterioration of morale and discipline. Contrary to the common opinion, the NKPA and CCF in Korea were dependent on formal, albeit relatively lean, logistical systems. Maximum use was made of captured supplies and items, particularly foodstuffs, requisitioned in areas near the frontlines, but in the final analysis the NKPA and CCF relied principally on war matériel obtained through "regular channels." The logistical systems of the NKPA and CCF in Korea differed significantly. The logistical doctrine and methods of both armies were quite flexible and changed, as did tactical organization, during the course of the war, mostly in the direction of the more rigid, but more efficient, Soviet model. In much the same way, the logistical organizations of the NKPA and CCF also exhibited considerable internal variation from unit to unit as well as considerable change over time, again in the direction of the Soviet model.

The efficiency of NKPA-CCF logistical support was directly affected by the ebb and flow of combat operations up and down the Korean peninsula. The farther south Communist forces advanced, the longer and more exposed became their lines of supply and the less efficient their overall logistical performance. The same was true, of course, for UNC forces moving in the opposite direction. In view of the extended supply lines required, the NKPA-CCF distribution system was extremely vulnerable and was thus the focal point of UNC efforts to degrade Communist combat potential. Again contrary to common opinion, both the NKPA and the CCF distribution systems relied principally on rail movement supplemented by motor transport at intermediate levels. For the most part, carts, pack animals, and human bearers were used only in the immediate area of the front (regimental level and below), for unit movements, and for supplementary operations in rear areas. From a UNC perspective, the inadequacy of NKPA-CCF motor transport at the lower levels was an important defect of the Communist logistical system in that reliance on frontline animal and man-pack transport restricted the tactical mobility and flexibility of the NKPA and CCF in combat operations, particularly their ability to shift forces rapidly or exploit breakthroughs.

The Communists compensated for a low level of logistical mechanization with extensive employment of manpower and extraordinary exertion. The NKPA and CCF in Korea also demonstrated great ingenuity and determination in working around UNC attempts to interdict their lines of communications and to destroy their logistical resources. They were particularly adept at passive air defense measures, including camouflage, and in the rapid restoration of destroyed and damaged fixed transport facilities (bridges, rail lines, and highways). Even so, until the last seven months of the war, the NKPA-CCF logistical systems were not able to deliver sufficient war matériel to frontline forces to permit them to sustain extended offensive operations. Until early 1953, most Communist offensive operations petered out within six to eight days due to the exhaustion of available food, ammunition, and other key supplies. However, the NKPA and CCF were able to supply their forces on the frontlines with the minimum amounts of essential supplies necessary to a strong static defense against UNC forces, and by early 1953 they were beginning to demonstrate a capability to stockpile sufficient supplies to support sustained offensives as well. By the end of active hostilities in July 1953, the NKPA-CCF had on hand in forward areas sufficient food, fuel, ammunition, and other supplies to support a general offensive of seventeen to twenty-four days duration. Despite over one million UNC interdiction sorties directed against their lines of communication, transport equipment, supply installations, and industrial facilities over a period of three years, the NKPA and CCF were stronger than ever when the Armistice was signed on 27 July 1953.

The Communist logistical situation at various times would have been complicated greatly by more sustained aggressive action on the part of UNC forces. The failure of UNC forces to maintain a high operational tempo after July 1951, and thus place constant pressure on the enemy, permitted the NKPA and CCF to stockpile supplies in periods of reduced combat. Static situations thus favored the NKPA-CCF in that to be effective, interdiction must be employed against an enemy using supplies at a high rate. In Korea, the NKPA-CCF were allowed to initiate or break off contact at will and thus could rest and build up supplies as they wished. The failure to maintain constant ground pressure on the Communist forces can be attributed to both the political and material constraints under which the UNC commanders operated, but the potential nemesis of the Communist distribution system, the UNC air interdiction program, was also restrained by the lack of adequate technology for detecting movement at night and under conditions of reduced visibility as well as by the limited number of suitable aircraft which could be applied to the interdiction effort. The constant improvement of NKPA-CCF anti-aircraft artillery coverage further restricted the UNC air interdiction effort. Although often cited as a critical restraint on UNC forces, the existence of a Communist supply base in Manchuria which was immune from attack was a relatively unimportant factor. Had the UNC air forces been able to attack the Manchurian bases, the end result of the UNC air interdiction effort would probably not have been materially affected.

Perhaps the final word in the story of the logistical support of North Korean and Chinese Communist forces in Korea should go to one of their opponents, Brigadier General Darr H. Alkire, who served as Deputy Commander for Matériel of the U.S. Far East Air Forces. In June 1951, General Alkire said that

It has frequently been stated by commanders in Korea that the one man they would like to meet when the war is over is the G-4 of the Communist forces. How he has kept supplies moving in the face of all obstacles is a real mystery. He has done it against air superiority, fire superiority, guts, and brawn.[1]

NOTE

1. Quoted by Robert Frank Futrell in *The United States Air Force in Korea, 1950–1953* (rev. ed., Washington: Office of Air Force History, 1983), 336–337.

Appendixes

Appendix A

NKPA-CCF Order of Battle in Korea

The determination of the enemy order of battle (OB) was a continuous process carried out by UNC intelligence agencies at all levels throughout the war. Very detailed OBs for both the NKPA and the CCF in Korea were developed from a variety of sources. Of course, the NKPA-CCF OBs fluctuated over the course of the war, and UNC intelligence estimates were not always accurate. It is obviously impractical to include here more than a few representative "snapshots" of what the NKPA and CCF OBs looked like at key points. Accordingly, OB information is provided only for the following dates: 25 June 1950 (the day the war began; NKPA only); 14 July 1951 (at the time truce talks began); and 27 July 1953 (the day the Armistice went into effect). The NKPA and CCF OBs presented here are necessarily abbreviated. The original OB documents should be consulted for detailed and more accurate information.

The following abbreviations are used in the OB tables:

Arty	Artillery
Bde	Brigade
CCF	Chinese Communist Forces
Div	Division
Inf	Infantry
NKPA	North Korean Peoples Army
Regt	Regiment
RR	Railroad
u/i	Unidentified

NKPA Order of Battle, 25 June 1950[1]

Major Command	Divisions and Brigades	Regiments
General Headquarters, NKPA		
I Corps		
II Corps		
	1st Infantry Division	2, 3, & 14th Inf; 1st Arty
	2nd Infantry Division	4, 6, & 17th Inf; 2nd Arty
	3rd Infantry Division	7, 8, & 9th Inf; 31st Arty
	4th Infantry Division	5, 16, & 18th Inf; 4th Arty
	5th Infantry Division	10, 11, & 12th Inf; 5th Arty
	6th Infantry Division	1, 13, & 15th Inf; 6th Arty
	7th Infantry Division	51, 53, & 54th Inf; 7th Arty
	10th Infantry Division	25, 27, & 29th Inf; u/i Arty
	13th Infantry Division	19, 21, & 23rd Inf; 13th Arty
	15th Infantry Division	48, 49, & 50th Inf; 15th Arty
	105th Tank Brigade	
	1st Border Constabulary Bde	
	2nd Border Constabulary Bde	
	3rd Border Constabulary Bde	
	5th Border Constabulary Bde	
	7th Border Constabulary Bde	
		776th Independent Inf Regt
		12th Motorcycle Regiment
		17th Motorcycle Regiment
Support Troops		
Service Troops		

Total NKPA Troops   approximately 135,000

NKPA Order of Battle, 14 July 1951[2]

Command/Division/Unit	Regiments	Strength
General Headquarters, NKPA		**540**
Frontline General Headquarters		**346**
Corps Troops		**11,867**
I Corps		
8th Infantry Division	81, 82, & 83rd Inf; 8th Arty	4,251
19th Infantry Division		4,459
47th Infantry Division	113, 123, & 124th Inf; 35th Arty	4,515
		13,225
II Corps		
2nd Infantry Division	4, 6 & 17th Inf; 2nd Arty	3,774
13th Infantry Division	19, 21, & 23rd Inf; 13th Arty	7,891
27th Infantry Division	172, 173, & 174th Inf; 25th Arty	2,174
		13,839
III Corps		
1st Infantry Division	2, 3, & 14th Inf; 1st Arty	7,727
15th Infantry Division	45, 48, & 50th Inf; 15th Arty	7,189
45th Infantry Division	89, 90, & 91st Inf; 51st Arty	7,367
		22,283
IV Corps		
4th Infantry Division	5, 18, & 29th Inf; 4th Arty	8,940
5th Infantry Division	10, 11, & 12th Inf; 5th Arty	8,968
105th Tank Division		4,184
26th Infantry Brigade		2,294
63rd Infantry Brigade		3,155
		27,541
V Corps		
6th Infantry Division	1, 13, & 15th Inf; 6th Arty	7,435
12th Infantry Division	30, 31, & 32nd Inf; 12th Arty	7,078
32nd Infantry Division		7,217
		21,730
VI Corps		
9th Infantry Division	85, 86, & 87th Inf; u/i Arty	6,829
17th Infantry Division		6,845
18th Infantry Division		9,323
23rd Infantry Brigade		5,205
		28,202

VII Corps

3rd Infantry Division	7, 8, & 9th Inf; 3rd Arty	6,845
7th Infantry Division	51, 53, & 54th Inf; 7th Arty	6,850
24th Infantry Division		9,286
37th Infantry Division	70, 71, & 76th Inf; 31st Arty	9,883
46th Infantry Division	158, 159, & 160th Inf; 66th Arty	9,804
		42,668

Line of Communications Troops   **2,270**

Guerrillas and Remnants   **7,300**

Replacements in Training   **30,000**

               Total NKPA Troops   **227,721**

CCF Order of Battle, 14 July 1951[3]

Major Command	Army/Division/Unit	Infantry Regiments	Strength
III Army Group (2nd Field Army)			
	10th Army		
	10th Army Troops		4,441
	28th Infantry Division	81, 82, & 83rd	8,420
	30th Infantry Division	88, 89, & 90th	8,903
			21,764
	11th Army		
	11th Army Troops		4,430
	32nd Infantry Division	94, 95, & 96th	8,989
	33rd Infantry Division	97, 98, & 99th	8,994
			22,413
	12th Army		
	12th Army Troops		4,345
	31st Infantry Division	91, 92, & 93rd	2,693
	34th Infantry Division	100,101, & 102nd	2,734
	35th Infantry Division	103, 104, & 105th	3,255
			13,027
	15th Army		
	15th Army Troops		4,479
	29th Infantry Division	85, 86, & 87th	2,402
	44th Infantry Division	130, 131, & 132nd	3,239
	45th Infantry Division	133, 134, & 135th	2,334
			12,454
	60th Army		
	60th Army Troops		4,280
	179th Infantry Division	535, 536, & 537th	2,503
	180th Infantry Division	538, 539, & 540th	2,622
	181st Infantry Division	541, 542, & 543rd	2,882
			12,287
	Total III Army Group		**81,945**
XIII Army Group (4th Field Army)			
	u/i Cavalry Division		2,149
	1st Artillery Division		6,967
	2nd Artillery Division		7,197
	5th Artillery Division		7,308
	8th Artillery Division		6,953
			30,574

39th Army		
39th Army Troops		4,156
115th Infantry Division	343, 344, & 345th	3,868
116th Infantry Division	346, 347, & 348th	4,433
117th Infantry Division	349, 350, & 351st	5,559
		18,016
40th Army		
40th Army Troops		4,242
118th Infantry Division	352, 353, & 354th	6,695
119th Infantry Division	355, 356, & 357th	6,595
120th Infantry Division	358, 359, & 360th	3,386
		20,918
47th Army		
140th Infantry Division	418, 419, & 420th	**9,365**
Total XIII Army Group		**78,874**

IX Army Group (3rd Field Army)		
u/i Cavalry Division		**4,222**
20th Army		
20th Army Troops		3,574
58th Infantry Division	172, 173, & 174th	1,541
59th Infantry Division	175, 176, & 177th	2,257
60th Infantry Division	178, 179, & 180th	2,906
		10,278
26th Army		
26th Army Troops		4,200
76th Infantry Division	226, 227, & 228th	3,923
77th Infantry Division	229, 230, & 231st	3,459
78th Infantry Division	232, 233, & 234th	5,602
		17,184
27th Army		
27th Army Troops		3,757
79th Infantry Division	235, 236, & 237th	4,106
80th Infantry Division	238, 239, & 240th	3,252
81st Infantry Division	241, 242, & 243rd	4,668
		15,783
37th Army		
37th Army Troops		3,784
109th Infantry Division	325, 326, & 327th	6,061
111th Infantry Division	331, 332, & 333rd	6,974
		16,819
Total IX Army Group		**64,286**

XIX Army Group (North China Field Army)

    63rd Army

63rd Army Troops		4,275
187th Infantry Division	559, 560, & 561st	2,951
188th Infantry Division	562, 563, & 564th	2,083
189th Infantry Division	565, 566, & 567th	1,994
		11,303
64th Army		
64th Army Troops		4,285
190th Infantry Division	568, 569, & 570th	2,647
191st Infantry Division	571, 572, & 573rd	3,494
192nd Infantry Division	574, 575, & 576th	3,435
		13,861
65th Army		
65th Army Troops		4,329
193rd Infantry Division	577, 578, & 579th	3,831
194th Infantry Division	580, 581, & 582nd	2,445
195th Infantry Division	583, 584, & 585th	3,980
		14,585
Total XIX Army Group		**39,749**

Support Troops	**unknown**
Service and Security Troops	**unknown**
Total CCF Troops in Korea	**264,854+**

NKPA Order of Battle, 27 July 1953[4]

Command/Division/Unit	Regiments	Strength
General Headquarters, NKPA		
21st Infantry Brigade		3,800
23rd Infantry Brigade		3,500
26th Infantry Brigade		5,000
		12,300
I Corps		
I Corps Troops		2,500
8th Infantry Division	81, 82, & 83rd Inf; 8th Arty	8,300
47th Infantry Division	113, 123, & 124th Inf; 35th Arty	9,000
		19,800
II Corps		
II Corps Troops		2,500
2nd Infantry Division	4, 6 & 17th Inf; 2nd Arty	9,500
13th Infantry Division	19, 21, & 23rd Inf; 13th Arty	9,500
27th Infantry Division	172, 173, & 174th Inf; 25th Arty	9,500
24th Infantry Brigade		8,000
		39,000
III Corps		
III Corps Troops		2,500
1st Infantry Division	2, 3, & 14th Inf; 1st Arty	7,200
15th Infantry Division	45, 48, & 50th Inf; 15th Arty	6,900
37th Infantry Division	70, 71, & 76th Inf; 31st Arty	7,800
45th Infantry Division	89, 90, & 91st Inf; 51st Arty	6,600
		31,000
IV Corps		
IV Corps Troops		2,500
4th Infantry Division	5, 18, & 29th Inf; 4th Arty	9,500
5th Infantry Division	10, 11, & 12th Inf; 5th Arty	9,500
10th Infantry Division	25, 27, & 33rd Inf; u/i Arty	7,000
		28,500
V Corps		
V Corps Troops		2,500
6th Infantry Division	1, 13, & 15th Inf; 6th Arty	9,500
12th Infantry Division	30, 31, & 32nd Inf; 12th Arty	9,500
46th Infantry Division	158, 159, & 160th Inf; 66th Arty	9,500
20th Infantry Brigade		3,000
22nd Infantry Brigade		3,000
25th Infantry Brigade		3,000
		40,000

VII Corps
    VII Corps Troops   2,500

VII Corps Troops		2,500
3rd Infantry Division	7, 8, & 9th Inf; 3rd Arty	6,900
7th Infantry Division	51, 53, & 54th Inf; 7th Arty	6,700
9th Infantry Division	85, 86, & 87th Inf; u/i Arty	8,000
	504th Reserve Regiment	2,300
		26,400

Support Troops

Mechanized Branch (including about 7 tank regiments)	5,200
29th Artillery Regiment	1,500
30th Artillery Regiment	1,500
18th Mortar Regiment	800
31st Mortar Regiment	800
u/i Mortar Regiment	800
16th Anti-Aircraft Artillery Division	5,500
21st Anti-Aircraft Artillery Regiment	800
22nd Anti-Aircraft Artillery Regiment	1,000
24th Anti-Aircraft Artillery Gun Regiment	800
32nd Anti-Aircraft Artillery Regiment	800
38th Anti-Aircraft Artillery Regiment	800
52nd Anti-Aircraft Artillery Battalion	300
54th Anti-Aircraft Artillery Battalion	300
55th Anti-Aircraft Artillery Battalion	300
57th Anti-Aircraft Artillery Battalion	300
Total Support Troops	**21,500**

Service Troops

General Headquarters Service Troops	13,500
Engineer Section (including 2 engineer regiments)	2,500
Signal Section (including 2 signal regiments)	4,000
Transportation Section	4,300
1st Railroad Recovery Brigade	7,000
2nd Railroad Recovery Brigade	7,000
Railroad Security Div 5, 6, 7, & 8th RR Security Regts	7,000
Total Service Troops	**43,300**

Total NKPA Troops	**263,800**

CCF Order of Battle, 27 July 1953[5]

Major Command	**Army/Division/Unit**	**Infantry Regiments**	**Strength**
III Army Group			
	12th Army		
	12th Army Troops		5,000
	31st Infantry Division	91, 92, & 93rd	10,800
	34th Infantry Division	100, 101, & 102nd	10,800
	35th Infantry Division	103, 104, & 105th	10,800
			37,400
	15th Army		
	15th Army Troops		5,000
	29th Infantry Division	85, 86, & 87th	10,800
	44th Infantry Division	130, 131, & 132nd	10,800
	45th Infantry Division	133, 134, & 135th	10,800
			37,400
	60th Army		
	60th Army Troops		5,000
	33rd Infantry Division	97, 98, & 99th	8,000
	179th Infantry Division	535, 536,& 537th	4,000
	180th Infantry Division	538, 539, & 540th	3,000
	181st Infantry Division	541, 542, & 543rd	2,000
			22,000
	Total III Army Group		**96,800**
IX Army Group			
	16th Army		
	16th Army Troops		5,000
	32nd Infantry Division	94, 95, & 96th	11,800
	46th Infantry Division	136, 137, & 138th	11,000
	47th Infantry Division	139, 140, & 141st	11,800
			39,600
	23rd Army		
	23rd Army Troops		5,000
	67th Infantry Division	199, 200, & 201st	6,200
	69th Infantry Division	205, 206, & 207th	9,600
	73rd Infantry Division	217, 218, & 219th	8,800
			29,600
	24th Army		
	24th Army Troops		5,000
	70th Infantry Division	208, 209, & 210th	7,800

72nd Infantry Division	214, 215, & 216th	5,000
74th Infantry Division	220, 221, & 222nd	8,300
		26,100

21st Army

21st Army Troops		5,000
61st Infantry Division	181, 182, & 183rd	10,800
62nd Infantry Division	184, 185, & 186th	10,800
63rd Infantry Division	187, 188, & 189th	10,800
		37,400

Total IX Army Group	**132,700**

XIII Army Group

1st Army

1st Army Troops		5,000
1st Infantry Division	1, 2, & 3rd	9,200
2nd Infantry Division	4, 5, & 6th	11,600
7th Infantry Division	19, 20, & 21st	9,900
		35,700

38th Army

38th Army Troops		5,000
112th Infantry Division	334, 335, & 336th	11,800
113th Infantry Division	337, 338, & 339th	11,800
114th Infantry Division	340, 341, & 342nd	11,800
		40,400

40th Army

40th Army Troops		5,000
118th Infantry Division	352, 353, & 354th	10,900
119th Infantry Division	355, 356, & 357th	11,000
120th Infantry Division	358, 359, & 360th	6,400
		33,300

46th Army

46th Army Troops		5,000
133rd Infantry Division	397, 398, & 399th	9,700
136th Infantry Division	406, 407, & 408th	11,400
137th Infantry Division	409, 410, & 411th	11,800
		37,900

47th Army

47th Army Troops		5,000
139th Infantry Division	415, 416, & 417th	10,800
140th Infantry Division	418, 419, & 420th	10,800
141st Infantry Division	421, 422, & 423rd	10,800
		37,400

```
50th Army
    50th Army Troops                                      5,000
    148th Infantry Division    442, 443, & 444th         10,800
    149th Infantry Division    445, 446, & 447th         10,800
    150th Infantry Division    448, 449, & 450th         10,800
                                                         37,400
```

Total XIII Army Group   **222,100**

XIX Army Group
```
    63rd Army
        63rd Army Troops                                  5,000
        187th Infantry Division    559, 560, & 561st     11,800
        188th Infantry Division    562, 563, & 564th     11,800
        189th Infantry Division    565, 566, & 567th     11,800
                                                         40,400
    64th Army
        64th Army Troops                                  5,000
        190th Infantry Division    568, 569, & 570th     11,800
        191st Infantry Division    571, 572, & 573rd     11,800
        192nd Infantry Division    574, 575, & 576th     11,800
                                                         40,400
    65th Army
        65th Army Troops                                  5,000
        193rd Infantry Division    577, 578, & 579th      8,400
        194th Infantry Division    580, 581, & 582nd     10,200
        195th Infantry Division    583, 584, & 585th      8,300
                                                         31,900
```

Total XIX Army Group   **112,700**

XX Army Group
```
    54th Army
        54th Army Troops                                  5,000
        130th Infantry Division    388, 389, & 390th      8,600
        134th Infantry Division    400, 401, & 402nd     11,800
        135th Infantry Division    403, 404, & 405th      3,900
                                                         29,300
    67th Army
        67th Army Troops                                  5,000
        199th Infantry Division    595, 596, & 597th      5,000
        200th Infantry Division    598, 599, & 600th      8,600
        201st Infantry Division    601, 602, & 603rd      4,300
                                                         22,900
```

68th Army
 68th Army Troops 5,000
 202nd Infantry Division 604,.605, & 606th 6,800
 203rd Infantry Division 607, 608, & 609th 5,200
 204th Infantry Division 610, 611, & 612th 5,900
 22,900

    Total XX Army Group **75,100**

Support Troops
 1st Motorized Artillery Div 25, 26, & 27th 6,300
 2nd Motorized Artillery Div 28, 29, 30, & 31st 6,300
 7th Motorized Artillery Div 11, 20, & 21st 6,300
 8th Motorized Artillery Div 45, 46, & 47th 12,000
 31st Antitank Division (-) 2,200
 32nd Antitank Division 3,400
 21st Rocket Division 3,300
 9th Independent Artillery Regiment 2,100
 10th Independent Artillery Regiment 2,100
 40th Artillery Regiment 2,100
 41st Artillery Regiment 2,100
 66th Army Artillery Regiment 2,100
 1st Tank Regiment 800
 6th Tank Regiment 800
 u/i Tank Regiment 800
 Anti-Aircraft Artillery Troops (4 regts and 43 bns) 10,000

    Total Support Troops **62,700**

Headquarters, Security, and Service Troops
 General Headquarters, CCF in Korea 5,000
 General Headquarters Rear Service Department 3,000
 Branch Units (5) 30,000
 Truck Regiments (18) 21,700

 Army Group Headquarters Administrative Personnel 18,000
 81st Chinese Railroad(?) Volunteer Force 4,500

   Total Headquarters, Security, and Service Troops **82,200**

    Total CCF Troops in Korea **784,300**

NOTES

1. Roy E. Appleman, *South to the Naktong, North to the Yalu* (Washington: Office of the Chief of Military History, Department of the Army, 1961), 11 and 263; Headquarters, Department of the Army, Office of the Assistant Chief of Staff, G-2, *North Korean Order of Battle* (Washington: Headquarters, Department of the Army, Office of the Assistant Chief of Staff, G-2, 1 September 1950).

2. General Headquarters, Far East Command, Military Intelligence Service, *Daily Intelligence Summary No. 3234*, 18 July 1951, Chart 2. *NB*: The figure given for "Line of Communications Troops" is obviously too low.

3. General Headquarters, Far East Command, Military Intelligence Section, *Daily Intelligence Summary, No. 3234*, 18 July 1951, Chart 1 (a and b). *NB*: No data given for General Headquarters, Support, or Service and Security units.

4. Headquarters, Eighth United States Army Korea, Office of the Assistant Chief of Staff, G-2, *Intelligence Estimate*, 27 July 1953, Annex P (Strengths and Subordination of Enemy Units), 2.

5. Headquarters, Eighth United States Army Korea, Office of the Assistant Chief of Staff, G-2, *Intelligence Estimate*, 27 July 1953, Annex P (Strengths and Subordination of Enemy Units), 2.

Appendix B

Characteristics of NKPA-CCF
Logistical Vehicles

The NKPA and CCF in Korea used a variety of motor vehicles both as prime movers for artillery and other heavy equipment and to move supplies. Most of the trucks used by the Communist forces in Korea were of Soviet manufacture, and the GAZ-51, GAZ-63, ZIS-150, and ZIS-151 were the most common types.[1] The GAZ type trucks were lighter and were most often assigned to transportation units, while the heavier ZIS models were favored for artillery prime movers. Captured U.S. Dodge and Ford trucks were also favored as prime movers due to their greater horsepower.[2] In many artillery units, the ZIS-150 was used to tow 75/76-mm guns and the ZIS-151 to tow 122-mm howitzers. In some cases, the lighter GAZ-63 was used to tow the 120-mm mortar and light artillery, antitank, and anti-aircraft artillery pieces.[3] Table B.1 displays the characteristics of the most commonly encountered trucks used by the NKPA and CCF in Korea.

Table B.1
Characteristics of Cargo Vehicles Used by the NKPA and CCF in Korea[4]

Model	Type	Weight (ST)	Height × Width × Length (inches)	Wheel Base (inches)	Maximum Speed (mph)	Cruise Range (miles)	Pay Load (ST)	Personnel Capacity
GAZ-51	4 × 2	3	83.8 × 86 × 210	131	44	260	2.2–2.7	12
GAZ-63	4 × 4	3.6	86 × 86 × 210	131	42	285	2.2	12
ZIS-5	4 × 2	3.4	85 × 88 × 238	150	37	110	3.3–4.4	12
ZIS-150	4 × 2	4.3	85 × 93.8 × 265	154	38	300	3.2–4.4	13
ZIS-151	6 × 6	4.5	90 × 92 × 270	165	41	413	3.8–5.0	16
US GMC	6 × 6				55	300	2.5–5.0	25
US Dodge	6 × 6				55	300	2.5–5.0	25

Gasoline was a critical item of supply and was strictly controlled by both the NKPA and CCF in Korea. It is believed that the GAZ-type trucks averaged about 13 kilometers per gallon and the ZIS-type trucks averaged about 7.5 kilometers per gallon.[5] Some vehicles were converted to charcoal burners, and such vehicles consumed about 200 kilograms of charcoal during an average nightly trip of about 30 miles.[6] Table B.2 gives the average fuel consumption data for the most commonly found NKPA-CCF vehicles.

Table B.2
Fuel Consumption of NKPA-CCF Vehicles[7]

Vehicle	Model	Type Fuel	Average Fuel Consumption	
			Miles Per Gallon	Gallons Per 100 Miles
Medium Tank	T-34/T-85	Diesel	1.33	75.00
76-mm SP Gun	SU-76	Gasoline	1.90	52.60
Truck Cargo (4×4)	GAZ-63	Gasoline	9.04	10.50
Truck Cargo (4×4)	GAZ-67B	Gasoline	14.60	6.80
Truck Cargo (4×2)	GAZ-51	Gasoline	10.70	9.30
Truck Cargo (4×2)	ZIS-150	Gasoline	7.90	13.00
Truck Cargo (6×6)	ZIS-151	Gasoline	5.00	20.00

Most of the NKPA and CCF trucks used in Korea were in generally poor condition, and tires were a particular problem. The practical effect of these deficiencies was to reduce the average load size. Artillery units seem to have had priority for maintenance and replacements, and thus vehicle condition was perhaps somewhat better in artillery units than in transportation truck units.

The Chinese were notorious for overloading their available vehicles despite strict orders to the contrary.[8] In most cases, U.S. vehicles could carry more supplies and U.S. standard loads were larger than those of the Chinese, who did not have loading racks built into their trucks and who did not practice the refined loading techniques used by UNC forces.[9] The typical load for a GAZ-51 truck was thirty bags of rice (at 60 kilograms per bag) or 1,800 kilograms of vegetables or ten drums of gasoline (at 155 kilograms per drum).[10] Other common loadings are included in Table B.3.

Table B.3
Common Load Configurations for NKPA-CCF Trucks in Korea[11]

Item	Container	Containers per Truckload	Weight of Container (lb)	Weight of Truckload (lb)
Crackers	50 3-lb cartons in a large wood box	20 boxes	150	ca. 3,000
Salt Pork	wood box	140 boxes	27.2	ca. 2,800
Chow Mein	8–9-lb sacks tied in bundles of five	60 bundles	40–45	ca. 2,440
Soy Sauce	55-gallon drum	10 drums	450	ca. 4,500
Pork Sausage	wood box	120–130 boxes	50	ca. 6,000
Salted Fish	wood box	70–80 boxes	ca. 75	ca. 6,000
Canned Meat	10-oz cans in wood box	80–100 boxes	ca. 60	ca. 6,000
Rice	straw sacks	30 sacks	132	ca. 3,960
Gasoline	55-gallon drums	10 drums	341	ca. 3,410
105-mm shell	3-pack	60 shells	100	ca. 6,000
60-mm mortar shell	12-round wood box	60 boxes	ca. 60	ca. 3,600
82-mm mortar shell	4-rd wood box	60 boxes	44	ca. 2,640
76-mm shell	2-rd wood box	40 boxes	66	ca. 2,640
120-mm mortar shell	carton	48 shells	ca. 40	ca. 1,920
122-mm projectile	each	36 projectiles	ca. 58	ca. 1,988

Sketch B.1
Soviet ZIS-5 4×2 Cargo Truck[12]

DUAL WHEELS

Sketch B.2
Soviet GAZ-51 4×2 Cargo Truck

GAS TANK

DUAL WHEELS

Sketch B.3
Soviet GAZ-63 4×4 Cargo Truck

TOOL BOX

GAS TANKS

Sketch B.4
Soviet ZIS-150 4×2 Cargo Truck

DUAL WHEELS

Sketch B.5
Soviet ZIS-151 6×6 Cargo Truck

SPARE TIRE

DUAL WHEELS

NOTES

1. "Enemy Motor Transport in North Korea," *USAFFE Intelligence Digest*, I, no. 9 (2 May 1953), 35.

2. Headquarters, Eighth United States Army, Assistant Chief of Staff G-2/Headquarters, United States Fifth Air Force, Assistant Chief of Staff A-2, *Supply and Transportation System of the Chinese Communist and North Korean Forces in Korea* ([Tokyo]: Headquarters, Eighth United States Army, Assistant Chief of Staff G-2/Headquarters, United States Fifth Air Force, Assistant Chief of Staff A-2, 23 September 1951), 94.

3. "Enemy Motor Transport in North Korea," 35.

4. General Headquarters, Far East Command, Military Intelligence Section, General Staff, *Material in the Hands of or Possibly Available to the Enemy in Korea* (APO 500: General Headquarters, Far East Command, Military Intelligence Section, General Staff, August 1951)196–205; "A Statistical Comparison of the Mobility of the US and Communist-Bloc Infantry Divisions in the Far East," *USAFFE Intelligence Digest*, VI, no. 4 (April 1956), 10, Chart 14; "Enemy Motor Transport in North Korea," 35; *Supply and Transportation System of the Chinese Communist and North Korean Forces in Korea*, 8–9 and 196–205; Headquarters, United States I Corps, G-2 Section, *CCF Logistical Capabilities: A Study of the Enemy Vehicular Effort on I Corps Front* ([Korea]: Headquarters, U.S. I Corps, 28 June 1952), 2.

5. "Enemy Motor Transport in North Korea," 37.

6. "Enemy Motor Transport in North Korea," 37.

7. "Petroleum, Oils and Lubricants Requirements for Communist Ground Forces, Far East," *USAFFE Intelligence Digest*, V, no. 4 (April 1955), 72 (Table V) based on DA Intelligence Research Project 6990, 15 January 1954, Figure 17. U.S. I Corps transportation units using the GMC 2.5-ton truck reported an overall rate of 5.6 mpg in Korea (see *CCF Logistical Capabilities*, 2).

8. *Logistical Data for the Chinese Communist Army*, 9; *CCF Logistical Capabilities*, Annex 2, page 3.

9. *Logistical Data for the Chinese Communist Army*, 9; *CCF Logistical Capabilities*, Annex 2, page 3.

10. "Enemy Motor Transport in North Korea," 35.

11. *Supply and Transportation System of the Chinese Communist and North Korean Forces in Korea* , 94–95; *CCF Logistical Capabilities*, Annex 2, page 1.

12. Illustrations of Soviet trucks are from General Headquarters, Far East Command, Military Intelligence Section, General Staff, *Material in the Hands of or Possibly Available to the Enemy in Korea* (APO 500: General Headquarters, Far East Command, Military Intelligence Section, General Staff, August 1951).

Abbreviations

AA	Anti-Aircraft
AAA	Anti-Aircraft Artillery
AAMG	Anti-Aircraft Machinegun
Admin	Administration; administrative
Adv	Advanced
Ammo	Ammunition; Class V supplies
Arty	Artillery
AT	Antitank
ATIS	Allied Translator and Interpreter Service
AU	Army Unit (UNC designator for NKPA-CCF units)
Avg	Average
AW	Automatic Weapons
B-26	U.S. light bomber
B-29	U.S. medium/heavy bomber
Basic Load	An amount of rations, POL, ammunition, etc. normally carried by a using unit; usually consists of one or more days of supply/fire depending on the commander's guidance
Bbl.	Barrel = 42 U.S. gallons
Bn	Battalion
Bo An Dae	North Korean Border Constabulary
Branch Unit	Major CCF logistical unit; also known as *Logistical Command*, *Logistical Base*, and *Rear Service Base Headquarters* (RSBH)
Ca.	Circa; about; approximately
Cav	Cavalry

CCA	Chinese Communist Army; the Chinese People's Liberation Army
CCF	Chinese Communist Forces (in Korea)
Cdr	Commander
CINCUNC	Commander-in-Chief, United Nations Command
Class I	Supply Class I: rations and forage
Class II	Supply Class II: individual clothing and equipment; administrative supplies
Class III	Supply Class III: petroleum products
Class IV	Supply Class IV: weapons and equipment; major end items; construction and barrier materials
Class V	Supply Class V: ammunition and explosives
Cloth	Clothing
Cmd	Command; command section
CO	Commander
Co	Company
Commo	Communications
Consumption Factor	A planning factor, usually expressed in terms of lb/man/day and representing one day's supply of a given commodity
Crypto	Cryptological
Ctr	Center
Dept	Department
Div	Division
Division Slice	A planning concept usually expressed as a number of men and representing the number of men in a type division plus a proportionate share of the men at higher echelons (corps, army, theater) providing support to the division
Do	North Korean province
Dodge	U.S. 2 1/2-ton 6×6 cargo truck
DOS/DOF	Days of Supply/Days of Fire; the amount of supplies/ammunition sufficient for one day's operations; may vary according to local conditions and the desires of the commander; usually applied to unit, rather than individual, quantities

Double-Tracked	A railroad term indicating that a line is capable of handling traffic in both directions simultaneously; literally two sets of tracks, often in parallel
DS	Direct Support; providing support directly to customers
EM	Enlisted men
Engr	Engineer
Eq	Equipment
Equip	Equipment
EUSA	Eighth United States Army
EUSAK	Eighth United States Army in Korea
FEAF	United States Far East Air Forces
FEC	United States Far East Command
Fin	Finance
FM	Field Manual
Forage	Subsistence for animals, usually grain and hay
GAZ-51	Soviet truck
GAZ-63	Soviet truck
GAZ-67b	Soviet light truck; similar to the U.S. jeep
Gd	Guard
GHQ	General Headquarters
GMC	General Motors Corporation (2 1/2-ton 6 × 6 cargo truck)
GS	General Support; providing support to other support units
Gun	North Korean county
HMG	Heavy Machinegun
Howz	Howitzer
HQ	Headquarters
Hvy	Heavy
Hwy	Highway
Inf	Infantry
Inland waterway	A system of rivers, canals, lakes, etc. capable of bearing water movements in ships, tugs, barges, steamboats, etc.
Inmun Gun	North Korean People's Army
Intell	Intelligence

Intend	Intendance; Quartermaster
INTSUM	Intelligence Summary
Kaoliang	Sorghum (milo); an important grain component of the CCF ration
Km	Kilometer (10 km = ca. 6 miles)
Lb	Pound or pounds
Line haul	Motor transport operations conducted over a line of communications; normally over 20 miles (32 km) one way
LMG	Light Machinegun
LOC	Line(s) of communication
Local haul	Motor transport operations conducted within a limited area; normally less than 20 miles (32 km) one way
Logistical Base	See *Branch Unit*
Logistical Command	See *Branch Unit*
LT	Long ton: a unit of weight equal to 2,240 lb avoirdupois (1016.106 kilograms); usually divided into 20 hundred-weight (112 lb each); also called a *gross ton*
Maint	Maintenance
Med	Medical
Metric ton	A unit of weight equal to 1,000 kilograms (2,204.62 lb avoirdupois)
MHAB	North Korean Military Highways Administration Bureau
MIG-15	Soviet jet fighter aircraft used by the North Koreans and Chinese
Mil	Military
MLR	Main Line of Resistance; the forward edge of the battle area
Mm	Millimeters
MND	North Korean Ministry of National Defense
MOD	Ministry of Defense
Mort	Mortar
Msgr	Messenger
MSR	Main Supply Route
MTON	Measurement ton: a unit of volume for cargo usually computed at 40 cubic feet but depending on the type of cargo; also called a *freight ton*, *stevedore ton*, or *ship ton*
Mtz	Motorized

Myon	North Korean district
Narrow Gauge	Railroad trackage with rails set less than 56.5 inches apart; 60 cm was a common railroad narrow gauge
NCO	Noncommissioned officer
NKA	North Korean Army
NKPA	North Korean People's Army
Obsvn	Observation
OEM	Officers and Enlisted Men
Opn(s)	Operation(s)
Ord	Ordnance
Org	Organization
Orgz	Organization
Pers	Personnel
PIR	Periodic Intelligence Report
PLA	Chinese People's Liberation Army
POL	Petroleum, oils, and lubricants; may be either in bulk or packaged (in drums)
POW/PW	Prisoner of War
PRC	People's Republic of China
Prov	Provisions; provisional
PX	Post Exchange; personal comfort supplies
QM	Quartermaster
Ration	An amount of food, etc. sufficient for one man for one day
Rcn	Reconnaissance
Recon	Reconnaissance
Regt	Regiment
RL	Rocket Launcher
ROK	Republic of Korea
ROKA	Republic of Korea Army
RR	Railroad
RSBH	See *Branch Unit*
RSD	Rear Services Department
RSS	Rear Service Section
Scty	Security
Sig	Signal

Single-Tracked	A railroad term indicating that a line is capable of handling traffic in only one direction at a time; literally one set of tracks
SMG	Submachinegun
Sortie	One mission or round trip by one aircraft
SP	Self-Propelled
ST	Short ton: a unit of weight equal to 2,000 lb avoirdupois (907.2 kilograms)
Standard Gauge	Railroad trackage with rails set 56.5 inches apart; U.S. railroads are standard gauge
Stockage Objective/	
Stockage Level	A quantity of supplies which it is desired to accumulate/has been accumulated at a storage area to support a given force; usually expressed in terms of days of supply/fire for the number of troops in the supported force; the stockage objective is the desired amount; the stockage level is the amount on hand
SU-76	Soviet self-propelled 76-mm gun
Sup	Supply
Svc	Service
T-34	Soviet medium tank
Tk	Tank
Tng	Training
TOE	Table of Organization and Equipment; a listing of authorized numbers of personnel and amounts of equipment by type
Tp	Telephone
Trans	Transportation; transport
Trk	Truck
UK	United Kingdom
UN	United Nations
UNC	United Nations Command
UOF	Unit of Fire; a concept used by Communist forces to forecast ammunition resupply requirements; an arbitrary quantity of ammunition, the amount of which is determined by the commander based on the tactical situation; similar to U.S. *Day of Fire/Basic Load*
U.S.	United States
USA	United States of America; United States Army
USAFFE	United States Army Forces, Far East

USSR	Union of Soviet Socialist Republics
Vet	Veterinary
WIS	Weekly Intelligence Summary
ZIS-5	Soviet truck
ZIS-150	Soviet truck
ZIS-151	Soviet truck

Symbols

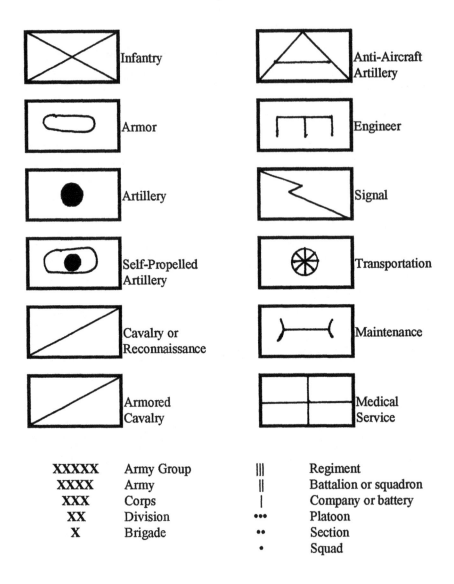

XXXXX	Army Group	|||	Regiment
XXXX	Army	||	Battalion or squadron
XXX	Corps			Company or battery
XX	Division	•••	Platoon
X	Brigade	••	Section
		•	Squad

Selected Bibliography

This bibliography includes studies, articles, books, official documents, and other materials which were found to be of substantial value in the composition of this book. In some cases, works which have not been cited, but which are pertinent to the general subject of NKPA-CCF logistics in the Korean War, are also included.

In the absence of access to North Korean and Chinese Communist documents relating to the logistical support of their forces during the Korean War, the present study has relied heavily on contemporary U.S. and UNC intelligence estimates, studies, orders of battle, and other documents. From 1950 to 1953 and for several years thereafter, the higher level U.S. and UNC headquarters concerned with the management of the war in Korea produced a large volume of material related to the size, organization, doctrine, and methods of the NKPA and CCF in Korea. Much of this material is contained in *Daily Intelligence Summaries (INTSUM)*, *Weekly Intelligence Summaries (WIS)*, *Periodic Intelligence Reports (PIR)*, and other intelligence documents produced by the offices of the Assistant Chief of Staff, G-2, at General Headquarters, United States Far East Command; Headquarters, United States Army Forces, Far East; and Headquarters, Eighth United States Army. The articles contained in the *Intelligence Digest* published by the G-2 Section of United States Far East Command (and continued by the G-2 Section, United States Army Forces, Far East) are an especially rich source of material on Communist logistical organizations, requirements, and methods during the Korean War. Of particular use in this study were the *History of the North Korean Army* published by the Military Intelligence Section of General Headquarters, Far East Command, and *Supply and Transportation System of the Chinese Communist and North Korean Forces in Korea* published by the Assistant Chief of Staff, G-2, Headquarters, Eighth United States Army; and the Assistant Chief of Staff, A-2, Headquarters, United States Fifth Air Force. One cautionary note is necessary regarding the accounts published by U.S. and UNC intelligence agencies during the Korean

War. The data contained in these documents are often unclear, uncertain, or inconsistent with other materials. The reason for such inaccuracy is, of course, that such materials were produced under the pressure of ongoing combat operations and thus reflect the lack of reliable intelligence regarding enemy order of battle, organization, and methods. In general, the FEC, USAFFE, and EUSAK materials published in 1953 are more accurate and complete than those published early in the war.

Headquarters, Department of the Army, also published a number of useful items, including a number of excellent handbooks on Korea and on the Chinese Communist forces. The Korean area handbooks contain basic geographical, climatological, and topological data as well as important information on industry, commerce, and government in both North and South Korea. Another excellent, semiofficial source is the collection of historical studies published by the Operations Research Office, Johns Hopkins University, for the United States Army in the 1950s. Most of the so-called "ORO" studies focus on U.S. and UNC activities, but many of them also include pertinent material on North Korean and Chinese Communist organizations and operations. Of particular value is the 1951 study by E. L. Atkins, H. P. Griggs, and Roy T. Sessums entitled *North Korean Logistics and Methods of Accomplishment.*

The official histories of the Korean War published by the various United States armed forces also provide excellent information on NKPA and CCF logistical activities. The official Army history volumes by Appleman, Hermes, Mossman, and Schnabel are excellent for background and comparative information. Perhaps the most useful official history is the Air Force history of the Korean War by Robert Frank Futrell, who deals extensively with the air interdiction effort. The official Navy history by James A. Field, Jr., is also valuable with respect to the air interdiction campaign.

There is no single reliable major study of North Korea, 1950–1953, or of the North Korean People's Army in the Korean War period. However, the series of captured documents and prisoner of war interrogation reports published by the Allied Translator and Interpreter Service of General Headquarters, Far East Command, are very useful for filling in gaps in our knowledge of basic North Korean government and military organization and methods. On the other hand, the Chinese People's Liberation Army and the Chinese Communist Forces in Korea have been the subject of several excellent books by civilian scholars such as George, Gittings, Griffith, Rigg, Spurr, and Whiting. I have relied heavily on these works for descriptions of CCF organization and logistical operations.

The present study is incomplete in one important respect. The North Korean and Chinese documents relating to the logistical support of the NKPA and CCF in Korea remain unavailable, and thus the story had to be told principally from the U.S./UNC perspective. This study might also have been improved by the use of still classified U.S./UNC materials. Although I have reviewed and used a large number of now declassified contemporary documents and studies, I have made no attempt to investigate those materials on enemy logistics contained in

U.S. and UNC official documents which still remain classified. Nor have I had access to any of the signals intelligence produced by U.S. and UN forces during the Korean War. It was decided early in the research phase of this project that classified materials would not be used in order to insure that the final product could receive the widest possible dissemination. When Western historians can gain access to NKPA and CCF documents as well as additional declassified U.S./UNC materials, this brief history of NKPA and CCF logistics in the Korean War will have to be fundamentally revised. Until that time, however, it may serve as a useful summary of the current open sources on the subject.

Appleman, Roy E. *South to the Naktong, North to the Yalu.* (United States Army in the Korean War). Washington: Office of the Chief of Military History, Department of the Army, 1961. *Official Army history.*

Arozian, John P. *An Analysis of North Korean LOC.* Washington: Defense Intelligence Agency, April 1980.

Atkins, E. L., H. P. Griggs, and Roy T. Sessums. *North Korean Logistics and Methods of Accomplishment.* (ORO Technical Memorandum ORO-T-8 [EUSAK]). Chevy Chase, MD: Operations Research Office, The Johns Hopkins University, 1951. 88 pages.

Black, R. B., W. A. Taylor, and William Neilson. *An Evaluation of Service Support in the Korean Campaign.* (ORO Technical Memorandum ORO-T-6 [FEC]). APO 500: Operations Research Office, The Johns Hopkins University, March 1951. 243 pages. *U.S./UN focus.*

Blair, Clay. *The Forgotten War: America in Korea, 1950–1953.* New York: Times Books, 1987. 1136 pages. *General history of the Korean War.*

Blanchard, Carroll H., Jr. *Korean War Bibliography and Maps of Korea.* Albany, NY: Korean Conflict Research Foundation, 1964. 181 pages.

Cagle, Malcolm W., and Frank A. Manson. *The Sea War in Korea.* Annapolis, MD: U.S. Naval Institute Press, 1957.

Carr, Gerard H. *The Chinese Red Army.* New York: Schocken, 1974.

Carter, Gregory A. *Some Historical Notes on Air Interdiction in Korea.* Santa Monica, CA: The RAND Corporation, September 1966.

Chilimuniya, Avrosimov, and Shih-ku-li-tieh-tzu. *Chinese Communist General Principles of Army Group Tactics.* 2 volumes. Manila: General Headquarters, Far East Command, Military Intelligence Section, General Staff, 1951. *Translation of a captured document outlining Soviet military doctrine as adapted by the PLA.*

Chou Ching-wen. *Ten Years of Storm.* New York: Holt, Rinehart and Winston, 1960. *Memoir of a Chinese Communist general.*

Cohen, Eliot A., and John Gooch, *Military Misfortunes: The Anatomy of Failure in War.* New York: Vintage Books, 1991. *Contains a chapter on the failure of U.S./UNC intelligence agencies to detect the infiltration of the CCF into Korea in October 1950.*

Collier, Harry H., and Paul Chin-Chih Lai. *Organizational Changes in the Chinese Army, 1895–1950.* 2nd edition. Taipei: Office of the Military Historian, May 1969. 414 pages.

Collins, J. Lawton. *War in Peacetime.* Boston: Houghton Mifflin, 1969. *Memoir of the U.S. Army Chief of Staff during the Korean War.*

Davison, W. Phillips, and Jean Hungerford. *North Korean Guerrilla Units.* (RAND-RM-550). Santa Monica, CA: The RAND Corporation, 21 February 1951. 7 pages.

Dean, William F. *General Dean's Story.* New York: Viking Press, 1954. *Memoir of the U.S. general who commanded the U.S. 24th Infantry Division in Korea in July 1950.*

Domes, Juergen. *Peng Te-huai: The Man and the Image.* Stanford, CA: Stanford University Press, 1985. *Biography of the CCF commander in Korea.*

Dowling, Patrick M., Thomas H. Tudor, and Theodore G. Schad. *The Vulnerability of Army Supply to Air Interdiction.* (ORO Technical Memorandum ORO-T-46 [FEC]). Chevy Chase, MD: Operations Research Office, The Johns Hopkins University, 1 April 1953. 326 pages. *U.S./UN focus, but contains some interesting material on NKPA-CCF countermeasures.*

Fehrenbach, T. R. *This Kind of War: A Study in Unpreparedness.* Revised edition. New York: Bantam Books, 1991. 684 pages. *Well-known general history of the Korean War.*

Field, James A., Jr. *History of United States Naval Operations: Korea.* Washington: U.S. GPO, 1962. *Official Navy history of the Korean War.*

Futrell, Robert Frank. *The United States Air Force in Korea, 1950–1953.* Revised edition. Washington: Office of Air Force History, 1983. *Official Air Force history of the Korean War.*

General Headquarters, Far East Command, Military Intelligence Section, Allied Translator and Interpreter Service. "Enemy Documents, Korean Operations," *ATIS Research Supplement*, Issue No. 5 (13 December 1950). 132 pages. *Consists of a translation of a manual entitled "Staff Department Field Manual" issued by National Defense Bureau, North Korean Democratic Republic, in 1949 (captured in the vicinity of Tuksong-dong, 12 August 1950).*

_____. "Enemy Documents, Korean Operations," *ATIS Research Supplement*, Issue No. 9 (10 April 1951). *Consists of a translation of a manual entitled "Combat Handbook" produced by General Staff Section, National Defense Ministry, North Korean Democratic Republic, in 1949 and captured at Pyongyang, 1 November 1950.*

_____. "Interrogation Reports—North Korean Forces: North Korean Logistics," *ATIS Research Supplement*, Issue No. 1 (19 October 1950), 17–27. *Important source of basic information.*

_____. "Interrogation Reports—North Korean Forces: Typical North Korean Infantry Division," *ATIS Research Supplement*, Issue No. 1 (19 October 1950), 3–15. *Important source of basic information.*

General Headquarters, Far East Command, Military Intelligence Section, General Staff. *History of the North Korean Army.* Tokyo: General Headquarters, Far East Command, Military Intelligence Section, General Staff, 31 July 1952. *Very useful.*

General Headquarters, Far East Command, Military Intelligence Section, General Staff. *FEC Daily Intelligence Summary.* Daily; 1950–1955. *Series includes important material on NKPA-CCF logistics. Individual issues are cited in the text but are not listed separately in this bibliography.*

_____. *FEC Intelligence Digest* Semimonthly; Issues nos. 1–36, 17 June 1951–2 December 1952. [Continued as *USAFFE Intelligence Digest*]. *Series includes important material on NKPA-CCF logistics. Individual articles are listed below by title under Headquarters, United States Army Forces, Far East (Advanced), Office of the Assistant Chief of Staff, G-2, USAFFE* Intelligence Digest.

_____. *Logistical Capability of Communist Forces in Korea to Support a Major Offensive.* APO 500: General Headquarters, Far East Command, Military Intelligence Section, Office of the Assistant Chief of Staff, J-2, 28 February 1953. *Important source.*

_____. *Material in the Hands of or Possibly Available to the Enemy in Korea.* APO 500: General Headquarters, Far East Command, Military Intelligence Section, General Staff, August 1951. 269 pages. *Contains illustrations of most Communist weapons and vehicles used in Korea.*

_____. *Uniform, Insignia, Equipment—North Korean Army.* Tokyo: General Headquarters, Far East Command, Military Intelligence Section, General Staff, August 1950. 52 pages.

General Headquarters, Far East Command, Military Intelligence Section, Intelligence Division. *Order of Battle Information, Chinese Communist Regular Ground Forces (China, Manchuria, and Korea).* Tokyo: General Headquarters, Far East Command, Military Intelligence Section, Intelligence Division, 9 December 1951.

General Headquarters, Far East Command, Military Intelligence Section, Theater Intelligence Division, Operations Branch. *Order of Battle Information: Chinese Communist Third Field Army.* Tokyo: General Headquarters, Far East Command, Military Intelligence Section, Theater Intelligence Division, Operations Branch, August 1950.

General Headquarters, Far East Command, Military Intelligence Section, Theater Intelligence Division, Order of Battle Branch. *Order of Battle Information: Chinese Communist Forces in Korea, Table of Organization and Equipment.* Tokyo: General Headquarters, Far East Command, Military Intelligence Section, Theater Intelligence Division, Order of Battle Branch, 30 October 1951.

George, Alexander L. *The Chinese Communist Army in Action: The Korean War and Its Aftermath.* New York: Columbia University Press, 1967. 255 pages.

Gittings, John. *The Role of the Chinese Army.* New York: Oxford University Press, 1967. 331 pages. *Excellent study.*

Goulden, Joseph C. *Korea: The Untold Story of the War.* New York: Times Books, 1982. *General history of the Korean War.*

Griffith, Samuel B., II. *The Chinese People's Liberation Army.* New York: McGraw-Hill Book Company for the Council on Foreign Relations, 1967. 394 pages. *Excellent study.*

Gunn, William A. *A Study of the Effectiveness of Air Support Operations in Korea.* (ORO Technical Memorandum ORO-T-13). APO 500: Operations Research Office, The Johns Hopkins University, 1951. 39 pages. *U.S./UNC focus.*

Harris, Frank J. *Training the Combat Rifleman in the Chinese Communist Forces and North Korean Army.* (ORO Technical Memorandum ORO-T-52 [FEC]). Chevy

Chase, MD: Operations Research Office, The Johns Hopkins University, March 1954.

Hastings, Max. *The Korean War.* New York: Simon and Schuster, 1987. *General history of the Korean War.*

Headquarters, Army Field Forces, G-2 Section. *Impressions of North Korean Divisions (Gained from Hasty Analysis of 252 Interrogations of Prisoners of War Received To-date).* Washington: Headquarters, Army Field Forces, 21 August 1950.

Headquarters, Army Service Forces, Office of the Director of Plans and Operations, Planning Division, Strategic Logistics Branch. *Ability of the Japanese to Maintain Themselves in China, Manchuria, and Korea.* (Report 13: *Economic Study*, Part 9). Washington: Headquarters, Army Service Forces, 21 October 1944. *Interesting background data.*

Headquarters, Department of the Army. *Area Handbook for Korea.* (DA Pamphlet No. 550-41). Washington: U.S. GPO, November 1964. 595 pages. *Essential basic information.*

Headquarters, Department of the Army. *Handbook on the Chinese Communist Army.* (DA Pamphlet No. 30-51). Washington: U.S. GPO, 1952. *Essential basic information.*

Headquarters, Department of the Army, Office of the Assistant Chief of Staff, G-2. *Estimate of the North Korean Capability to Reinforce Their Organized Forces by the Spring of 1951.* (Intelligence Staff Study No. 6018). Washington: Headquarters, Department of the Army, Office of the Assistant Chief of Staff, G-2, 16 October 1950. *Contemporary study of North Korean capabilities after Inchon.*

_____. *North Korean Order of Battle.* (Intelligence Research Project No. 5942). Washington: Headquarters, Department of the Army, Office of the Assistant Chief of Staff, G-2, 1 September 1950. *One of the few available documents on the NKPA in 1950.*

_____. *The Pre-Inchon North Korean People's Army.* (Intelligence Research Project No. 6231). Washington: Headquarters, Department of the Army, Office of the Assistant Chief of Staff, G-2, 5 March 1951. *Contemporary study of North Korean order of battle at the start of the Korean War.*

_____. *Area Analysis Data.* Irregular; June 1950–September 1953. *Series includes important material on NKPA-CCF logistics.*

_____. *Intelligence Review.* Monthly; June 1950–September 1953. *Series includes important material on NKPA-CCF logistics. Important individual articles listed immediately below.*

_____. "Artillery in the Chinese Communist Army," *Intelligence Review*, 195 (August 1952), 34.

_____. "Chinese Communist Army Develops into Effective Force of 3,500,000," *Intelligence Review*, 201 (February 1953), 86 and 95.

_____. "The Communist Forces' Logistic Movement in Korea," *Intelligence Review*, 191 (April 1952), 16–17.

_____. "The Communists' Military Buildup in North Korea," *Intelligence Review*, 196 (September 1952), 20.

_____. "Increased Firepower in Chinese Communist Infantry Units," *Intelligence Review*, 198 (November 1952), 38–42.

Headquarters, Department of the Army, Office of the Assistant Chief of Staff, G-2. "Munitions Production in Communist China," *Intelligence Review*, 184 (September 1951), 47–49.

_____. "Soviet Armament Aid to Korea," *Intelligence Review*, 200 (January 1953), 9.

_____. *Korea—Basic Intelligence Summary (Tentative)*. Washington: Headquarters, Department of the Army, Office of the Assistant Chief of Staff, G-2, 18 July 1950. 72 pages. *Forerunner of the area handbook.*

_____. *Korea Handbook*. Washington: Headquarters, Department of the Army, Office of the Assistant Chief of Staff, G-2, September 1950. 118 pages. *Essential data.*

_____. *Weekly Intelligence Reports*. Weekly; nos. 1–75 (25 February 1949–28 July 1950). *Series includes important material on NKPA-CCF logistics.*

Headquarters, Department of the Army, Office of the Assistant Chief of Staff for Intelligence. *Logistical Data for the Chinese Communist Army*. Washington: Headquarters, Department of the Army, Office of the Assistant Chief of Staff for Intelligence, 1959. *Excellent data for post-Korean War period but useful indicator of the situation, 1950–1953.*

Headquarters, Eighth United States Army. *Combat Information Bulletin No. 1*. Korea: Headquarters, Eighth United States Army, 1950. *Series includes important material on NKPA-CCF logistics.*

_____. *Command Report*. Monthly; June 1950–September 1953. *Series includes important material on NKPA-CCF logistics.*

Headquarters, Eighth United States Army, Office of the Assistant Chief of Staff, G-2. *Intelligence Estimate, 27 July 1953*. APO 301: Headquarters, Eighth United States Army, Office of the Assistant Chief of Staff, G-2, 27 July 1953. *Very useful summary of the situation at the time the Armistice went into effect.*

Headquarters, Eighth United States Army, Assistant Chief of Staff G-2/Headquarters, United States Fifth Air Force, Assistant Chief of Staff A-2. *Supply and Transportation System of the Chinese Communist and North Korean Forces in Korea*. Tokyo: Headquarters, Eighth United States Army, Assistant Chief of Staff G-2/Headquarters, United States Fifth Air Force, Assistant Chief of Staff A-2, 23 September 1951. 108 pages. *Important source, but must be used with care inasmuch as some data collected early in the Korean War later proved inaccurate.*

Headquarters, Eighth United States Army in Korea. *Armor Bulletin No. 5*. Korea: Headquarters, Eighth United States Army Korea, June 1952. *Series includes some important material on NKPA-CCF logistics.*

Headquarters, Eighth United States Army Korea, Historical Section and Eighth Army Historical Service Detachment (Provisional). *Logistical Problems and Their Solutions*. APO 301: Headquarters, Eighth United States Army Korea, 1952. 105 pages. *U.S./UN focus.*

Headquarters, Eighth United States Army in Korea, Office of the Assistant Chief of Staff, G-2. *Periodic Intelligence Report*. Irregular; June 1950–September 1953. *Series includes important material on NKPA-CCF logistics.*

_____. *Weekly Intelligence Summary*. Weekly; July 1950–September 1953. *Series includes important material on NKPA-CCF logistics.*

Headquarters, Eighth United States Army in Korea, Office of the Assistant Chief of Staff, G-2. "Statistical Summary on Friendly and Enemy Personnel and Materiel," Inclosure No. 5 to EUSAK G-2 *Weekly Intelligence Summary No. 6*, 6 September 1953.

Headquarters, Eighth United States Army in Korea, Office of the Assistant Chief of Staff, G-2, Order of Battle Branch. *CCF Army Histories*. Korea: Headquarters, Eighth U.S. Army in Korea, Office of the Assistant Chief of Staff, G-2, Order of Battle Branch, 1 December 1954. *Very useful.*

Headquarters, Eighth United States Army in Korea, Office of the Assistant Chief of Staff, G-2, Research and Analysis Branch. *Weaknesses of the Communist Forces in Korea*. (Staff Study). APO 301: Headquarters, Eighth United States Army, Office of the Assistant Chief of Staff, G-2, Research and Analysis Branch, 1 October 1952. 16 pages.

Headquarters, Far East Air Forces. *Report on the Korean War.* 2 volumes. Tokyo: Headquarters, Far East Air Forces, 26 March 1954. *Official report; important for data on the UNC air interdiction effort.*

Headquarters, United States Air Force. *Air Intelligence Digest.* Monthly; June 1950–September 1953. *Series includes important material on NKPA-CCF logistics.*

Headquarters, United States Army Forces, Far East (Advanced), Office of the Assistant Chief of Staff, G-2. *Chinese Communist Ground Forces in Korea: Tables of Organization and Equipment.* APO 500: Headquarters, United States Army Forces, Far East (Advanced), Office of the Assistant Chief of Staff, G-2, 1 March 1953.

_____. *Chinese Communist Ground Forces in Korea: Unit and Personality List.* APO 500: Headquarters, United States Army Forces Far East (Advanced), Office of the Assistant Chief of Staff G-2, 20 March 1953.

_____. *Chinese Communist Ground Forces in Korea: Unit and Personality List.* APO 500: Headquarters, United States Army Forces Far East (Advanced), Office of the Assistant Chief of Staff G-2, 30 November 1953.

_____. *USAFFE Intelligence Digest.* Bimonthly, then monthly. January 1953–April 1956+ [Continues *FEC Intelligence Digest*]. *Contains very important material on NKPA and CCF logistics. The more important articles from the* FEC/ USAFFE Intelligence Digest *are listed immediately below.*

_____. "Armor Support in the Chinese Communist Ground Forces," *USAFFE Intelligence Digest*, V, no. 3 (March 1955), 21–40.

_____. "Artillery Regiment, Infantry Division, Chinese Communist Ground Forces," *USAFFE Intelligence Digest*, V, no. 2 (February 1955), 1–8.

_____. "Artillery Support in Chinese Communist Ground Forces," *USAFFE Intelligence Digest*, V, no. 2 (February 1955), 9–32.

_____. "The BAM Railroad Today—A Reconsideration of Trans-Siberian Rail Alternates," *USAFFE Intelligence Digest*, V, no. 10 (October 1955), 11–14.

_____. "Camouflage as Employed by Communist Forces in Korea," *USAFFE Intelligence Digest*, IV, no. 2 (April 1954), 15–32.

_____. "Capability of the Soviet Far Eastern Rail Net," *USAFFE Intelligence Digest*, VI, no. 4 (April 1956), 12–21.

_____. "The Chinese Communist Army—Two Years After Korea," *USAFFE Intelligence Digest*, V, no. 9 (September 1955), 35–42.

Headquarters, United States Army Forces, Far East (Advanced), Office of the Assistant Chief of Staff, G-2. "Chinese Communist Army and North Korean Army Logistics and Class Supply," *USAFFE Intelligence Digest*, VI, no. 4 (April 1956), 49–68.

_____. "Chinese Communist Army Supply System," *USAFFE Intelligence Digest*, IV, no. 4 (June 1954), 31–46.

_____. "Chinese Communist Capability to Reinforce North Korea," *USAFFE Intelligence Digest*, IV, no. 6 (August 1954), 19–22.

_____. "The Chinese Communist Field Army," *USAFFE Intelligence Digest*, V, no. 10 (October 1955), 1–6.

_____. "Chinese Communist Forces Deployment in Korea," *USAFFE Intelligence Digest*, IV, no. 8 (October 1954), 23–24.

_____. "The Chinese Communist Forces Winter Uniform from 1950 to 1954," *USAFFE Intelligence Digest*, IV, no. 6 (August 1954), 27–34.

_____. "The Chinese Communist Ground Forces," *USAFFE Intelligence Digest*, IV, no. 7 (September 1954), 17–24.

_____. "Chinese Communist Ground Forces: Order of Battle Estimate on Field Forces—Trends and Apparent Changes in Organization," *USAFFE Intelligence Digest*, I, no. 12 (17 June 1953), 23–46.

_____. "Chinese Communist Munitions Facilities," *USAFFE Intelligence Digest*, II, no. 7 (17 October 1953), 7–25.

_____. "Chinese Communist Road and Rail Reinforcement Capabilities in Korea," *USAFFE Intelligence Digest*, VI, no. 2 (February 1956), 13–19.

_____. "Chinese Rail Net—Still A Major Military Weakness," *USAFFE Intelligence Digest*, V, no. 7 (July 1955), 1–6.

_____. "Civil Air Transport in Communist China," *USAFFE Intelligence Digest*, V, no. 3 (March 1955), 43–46.

_____. "Communist China's Logistical Hurdle: The Sino-Soviet Frontier," *USAFFE Intelligence Digest*, V, no. 9 (September 1955), 1–5.

_____. "Comparison Between North Korean and Republic of Korea Armies," *USAFFE Intelligence Digest*, V, no. 6 (June 1955), 49–62.

_____. "Current Intelligence: Indications and Capabilities, 25 June 1955," *USAFFE Intelligence Digest*, V, no. 7 (July 1955), v–vi.

_____. "Current Intelligence: Indications and Capabilities, 25 June to 25 September 1955," *USAFFE Intelligence Digest*, V, no. 10 (October 1955), vi–viii.

_____. "Current Intelligence: Indications and Capabilities, 25 September to 25 December 1955," *USAFFE Intelligence Digest*, VI, no. 1 (January 1956), 1–7.

_____. "Current Status and Adequacy of Chinese Communist Railroads," *USAFFE Intelligence Digest*, IV, no. 3 (May 1954), 3–8.

_____. "Effect of the Armistice on Enemy Logistics in North Korea, Part I: Enemy Transport Facilities," *USAFFE Intelligence Digest*, IV, no. 6 (August 1954), 3–18.

_____. "Effect of the Armistice on Enemy Logistics in North Korea, Part II: Enemy Supply System and Logistics Requirements in North Korea," *USAFFE Intelligence Digest*, IV, no. 8 (October 1954), 25–32.

_____. "Enemy Artillery Capabilities," *USAFFE Intelligence Digest*, I, no. 8 (17 April 1953), 25–31.

Headquarters, United States Army Forces, Far East (Advanced), Office of the Assistant Chief of Staff, G-2. "Enemy Motor Transport in North Korea," *USAFFE Intelligence Digest*, I, no. 9 (2 May 1953), 29–49.

_____. "The Enemy Supply System in North Korea," *USAFFE Intelligence Digest*, II, no. 4 (2 September 1953), 15–34.

_____. "Far East Trends, January–June 1955," *USAFFE Intelligence Digest*, V, no. 7 (July 1955), 17–20.

_____. "Food Supply in the Communist Far East," *USAFFE Intelligence Digest*, VI, no. 1 (January 1956), 13–16.

_____. "Foreign Aid and Reconstruction in North Korea," *USAFFE Intelligence Digest*, V, no. 6 (June 1955), 11–26.

_____. "Grain Stockpiling in Communist China," *USAFFE Intelligence Digest*, II, no. 5 (17 September 1953), 13–26.

_____. "Histories of Chinese Communist Forces Army Groups Active in Korea, Part I: III CCF Army Group," *USAFFE Intelligence Digest*, I, no. 1 (2 January 1953), 31–37.

_____. "Histories of Chinese Communist Forces Army Groups Active in Korea, Part II: Ninth Army Group," *USAFFE Intelligence Digest*, I, no. 3 (2 February 1953), 32–37.

_____. "Histories of Chinese Communist Forces Army Groups Active in Korea, Part III: Thirteenth Army Group," *USAFFE Intelligence Digest*, I, no. 4 (17 February 1953), 26–38.

_____. "Histories of Chinese Communist Forces Army Groups Active in Korea, Part IV: Nineteenth Army Group," *USAFFE Intelligence Digest*, I, no. 5 (2 March 1953), 27–32.

_____. "Histories of Chinese Communist Forces Army Groups Active in Korea, Part V: Twentieth CCF Army Group," *USAFFE Intelligence Digest*, I, no. 6 (17 March 1953), 23–26.

_____. "Individual Histories, Chinese Communist Support and Service Units," *FEC Intelligence Digest*, 26 (2 July 1952), 44–54.

_____. "Industrial Progress in Manchuria," *USAFFE Intelligence Digest*, IV, no. 2 (April 1954), 53–64.

_____. "Internal Transport Systems of North Vietnam—Their Military Significance," *USAFFE Intelligence Digest*, VI, no. 2 (February 1956), 1–12.

_____. "The Logistical Capability of the Chinese Communist Ground Forces on the Offshore Front," *USAFFE Intelligence Digest*, V, no. 11 (November 1955), 8–14.

_____. "Manchurian Highway Logistic Capabilities," *USAFFE Intelligence Digest*, IV, no. 1 (March 1954), 51–58.

_____. "Manpower in North Korea," *USAFFE Intelligence Digest*, V, no. 4 (April 1955), 11–18.

_____. "Medical Support in North Korea," *USAFFE Intelligence Digest*, II, no. 11 (17 December 1953), 7–46.

_____. "Military Supply in North Korea," *USAFFE Intelligence Digest*, V, no. 10 (October 1955), 40–44.

_____. "North Korean Railroad Security Division," *USAFFE Intelligence Digest*, I, no. 2 (17 January 1953), 25–29.

Headquarters, United States Army Forces, Far East (Advanced), Office of the Assistant Chief of Staff, G-2. "North Korean Underground Industry," *USAFFE Intelligence Digest*, II, no. 5 (17 September 1953), 1–12.

_____. "North Korean-Manchurian Electric Power Transmission to Eastern Siberia," *USAFFE Intelligence Digest*, II, no. 6 (2 October 1953), 13–14.

_____. "Order of Battle, Communist Ground Forces, Far East, April 1952," *FEC Intelligence Digest*, 21 (2 April 1952), 47–69.

_____. "Pattern of Enemy Frontline Activities, 1 September 1952 to Date," *USAFFE Intelligence Digest*, I, no. 8 (17 April 1953), 7–13.

_____. "Petroleum, Oils and Lubricants Requirements for Communist Ground Forces, Far East," *USAFFE Intelligence Digest*, V, no. 4 (April 1955), 67–74.

_____. "POL Vulnerability, Soviet Far East," *USAFFE Intelligence Digest*, VI, no. 4 (April 1956), 23–30.

_____. "Railroads and Highway Transport in North Korea and Their Impact on Enemy Logistics," *USAFFE Intelligence Digest*, I, no. 13 (2 July 1953), 25–45.

_____. "Recent Developments in the Chinese Communist Economy," *USAFFE Intelligence Digest*, V, no. 3 (March 1955), 41–42.

_____. "Reconstruction in North Korea," *USAFFE Intelligence Digest*, IV, no. 2 (April 1954), 33–40.

_____. "Selected Intelligence Items during Period 16 June–30 June 1952," *FEC Intelligence Digest*, 26 (2 July 1952), iii, v–vi, 17–19, and 44–54.

_____. "Soviet Artillery Developments," *USAFFE Intelligence Digest*, V, no. 10 (October 1955), 7–10.

_____. "Soviet Assistance to North Korean Forces Subsequent to 1948," *USAFFE Intelligence Digest*, I, no. 11 (2 June 1953), 23–28.

_____. "A Statistical Comparison of Communications in the U.S. and Communist-Bloc Infantry Divisions in the Far East," *USAFFE Intelligence Digest*, VI, no. 2 (February 1956), 1–12.

_____. "A Statistical Comparison of the Mobility of the U.S. and Communist-Bloc Infantry Divisions in the Far East," *USAFFE Intelligence Digest*, VI, no. 4 (April 1956), 1–11.

_____. "A Statistical Comparison of U.S. and Communist Bloc Infantry Divisions in the Far East," *USAFFE Intelligence Digest*, V, no. 11 (November 1955), 1–7.

_____. "Transportation Developments in Communist China," *USAFFE Intelligence Digest*, II, no. 7 (17 October 1953), 49–54.

Headquarters, United States Army Forces, Far East, and Eighth United States Army (Rear), Office of the Assistant Chief of Staff, G-2. *Order of Battle Handbook—Chinese Communist Forces, Korea, and the North Korean Army.* APO 343: Headquarters, United States Army Forces, Far East, and Eighth United States Army (Rear), Office of the Assistant Chief of Staff, G-2, 1 January 1956. 71 pages.

_____. *Principal North Korean Army Personalities.* APO 343: Headquarters, United States Army Forces, Far East, and Eighth United States Army (Rear), Office of the Assistant Chief of Staff, G-2, 1 January 1957.

Headquarters, United States Army Forces Far East (Advanced), and Eighth United States Army (Rear). *Logistics in the Korean Operations.* 4 volumes. Tokyo: Headquarters, United States Army Forces Far East (Advanced), and Eighth United States Army (Rear), December 1955. *U.S./UN focus.*

Headquarters, United States Army Forces Far East (Advanced), and Eighth United States Army (Rear). *Chinese Communist Ground Forces: Tables of Organization and Equipment.* APO 343: Headquarters, United States Army Forces, Far East (Advanced), and Eighth United States Army (Rear), Office of the Assistant Chief of Staff, G-2, 1955.

_____. *Intelligence Estimate Korea (March 1955).* APO 343: Headquarters, United States Army Forces, Far East (Advanced), and Eighth United States Army (Rear), Office of the Assistant Chief of Staff, G-2, 3 March 1955.

Headquarters, United States Army Pacific, Office of the Assistant Chief of Staff, G-2. *Tables of Organization and Equipment—Chinese Communist Ground Forces.* APO 958: Headquarters, United States Army Pacific, Office of the Assistant Chief of Staff, G-2, 1958.

Headquarters, United States I Corps, G-2 Section. *CCF and NK Code Numbers, Code Names, Personalities, Road Markers.* 7 sections. Korea: Headquarters, United States I Corps, G-2 Section, February 1952.

_____. *CCF Logistical Capabilities: A Study of the Enemy Vehicular Effort on I Corps Front.* Korea: Headquarters, United States I Corps, G-2 Section, 28 June 1952. 19 pages. *Interesting detailed study.*

Headquarters, United States IX Corps. *Combat Notes Nos. 1–3.* Korea: Headquarters, United States IX Corps, 14 April and 7–12 June 1951. *Series includes important material on NKPA-CCF logistics.*

Headquarters, United States IX Corps, G-2 Section. *Enemy Tactics, Techniques and Doctrine.* Korea: Headquarters, United States IX Corps, September 1951.

Headquarters, United States X Corps. *Organization Charts, Strength of Units, Weapons Tables, Korea, April 1953.* Korea: Headquarters, United States X Corps, April 1953.

Hermes, Walter G. *Truce Tent and Fighting Front.* (United States Army in the Korean War). Washington: Office of the Chief of Military History, Department of the Army, 1966. *Official Army history.*

Huston, James A. *Guns and Butter, Powder and Rice: U.S. Army Logistics in the Korean War.* Selinsgrove, PA: Susquehanna University Press, 1989. 492 pages. *Best study of U.S. Army logistics in the Korean War; includes important chapter on NKPA-CCF logistics.*

_____. "Korea and Logistics," *Military Review*, 36, no. 2 (February 1957), 18–32. *U.S. focus.*

Jones, Helen Dudenbostel, and Robin L. Winkler (Eds.). *Korea: An Annotated Bibliography of Publications in Western Languages.* Washington: The Library of Congress, Reference Department, August 1950. 155 pages.

Kahn, Lessing A. *A Preliminary Investigation of Chinese and North Korean Soldier Reactions to UN Weapons in the Korean War.* (ORO Technical Memorandum ORO-T-14 [FEC]). Chevy Chase, MD: Operations Research Office, The Johns Hopkins University, February 1952.

Kahn, Lessing A., and others. *A Study of North Korean and Chinese Soldiers' Attitudes Toward the Korean War.* (ORO Technical Memorandum ORO-T-34 [FEC]). Chevy Chase, MD: Operations Research Office, The Johns Hopkins University, 1953. 93 pages.

Kuo Mo-jo (Ed.). *A Volunteer Soldier's Day: Recollections by Men of the Chinese People's Volunteers in the War to Resist U.S. Aggression and Aid Korea.* Peking: Foreign Languages Press, 1961. 400 pages.

MacArthur, Douglas. *Reminiscences.* New York: McGraw-Hill, 1964. 438 pages. *Memoir of the CINCUNC.*

Mark, Eduard. *Aerial Interdiction: Air Power and the Land Battle in Three American Wars.* Washington: Center for Air Force History, 1994.

Marshall, S. L. A. *CCF in the Attack, Part II: A Study Based on the Operations of 1st Marine Division in the Koto-ri, Hagaru-ri, Yudam-ni Area, 20 November–10 December 1950.* (ORO Staff Memorandum ORO-S-34 [EUSAK]). APO 500: Operations Research Office, The Johns Hopkins University, 1951. 23 pages.

Montross, Lynn, and others. *U.S. Marine Operations in Korea, 1950–1953.* 5 volumes. Washington: Historical Branch, G-3, Headquarters, United States Marine Corps, 1954–1972. *Official Marine Corps history.*

Mossman, Billy C. *Ebb and Flow, November 1950–July 1951.* (United States Army in the Korean War). Washington: Center of Military History, United States Army, 1990. 551 pages. *Official Army history.*

_____. "The Effectiveness of Air Interdiction during the Korean War." (CMH Draft Study No. 2-3.7 AD.H). Washington: Office of the Chief of Military History, Department of the Army, March 1966. 33 pages. *Contains useful statistical data.*

O'Ballance, Edgar. *The Red Army of China: A Short History.* New York: Frederick A. Praeger, 1963. 232 pages.

Peng Dehuai [Peng Teh-huai]. *Memoirs of a Chinese Marshal (1898–1974).* Peking: Foreign Language Publishing House, 1984. *Memoir of the CCF commander in Korea.*

PLA Unit History. Mimeo ed. Taipei: published under the auspices of the United States Army Chief of Military History, ca. 1963. *Brief histories of PLA units.*

"Railroad Repair and Reconstruction by NKPA and CCF," *Engineer Intelligence Notes,* No. 17 (June 1952), 1 and 9 [prepared by Army Map Service, Corps of Engineers].

Rees, David. *Korea: The Limited War.* New York: St. Martin's Press, 1964. *General history of the Korean War.*

Republic of China, Ministry of Information. *China Handbook.* New York: Macmillan, 1950. *Contains some useful background material.*

Ridgway, Matthew B. *The Korean War.* Garden City, NY: Doubleday, 1967. *Memoir of U.S. general who commanded in Korea.*

Rigg, Robert B. *Red China's Fighting Hordes.* Revised edition. Harrisburg, PA: The Military Service Publishing Company, 1952. 378 pages. *Interesting account by an Army officer with first-hand knowledge of the PLA.*

Schnabel, James F. *Policy and Direction: The First Year.* (United States Army in the Korean War). Washington: Office of the Chief of Military History, Department of the Army, 1972. *Official Army history.*

Shreve, Robert O., Mary J. O'Brien, Alvin D. Coox, Owen F. Mattingly, and William H. Sutherland. *Combat Zone Logistics in Korea.* (ORO Technical Memorandum ORO-T-15 [FEC]). APO 500: Operations Research Office, Johns Hopkins University, March 1952. 200 pages. *U.S./UN focus.*

Sleeper, Raymond S. "Korean Targets for Medium Bombardment," *Air University Quarterly Review,* 4, no. 3 (Spring 1951), 18–31.

Spurr, Russell. *Enter the Dragon: China's Undeclared War Against the United States in Korea, 1950–51*. New York: Newmarket Press, 1988. 335 pages.

Stokesbury, James L. *A Short History of the Korean War*. New York: Quill/William Morrow, 1988. 276 pages. *Good brief general history of the Korean War.*

"The Story of 'Operation Strangle,' " *Air Intelligence Digest*, 5, no. 1 (January 1952), 4–10. *About the UNC air interdiction campaign.*

Summers, Harry G., Jr. *Korean War Almanac*. New York: Facts on File, 1990. 330 pages. *Useful.*

United States Air Force Academy Library. *A Revolutionary War: Korea and the Transformation of the Postwar World*. (Special Bibliography Series No. 84). USAFA, CO: United States Air Force Academy Library, October 1992. 84 pages.

United States Central Intelligence Agency. *National Intelligence Survey—North Korea*. (NIS 41A). Washington: Central Intelligence Agency, ca. 1959.

United States Department of the Navy, Office of Naval Intelligence. *Port Logistics Summary, Korea* (28 June 1950; Serial 51–50).

United States Department of State. *The Conflict in Korea*. Washington: U.S. GPO, 1951.

_____. *North Korea: A Case Study of a Soviet Satellite*. Washington: U.S. GPO, 20 May 1951.

_____. *United States Policy in the Korean Conflict, July 1950–February 1951*. Washington: U.S. GPO, 1951.

_____. *United States Policy in the Korean Crisis*. Washington: U.S. GPO, 1950.

United States Military Academy, Department of Military Art & Engineering. *Operations in Korea*. West Point, NY: United States Military Academy AG Printing Office, April 1954. 50 pages. *Brief operational history of the Korean War from the U.S./UNC perspective.*

United States Office of Strategic Services, Research and Analysis Branch, Far East Section. *Korea Economic Survey*. (Research and Analysis No. 774). Washington: Office of Strategic Services, 1942. 128 pages. *Contains some useful background material.*

United States Senate, Committee on Armed Services. *Military Situation in the Far East: Hearings before the Committee on Armed Services and the Committee on Foreign Relations, United States Senate, Eighty-second Congress, First Session, to Conduct an Inquiry into the Military Situation in the Far East and the Facts Surrounding the Relief of General of the Army MacArthur from His Assignments in That Area*. 5 volumes. Washington: U.S. GPO, 1951. *Major collection of primary source material.*

United States War Department, Military Intelligence Division. *Terrain Handbook—Korea*. (MID No. 461). Washington: U.S. GPO, 18 September 1945. 162 pages. *A forerunner of the area handbook for Korea.*

Whiting, Allen S. *China Crosses the Yalu: The Decision to Enter the Korean War*. (RAND Study). New York: Macmillan, 1960. *Excellent study.*

Index

About the Author

CHARLES R. SHRADER, an independent historian and consultant, lives in Carlisle, Pennsylvania. A Vietnam veteran, he retired from the United States Army in 1987 as a lieutenant colonel. He is the author of *Amicide: The Problem of Friendly Fire in Modern War* (1982) and *U.S. Military Logistics, 1607–1991: A Research Guide* (Greenwood, 1992). The general editor of *Reference Guide to United States Military History*, he currently serves as executive director of the Society for Military History.

Lightning Source UK Ltd.
Milton Keynes UK
UKOW05n1342050117

291447UK00001B/53/P

9 780313 295096